TIME CAPSULE/1945

A HISTORY OF THE YEAR CONDENSED FROM THE PAGES OF TIME

TIME-LIFE BOOKS, NEW YORK

TIME/1945

EDITORS *Henry R. Luce, Manfred Gottfried*
MANAGING EDITOR *T. S. Matthews*
SENIOR EDITORS *Roy Alexander, Whittaker Chambers,*
John Osborne, Content Peckham, Dana Tasker
ASSOCIATE EDITORS *James Agee, Robert W. Boyd Jr.,*
Otto Fuerbringer, Thomas Griffith, Frederick Gruin,
Ernest C. Havemann, Hillis Mills, Duncan Norton-Taylor,
Joseph Purtell, Williston Rich, Robert Sherrod,
Walter Stockly, Leon Svirsky, John Walker, Max Ways,
Eleanor Welch

EDITOR *Maitland A. Edey*
EXECUTIVE EDITOR *Jerry Korn*
TEXT DIRECTOR *Martin Mann*
ART DIRECTOR *Sheldon Cotler*
CHIEF OF RESEARCH *Beatrice T. Dobie*

SERIES EDITOR *John Dille*
ASSISTANT *Lee Greene*
RESEARCHER *Lea Guyer*
DESIGNER *Arnold Holeywell*
ASSISTANT DESIGNER *John M. Woods*
COPYREADER *Rosemarie Conefrey*

PUBLISHER *Rhett Austell*

COVER ILLUSTRATION *Lou Lomonaco*

EVENTS OF THE YEAR

Editors' Note

The year 1945 saw the end of World War II and the deaths of three of the leading figures in the drama: Adolf Hitler, a suicide in his Berlin bunker, Benito Mussolini, murdered by a group of Italian partisans, and President Franklin Roosevelt, stricken by a cerebral hemorrhage. The news of Roosevelt's death is recounted in the Presidency section. Then, because of the way TIME CAPSULES are organized, his name crops up again in later sections of the volume that report on the President's varied activities before his death. The same is true of the military victories in Europe and Japan, which are first reported on briefly in the Presidency section, on pages 21 and 25, and are later explained in greater detail in a separate Battlefronts section, beginning on page 88.

■

TIME CAPSULE/1945 is one of a series of volumes, each adapted and condensed from a year's contents of TIME, the Weekly Newsmagazine. The words, except for a few connecting passages, are those of the magazine itself, and therefore reflect the flavor, the attitudes and the state of knowledge of the day—sometimes innocent, sometimes opinionated, sometimes prescient. The book is divided, like the magazine, into departments, and is organized so that each department forms a chronological chapter for the entire year. The dates in the margin are the issue dates of the magazine.

U.S. AT WAR

The Presidency

In this, the last year of Franklin Roosevelt's life, he was just beginning his fourth term in office. The nation was hearing persistent rumors that the President was seriously ill, but these reports were discounted by the White House and in February President Roosevelt undertook an arduous trip to Yalta to confer with Stalin and Churchill on the postwar partition of Germany. Two months later he suffered a fatal hemorrhage and the office passed to Vice President Harry S. Truman, a one-time railroad timekeeper and haberdasher from Missouri who had served two terms in the U.S. Senate and created a nationwide reputation as chairman of a Senate committee investigating the war effort.

JAN. 1 **AT EASE:** For 20 days, as Franklin Roosevelt relaxed at Warm Springs, Ga., Washington, D.C. seemed more & more like an empty stage. Last week, back at the White House, the President faced newsmen, who arrived full of questions and left nearly empty of answers. Franklin Roosevelt had gained a few pounds, and he had more color. Also he had adopted a new word—contentious—and used it freely as he fended off questions. Elizabeth May Craig, Washington correspondent of a string of Maine newspapers, tossed it back at him: "I have a contentious question, Mr. President, but I would like a serious answer. Are you going to the right or to the left?"

The President said he was going down the old line, a little left of center. That was true eleven and a half years ago, he added, and it still holds.

JAN. 15 **STATE OF THE NATION:** To the reassembled Congress, Franklin Roosevelt sent his twelfth annual message on the state of the nation. The President asked for universal military training as something which he thought was needed to insure against World War III. And he recommended a reduction of taxes after V-E day, Congressional consideration of a vast new postwar building program of houses, roads and airports.

He ended on a note of cautious hope: "This new year can be the greatest year of achievement in human history. 1945 can see the final ending of the Nazi-Fascist reign of terror in Europe. 1945 can see the closing in of the forces of retribution against Japan. Most important of all, 1945 can and must see the substantial beginning of the organization of world peace."

FOR THE FOURTH TIME: Snow fell the night before, turning JAN. 29 to sleet in the morning. On the White House lawn, most of the 13 Roosevelt grandchildren were out early in their snowsuits, coasting on the gentle slopes. Late in the morning the crowd began to gather. It came in overcoats and galoshes, sloshed about in mud and slush.

Promptly at noon the short and simple fourth-term inauguration began. Neat, grey Harry Truman, onetime Senator from Missouri, stepped forward and took the oath as Vice President. Then came that dreadful moment when Franklin Roosevelt must rise in public. Those on the portico could see what a supreme effort it takes to hoist himself up. Spurning a cape, he walked to the black podium, bare-headed and in a blue suit. His big shoulders and his suntanned face with the resolute jaw were all that was visible to the crowd below.

As the applause died down, Franklin Roosevelt placed his right hand on the same page of his old family Bible where it has rested at his previous inaugurations: the 13th Chapter of 1st Corinthians, which ends: *And now abideth faith, hope, charity, these three; but the greatest of these is charity.* His repetition of the oath, after it had been intoned by Chief Justice Harlan Fiske Stone, was clear and firm, ending with the familiar *so help me God.*

The President's remarks that day were on the kind of world that will follow the peace:

"We have learned lessons—at a fearful cost—and we shall profit by them. We have learned that we cannot live alone, at peace. We have learned that we must live as men, and not as ostriches, nor as dogs in the manger. We have learned the simple truth, as Emerson said, that 'the only way to have a friend is to be one.'"

The speech over, the President went back inside, to the Red

President Roosevelt, previewing the end of World War II, calls for universal military service to prevent World War III.

Room. Also inside streamed 2,000 invited guests for luncheon. It was the biggest reception of the twelve Roosevelt years in the White House, but it was also spare. The President had wanted chicken à la king. But he was overruled by the house-keeper, who settled for chicken salad. The rest of the lunch: hard rolls without butter, unfrosted pound cake, coffee.

Lunch lasted well into the afternoon, and was shortly followed by tea for "all those who didn't come to lunch." In the interval, Eleanor Roosevelt was discovered in a corner, teaching Bess Truman how to make entertaining less tiring by relaxing the knees. "I've learned from long experience," said Eleanor Roosevelt. For dinner that night the Roosevelts had their first rib roast in months.

FEB. 19 **TO YALTA:** For his second conference of the Big Three [the first was at Teheran in 1943] and his ninth with Winston Churchill, the President departed from Washington shortly after his inauguration. He appeared at Malta on a spotless U.S. battleship. He was wearing an old-fashioned tweed cap. There he was met by Winston Churchill. The President and Prime Minister then boarded planes for a night flight to a secret Crimean airport, and their meeting with Joseph Stalin at Yalta.

The Germans had wrecked the little city so badly that Russian workmen had to rush temporary restorations to house some of the Big Three staffs. The white stone palace where President Roosevelt stayed was built in 1911 for the last of the Romanovs.

As at Teheran, the eight days at Yalta were not all work. Roosevelt and Churchill talked, ate, drank together before Marshal Stalin joined them. Then, between working sessions, came the toasts. One of Stalin's toasts named the gathering for history: "The Crimea Conference."

SENSITIVE DE GAULLE: In the first days after Yalta, the major FEB. 26 test of the Yalta doctrine was France. The Crimea declaration made it clear that the Big Three did not yet rate France as one of the trustees, even in western Europe.

The French rebelled, and France's provisional leader, General de Gaulle, pointedly announced that France would handle its own empire. Finally, he declined to leave Paris for an aftermath session with President Roosevelt, who had hoped to pause in North Africa on his way home and soothe the General. If Roosevelt wanted to see him, said De Gaulle, the President would have to come to Paris.

TO CONGRESS: On the long voyage home Franklin Roosevelt MARCH 12 had made a decision to report to Congress on Yalta as soon as possible. Thirty-six hours after his return, he went to the House chamber for his first appearance there in 26 months. He had made a decision to leave his leg braces at home. There was a momentary hush as he came into the chamber in an armless wheel chair. Then there was an ovation. The President slipped into a red plush chair in the well of the House, behind a table lined with a dozen microphones.

He began by frankly noting what everyone had wondered about: "I hope you will pardon me for the unusual posture of sitting down, but I know you will realize it makes it a lot easier for me in not having to carry about ten pounds of steel around the bottom of my legs and also because of the fact that I have just completed a 14,000-mile trip."

Thus Franklin Roosevelt set the tone for what may come to be one of the most historic speeches of his career. It was a confidential, informal speech, all but devoid of the ringing Roosevelt oratorical tone. There was none of the usual recrimination, reprimand or warning. At one point the President's voice seemed to give way, as his throat got hoarse. He sipped water, and continued.

In his 54-minute speech the President touched on many matters. He said that Yalta had not only achieved unanimous action but, more important, unity of thought between the Big Three. One of his ad-libs was a roundhouse swing at "prima donnas"—"there are a great number of prima donnas in the world"—which many interpreted as a swat at Charles de Gaulle, who had refused to meet him at Algiers on the President's way home.

The gist of his speech, the whole purpose of his appearance, came out when he said: "There will soon be presented to the U.S. Senate and to the American people a great decision which will determine the fate of the United States—and of the world—for generations to come. There can be no middle ground here. We shall have to take the responsibility for world collaboration, or we shall have to bear the responsibility for another world conflict."

MARCH 19 **FINGERNAIL:** Returning refreshed from Hyde Park, Franklin Roosevelt plunged into a full week. First he set out resolutely to repair some of the damage done to U.S.-French relations. Greeting a group of visiting French correspondents, he spoke a few words of Rooseveltian French to them, then told them (in Rooseveltian English) how sorry he was he had not got to France on his way home from Yalta. In glowing terms, he recalled the days of his youth, when he had bicycled through the French countryside.

As the correspondents beamed, Franklin Roosevelt told them they should pay no attention to all those stories of friction between himself and General de Gaulle. The differences between himself and the General, the President added with a gesture, were no bigger than a fingernail.

APRIL 23 **"ROOSEVELT IS DEAD":** The news came to people in the hot soft light of the afternoon, in taxicabs, along the streets, in offices and bars and factories. In a Cleveland barbershop, 60-year-old Sam Katz was giving a customer a shave when the radio stabbed out the news. Sam Katz walked over to the water cooler, took a long, slow drink, sat down and stared into space for nearly ten minutes. Finally he got up and painted a sign on his window: "Roosevelt Is Dead." Then he finished the shave.

Everywhere, to almost everyone, the news came with the force of a personal shock. A woman in Detroit said: "It doesn't seem possible. It seems to me that he will be back on the radio tomorrow, reassuring us all that it was just a mistake."

It was the same through that evening, and the next day, and the next; the hand-lettered signs in the windows of stores: "Closed out of Reverence for F.D.R."; the unbroken, 85-hour dirge of the nation's radio; the typical tributes of typical Americans in the death-notice columns of their newspapers. Said one: "A Soldier Died Today."

AFTERNOON AT WARM SPRINGS: Bad weather had held up the plane which brought the President's daily mail from Washington, so it was late that morning before Mr. Roosevelt got down to work. He sat beside the fireplace in the cozy, cluttered living room of the cottage at Warm Springs—the Little White House—while his secretary helped him sort through the mail. At one end of the room his cousins Laura Delano and Margaret Suckley sat chatting.

There were a lot of things to sign—several State Department nominations, some postmasters' appointments, some citations for the Legion of Merit, the bill to extend the life of the Commodity Credit Corp. When he got to the bill, Franklin Roosevelt grinned at Bill Hassett, spoke the words that always made his secretary smile back: "Here's where I make a law."

Mrs. Elizabeth Shoumatoff, a portrait painter, came in. She had once done a portrait of Franklin Roosevelt and now was anxious to do another. She had driven down from her Long Island home several days before and had been making sketches. Hassett gingerly collected the papers, letting the President's signatures dry. "Don't mind me," Hassett remarked. "I'm waiting for my laundry to dry."

The President laughed. Mrs. Shoumatoff remembered afterwards: "He was so gay."

Mr. Hassett left, leaving a stack of state papers within easy reach of the President's chair. The artist sketched while the President unconcernedly shuffled his papers.

Utter weariness had kept him close to the cottage ever since he had arrived in Warm Springs, a little less than two weeks ago. He had seen few people. But this afternoon he was going to a barbecue. In the evening, the polio patients at his beloved Warm Springs Foundation were going to give a minstrel show for him. He was looking forward to both affairs.

Miss Suckley glanced his way. He had suddenly slumped sideways in his chair and, alarmed, she ran across the room to him. She heard him mutter: "I have a terrific headache." The women stood aghast at what they saw. The President fainted.

They called his Negro valet. Big Arthur Prettyman, veteran of 20 years in the Navy, was accustomed to helping the crippled President around. With the help of "Joe," a Filipino mess boy, he lifted the unconscious man in his arms and carried him into the bedroom.

There, in the small, plain room with its paneled walls and scatter rugs and the picture of a ship and a ticking brass chronometer, doctors found the stricken President. They untied his tie, took off his grey suit and put pajamas on him. But there was little they or anyone else could do. He had suffered a massive cerebral hemorrhage. They could only wait and pray.

The shadows of the pines grew longer. In the bedroom of the Little White House one of the physicians looked at the time. It was 3:35. Death, at that moment, had come to Franklin Delano Roosevelt.

THE LONGEST DAY: Mrs. Roosevelt, as guest of honor, arrived at the Sulgrave Club tea for the benefit of Washington's children's clinics "with a very light heart." She had heard from Warm Springs that the President had eaten a good breakfast and was feeling fine. The anxiety which she had borne so long was eased a little. She sat down next to Mrs. Woodrow Wilson. Soon afterwards, she was told that she was wanted on the telephone.

Mrs. Roosevelt rose and left the room. She returned after a few moments to apologize for leaving "in this way," and rode back to the White House. In her sitting room on the second floor, surrounded by hundreds of cherished photographs of her family and friends, she faced Press Secretary

Stephen Early and Vice Admiral Ross T. McIntire, the President's personal physician. "The President," said Early, "has slept away."

"I am more sorry for the people of the country and the world," Mrs. Roosevelt said after a moment, "than I am for us."

Steve Early telephoned Mr. Truman. Soon the Vice President came up to the sitting room. "The President has passed away," Mrs. Roosevelt told him. When Harry Truman choked, "What can I do?" she answered: "Tell us what we can do. Is there any way we can help you?"

Later, she changed to a black dress and strode with her usual determined gait to the waiting limousine and enplaned for Georgia. In the dark morning hours, Eleanor Roosevelt walked into the little white cottage on Pine Mountain. Silent and alone, she went in to her husband.

Miss Delano and Miss Suckley rode with her in the car which took them down to the railroad later that morning. The black dog the President called "Pup"—the Scottie Fala— lay at her feet. Just ahead of their car rolled the hearse. It was the President's invariable custom, whenever he left Warm Springs, to drive past the Foundation administration building and shout goodbye to the polio patients in wheel chairs.

Now, in the day's hot brightness, the procession rolled slowly into the driveway in front of Georgia Hall. Eleanor Roosevelt looked out at the tense faces of the cripples. The procession stopped and she saw Graham Jackson, a Negro accordionist who had performed for the President many times. He stepped up beside the hearse and began to play. It was "Going Home," one of the President's favorites.

A photographer aimed his camera at her. She lifted her hand and framed the word, "Please," and he lowered his camera. The procession crawled on.

The special train waiting to carry them north was at the little wooden station. Soldiers lifted the flag-draped casket into the last car. The band played on & on; the drums echoed hollowly in the hot valley. Leaning on Steve Early's arm, with Fala trailing them, she went steadily aboard.

The train rumbled on, past fields where farmers tied their mules and stood at the fences with their hats off—into Charlotte, N.C., where more thousands stood, bareheaded and

A Washington, D.C. woman waves goodbye as FDR's body passes. "I am more sorry for the people of the country," said Mrs. Roosevelt, "than I am for us."

staring, where she heard Negroes singing spirituals. The train rolled on through the dark hills of Virginia, into the nation's capital at last and toward the end of Eleanor Roosevelt's longest day.

BUGLER–SOUND TAPS: In the capital's hush every sound was audible—the twitter of birds in new-leafed shade trees; the soft, rhythmic scuffing of massed, marching men; the clattering exhaust of armored scout cars moving past. And the beat of muffled drums. As Franklin Roosevelt's flag-draped coffin passed slowly by on its black caisson, the hoofbeats of the white horses, the grind of iron-rimmed wheels on pavement overrode all other sounds.

Men stood bareheaded. An elderly weeping Negro woman sat on the curb, rocking and crying: "Oh, he's gone. He's gone forever. I loved him so. He's never coming back."

At last, the caisson ground up the graveled White House drive. The coffin was carried out of sight into the executive mansion. It was put in the East Room.

Franklin Roosevelt's wheel chair stood near the wall. The warm, flower-scented room filled with Franklin Roosevelt's family and friends, the top men of the U.S., representatives of the foreign world—the new President, Harry Truman, the Cabinet, Britain's Anthony Eden, Russia's Andrei Gromyko.

The pianist struck a chord, the mourners stood to sing the hymn, "Eternal Father, Strong to Save."

Mrs. Roosevelt listened, pale but dry-eyed, beside her son, Brigadier General Elliott Roosevelt, her daughter, Mrs. Anna Roosevelt Boettiger. But many near her could not control themselves. Harry Hopkins, who had hurried East from the Mayo Clinic, stood almost fainting beside his chair, white as death and racked by sobs.

That night, aboard a special train again, the President's body traveled to Hyde Park. In the green-hedged garden of the ancestral home two carloads of flowers lay heaped beside the open grave. The Rev. Dr. W. George W. Anthony, a white-haired clergyman, spoke the Episcopal burial service:

"We commit his body to the ground; earth to earth, dust to dust. . . . Blessed are the dead who die in the Lord. . . . Lord have mercy on us. Christ, have mercy on us. . . ."

A squad of West Point cadets raised rifles at the graveside, fired a volley, then another and another. A bugle sounded the long notes of taps. The grey-clad cadets swung smartly away. The crowd slowly scattered.

After a while Eleanor Roosevelt walked back through a wide opening in the hedge. She stood alone, silently watching the workmen shoveling soil into her husband's grave. Then, silent and alone, she walked away again. On her black dress she wore the small pearl fleur-de-lis which he had given her as a wedding present.

UNWELCOME SECRET: Months ago, persistent rumors were circulating in Washington that the President was in grave physical condition. In newsreels, the well-fleshed, strong face had begun to look wasted and faintly wistful, and sometimes the firm jaw quivered unaccountably. The ringing radio voice seemed now & then to drag with weariness.

In January, U.S. secret servicemen were told that the President was in serious ill health. They picked a bodyguard for Vice President Harry Truman, told it to stand by for a sudden call to duty. The call came about March 1. The Truman bodyguard was told that President Roosevelt might go at any time. They were ordered to take up a day & night watch on the Vice President. Last Thursday night they became the President's bodyguard.

THE THIRTY-SECOND: With hardly a care on his mind, Harry Truman had left his spacious, picture-lined office in the Senate Office Building, walked over to visit Speaker Sam Rayburn in the Capitol. In his two and a half months as Vice President, Harry Truman had not been invited to sit in with the policy-makers; he had continued to hobnob with his Congressional cronies. Sam Rayburn had just poured the Vice President a drink of bourbon and tap water when there was a call from the White House. Steve Early was on the wire. As he listened, Harry Truman's face turned pale. He left abruptly, saying not a word. But his sudden action spoke loudly enough. Said Sam Rayburn before the Vice President got to the door: "We'll all stand by you, Harry."

The White House was in confusion. Cabinet members and heads of war agencies had arrived, grave and solemn-faced. Except for Steve Early, the White House secretariat had collapsed with grief. Shortly before 7 p.m. the Trumans, the Cabinet members and other bigwigs gathered in the green-walled Cabinet Room. Harry Truman, not quite at ease, sat down nervously in a brown leather chair. When Chief Justice Harlan Fiske Stone strode in, Harry Truman rose, clasped a Bible between his hands, stood stiffly. It took just one minute for the oath to be administered, and Harry Truman, 60, the neat, slim, spectacled man from Missouri, became the 32nd man to be President of the U.S.

He plunged finally into work. The great mahogany desk in the oval study had been cleared of all of Franklin Roosevelt's crowding knickknacks. On it lay only a Bible, a thesaurus, and a leather-bound pictorial history of the U.S. In rapid order, President Truman had a 45-minute conference with Secretary of State Stettinius, then a 48-minute session with the war leaders. At noon he broke his first precedent: he went up to Capitol Hill for lunch.

Lunch over, Harry Truman showed another side of his character. Spotting newsmen waiting outside, he shook hands all around and asked: "Did you ever have a bull or a load of hay fall on you? If you have, you know how I felt last night. I felt as if two planets and the whole constellation had fallen on me. I don't know if you boys pray, but if you do, please pray God to help me carry this load."

Upon what sort of man had this load fallen?

Son of a Missouri farmer, Harry Truman went no farther than high school before setting to work. He was a timekeeper for the Santa Fe Railroad in Kansas City, wrapped papers for the *Star,* clerked in a bank. Then he went back to the farm until World War I swept him in. A longtime National Guardsman, he went to France a captain, won commendation for his coolness under fire and returned a major. From then on, Harry kept up his citizen-soldier interest in the Army, still holds a colonel's commission in the Army Reserve. He is the first ex-soldier to sit in the White House since Theodore Roosevelt.

After World War I, Harry Truman soon sank back into anonymity. With a war comrade he opened a haberdashery: it failed. He went into politics, became a county judge (an administrative, not a judicial post). He probably would have remained a minor politician except for a lucky break given him by Kansas City's late Boss Pendergast. In 1934, as a fine magisterial whim, Boss Tom made unknown Harry Truman a U.S. Senator. With Pendergast's control of the state, it was as simple as that. In 1940, Senator Truman won re-election. In his second term, the war came: what he did about it made him a national figure.

With a long memory for the waste of World War I, with a veteran's patriotism and a politician's shrewd eye for the main chance, Harry Truman organized the Senate investigating committee which soon bore his name. Overnight, he became the watchdog of the war effort, scourging shortages, prodding production, forcing the manufacturers, the Army & Navy to toe the mark. By the summer of 1944, Harry Truman's record made him a Vice Presidential possibility. And with almost complete unanimity, Harry Truman's friends—in Washington and across the land—agreed last week that he "would not be a great President."

THE FIRST TEN DAYS: In a few breathless days, the U.S. people APRIL 30 got an idea of how their new President would carry on: Harry Truman was quick, decisive, seemed to have a talent for working hard without getting confused or losing his temper.

Within a few days U.S. citizens grew accustomed to pictures of Harry Truman's neat, compact figure striding briskly across the street from Blair House and up the grey, curving driveway, into the executive offices at the White House. Once, when traffic halted to let the President pass, a cab driver yelled: "Good luck, Harry!" Harry Truman grinned and waved.

In the White House he upset the whole routine. An inordinately early riser, he was at his desk at 8:30, began his day's appointments promptly at 9:30. No matter how crowded the list, he kept the schedule running on time, a feat which loquacious Franklin Roosevelt had seldom been able to do.

One thing Harry Truman could not quite get used to: the office comforts of being President. He had presented to Eleanor Roosevelt the desk at which the late President had worked, and for himself had taken the old, dark red mahogany desk which had been used by Presidents Theodore Roosevelt, Taft, Wilson, Harding, Coolidge and Hoover. On the desk was a little oak plaque with three black buttons on it, to summon secretaries and stenographers. But whenever Harry Truman wanted a stenographer he would jump up, rush to the door and say, "Look, I want to dictate a few letters."

STORY OVER: Down from the walls of the oval White House study came Franklin Roosevelt's Currier & Ives prints, his ship's clock. After the final packing was done—there were 1,000 boxes and bundles in all—secret servicemen, White House office workers and servants came to Mrs. Roosevelt's upstairs study to say goodbye. She thanked them, her voice warm, her face strained. In the early evening, she put on her coat and hat. In the White House rooms past which she walked, the outlines of vanished pictures showed on bare walls.

Two black limousines took Mrs. Roosevelt and her family out through the gate in a drizzling rain, headed for the Union Station. That night in Manhattan the usual knot of reporters awaited her. She spoke only four words. "The story," she said, "is over."

MAY 14 **VICTORY IN EUROPE:** In Washington, in the chill grey morning, President Harry Truman entered the oval study, flanked by his family, his aides, his Cabinet. It was his 61st birthday. But it was also the end of a war. Anticipating the historic occasion, he had his speech ready for a week. In undramatic fashion, which served to emphasize the anticlimactic nature of the occasion, he first read his speech to 200 newsmen. Then, at 9 a.m., he went on the radio. In a clear and quiet voice, he announced the victory in Europe: "The Allied armies, through sacrifice and devotion and with God's help. . . ."

"FIDDLESTICKS": This week the White House flag was run up MAY 21 to full staff. The official period of mourning for Franklin Roosevelt was over, and Harry S. Truman had ended his first month as President. He also had moved across the street from Blair House, and the White House began to reflect the easy informality of the brisk Midwesterner's family life.

For the Trumans' first weekend in the White House came the President's 92-year-old mother, Mrs. Martha Truman. Harry Truman had sent the big presidential transport plane to Missouri to bring Mrs. Truman to Washington for Mother's Day. Jolly and chipper, the President's mother thoroughly enjoyed her first flight. At the capital, she was greeted by her son, then stepped into a swarm of cameramen. A little flustered at first, she quickly regained composure, said to the President: "Oh, fiddlesticks. If I'd known that, I wouldn't have come."

"I'D RATHER HAVE THAT MEDAL": On the White House JUNE 25 appointment list were five notable callers—three marines and an Army private—who were to be decorated by the President

Wearing a gaudy Indian sweater, President Truman goes fishing in Puget Sound. The wind is cool, the day bright, the catch poor.

—and volcanic General George Smith Patton Jr., who was making a courtesy call on his return from Europe.

Patton, who usually wears at least one ivory-handled revolver, made news by going in unarmed. But he took his riding crop along, waved it rakishly at the cheering White House staff. The other fighting men got the Congressional Medal of Honor. Reading the citations, Harry Truman got stuck when he came to "Peleliu Island," called on a Marine major to pronounce it. Next time he reached the same name, the President got grins all around by ducking the pronunciation, substituting the phrase "on that same island named a while ago."

Said onetime Artilleryman Harry Truman to the medal winners: "I congratulate you. I'd rather have that medal than be President."

JULY 2 **INNOCENT MERRIMENT:** The capital had been hot and steamy. But now, off in the cool Northwest evening, Harry Truman could see the dark green of fir forests, the snowy, glacier-scarred bulk of Mount Rainier. When the plane landed at McChord Field in Tacoma, his old Senate friend, Washington's Governor Mon Wallgren, was waiting. Then, for five days, Harry Truman forgot the cares of office.

Rummaging in the Governor's closet, he appropriated a battered hat, an exclamatory sweater knitted by Vancouver Island Indians. He rose early to stroll on the wide lawns, sometimes played the piano before breakfast. Going to the Capitol, he sat down at an organ under the lofty dome, launched into Beethoven's *Minuet in G* and the *Blackhawk Waltz.* Then, with the Governor and Press Secretary Charlie Ross, he sang *Peggy O'Neil* and *Melancholy Baby.*

One day he drove an open car up Puget Sound to a famed stretch of salmon water. No fisherman, the President hauled in nothing but a dogfish. But the wind was cool, the day bright, and a nearby fisherman presented him with a 12-lb. king salmon. This week, rested and refreshed, he took off the gaudy Indian sweater, prepared to fly to San Francisco and take up again the burdens of the Presidency.

SIGNING THE CHARTER: In San Francisco, Harry Truman would witness the scene which, perhaps above all others, Franklin Roosevelt most wanted to see: the signing of the

World Charter setting up the United Nations. A world organization to keep the peace was now a fact—and the U.S., barring an almost unbelievable change in official climate would be a member. There would be criticism and strictures. But an Associated Press poll of 75 Senators found none definitely against it.

ON TO POTSDAM: Before he left for the Big Three meeting at JULY 9 Potsdam, the President had had a busy fortnight in the field of foreign relations. Out of it had come:

¶ Assurance of Senate ratification of the new world charter.

¶ An informal vote of confidence from the U.S. public: the Gallup poll reported that 87% of U.S. citizens approve the way he has handled his job. (President Roosevelt's wartime high: 84%, right after Pearl Harbor.)

¶ An important Cabinet shift. The President dismissed earnest, young Edward R. Stettinius Jr. as Secretary of State, made him the U.S. representative on the World Security Council. To replace him, the President chose South Carolina's former Senator James Francis Byrnes, 66.

MISSOURIAN ABROAD: On Sunday Harry Truman, President JULY 23 of the U.S., landed at Potsdam. On Monday he sat down at the conference table with Joseph Stalin and Winston Churchill in a refurbished castle once owned by Kaiser Wilhelm.

The man from Missouri had crossed the Atlantic on the cruiser *Augusta* in eight leisurely days, had had plenty of time to fix in his mind the definite offers he would carry to the conference: friendly help in reconciling the differences between America's European friends; practical help in putting Europe back on its feet.

He had disembarked at Antwerp, had boarded the same plane in which Franklin Roosevelt had flown to other Big Three meetings. The devastated areas of northeastern France and northwestern Germany unrolled before him. Over the wastes of Berlin, over the roofless houses and the crumbling church towers, his pilot banked and circled.

U.S., British and Russian guards lined the roads from the airfields; the cavalcade of cars rolled behind motorcycle escorts to the thickly guarded compound where the Big Three and their aides will live. Several miles from the compound was the meeting place of the Big Three. There, on the castle grounds the Russians had planted a courtyard with red flowers in the shape of a huge red star. Inside was a dark-paneled main room, furnished with a crimson carpet overlaid with a red and purple Oriental rug, a 12-ft. circular table.

Here the Big Three would meet to decide the fate of nations. It was a long way from Missouri, a long way from the U.S. —whence, for the first time since Woodrow Wilson, a U.S. President had come to try for peace.

AUG. 13 **BIRTH OF AN ERA:** A new era was born—the age of atomic force. Like many an epoch in man's progress toward civilization, it was wombed in war's destruction. The birth was announced one day this week by the President of the United States. His words:

"Sixteen hours ago an American airplane dropped one bomb on Hiroshima, an important Japanese army base [see page 110]. That bomb had more power than 20,000 tons of TNT. It is an atomic bomb. It is a harnessing of the basic power of the universe. What has been done is the greatest achievement of organized science in history."

Thus to the U.S., already great in military and scientific prowess, had come man's most destructive weapon. To the U.S. Army Air Forces had been given the means for complete destruction of Japan, for one atomic bomb dropped from one plane can wreak the same destruction as 2,000 B-29s.

Once again President Truman applied the psychological squeeze on the Japanese: "If they do not now accept our terms, they may expect a rain of ruin from the air, the like of which has never been seen on this earth."

AUG. 20 **THE SURRENDER:** Friday morning the President was up early as usual and was about to leave his rooms in the White House when a War Department messenger arrived with a radio dispatch. The President took the piece of paper and read:

"In obedience to the gracious command of His Majesty the Emperor. . . ."

Three years, eight months, three days and 75,000 American lives after Pearl Harbor, the Japs were beaten. They knew it, and they wanted to quit "as quickly as possible."

Harry Truman, President for four months, still got a thrill out of great events and his part in them. The bright hazel eyes of the plain man from Missouri raced down the yellow page:

"The Japanese Government are ready to accept the terms enumerated at Potsdam on July 26, 1945 with the understanding that the said declaration does not comprise any demand which prejudices the prerogative of His Majesty as a sovereign ruler. The Japanese Government hope sincerely that this. . . ."

There, broken in mid-sentence, it ended. It was unofficial: a dispatch broadcast by Radio Tokyo, picked up by listening monitors on the Pacific Coast, and teletyped to Washington. It was nothing that a President could formally discuss with his Allies, or reply to.

Across the world, over the uncertain radio channels between Tokyo and Europe, the same message in diplomatic code creaked along via the neutral governments of Sweden and Switzerland. While the world throbbed with the known news, the President went on with his day's work.

His first scheduled caller was Representative Mike Mansfield of Montana, a Congressional authority on Asiatic affairs. Afterward, Mansfield felt free to say publicly that the U.S. should not and could not guarantee to leave intact "the prerogatives of His Majesty as a sovereign ruler."

Truman talked over that condition with other callers. He was inclined to make no concessions whatsoever to His Majesty the Emperor. Suddenly, the Imperial issue was the issue of the Pacific peace. Upon it, the life or death of many men was about to turn. The "prerogatives" which the victors were asked to preserve included four main powers:

¶ The Emperor is the central authority of civil government.
¶ He is supreme commander of the Army and Navy.
¶ He is head of the state religion (Shinto).
¶ He has supreme authority in foreign affairs, declarations of war, the making of treaties (including treaties of surrender).

The official version limped in at last. Truman now had something to discuss through diplomatic channels and he left the communications to Jimmy Byrnes and his State Department. Some 27 hours after Tokyo's surrender offer had first been heard, transmitters in San Francisco, Honolulu, Saipan were broadcasting Secretary of State Byrnes' note:

"From the moment of surrender the authority of the Emperor and the Japanese Government to rule the state shall be subject to the supreme commander of the Allied powers, who will take such steps as he deems proper to effectuate the surrender terms.

"The Emperor will be required to authorize and insure the signature of the surrender terms and shall issue his commands to all the Japanese military, naval and air authorities to cease active operations and to surrender their arms.

"The ultimate form of government of Japan shall, in accordance with the Potsdam declaration, be established—by the freely expressed will of the Japanese people.

"The armed forces of the Allied powers will remain in Japan until the purposes set forth in the Potsdam declaration are achieved."

The official version of this answer was 17 hours on the diplomatic route from Washington to Tokyo. Meanwhile, the Japanese press and domestic radio prepared the Japanese people both for surrender and for a finish fight.

On the fourth day, the President called in reporters. Said he: "I have received this afternoon a message from the Japanese Government, a full acceptance of unconditional surrender."

AUG. 27 **HISTORIC WEEK:** The week of the war's end was, in many ways, the true beginning of the Truman Presidency. The military tasks which Harry Truman had inherited were done. The crisis of peace had arrived—and Harry Truman was on his own.

On Surrender Day, the President was up at 7:15 a.m. As the tenseness grew, hour by hour, as Jimmy Byrnes made hurried trips in & out of the White House side door, Harry Truman outwardly seemed to be the calmest man in Washington. He found time to chat with the aging (51) but still boyish Duke of Windsor, who just wanted to say hello. When the big news came at last, the President called his Cabinet and the top men of the war bureaus. As the official family gathered in the Oval Room, the President beamed his greetings.

Mrs. Truman, in grey, sat quietly nearby. In a fresh-pressed, double-breasted blue suit, the President stood, glanced at the clock. It was a few seconds before 7 p.m.—the hour agreed upon with London and Moscow for the announcement of Japan's surrender. There was no flutter in Harry Truman's matter-of-fact voice as he read the message from Tokyo.

In a moment, outside in Pennsylvania Avenue, there was a roaring chant: "We want Truman!" The President quickly obliged. He and Mrs. Truman went out to the columned portico, then down the green lawn to within 25 feet of the shouting thousands behind the iron fence. The Trumans smiled and waved, then returned to the White House. But the crowd still wanted Truman. President and First Lady made a second appearance on the porch. The President spoke: "Ladies and gentlemen. This is a great day. This is the day when we can start on our real task of implementation of free government in the world." Soberly, he reminded the crowd of the emergency ahead. "It is going to take the help of all of us to do it."

Then happy Harry Truman had two telephone calls to make: 1) to his 92-year-old mother in Grandview, Mo., to make personal the news she had heard on the radio; 2) to Eleanor Roosevelt, to say that he wished Franklin Roosevelt could have been in Washington that day.

AFTER $40 BILLION WORTH: For almost an hour President Truman listened hard to the arguments for extension of Lend-Lease. There were reasons for an immediate decision: 1) China had made a formal request for extension; 2) Charles de Gaulle, reaching Washington this week, would doubtless bring up the question; 3) Britain could not buy heavily in the U.S. market without help in putting its own economy in order; 4) Russia had already asked for $6 billion of postwar credits.

Harry Truman heard the sum-up of his advisers—Secretary of State Jimmy Byrnes, Treasury Secretary Fred Vinson, War Mobilizer John Snyder, Fleet Admiral William Leahy. Then the President spoke his mind: he was dead set against the U.S. adding to its reputation as a Santa Claus; he wanted Lend-Lease cut to a minimum now, liquidated as quickly as possible.

Thus began the end of the unprecedented device by which Franklin Roosevelt, nine months before U.S. entry into the war, began to furnish munitions, food, tools and services to nations who became U.S. allies. By this week the horn of U.S. plenty had poured out about $40 billion worth of Lend-Lease.

SEPT. 3 **LE NOUVEAU CHARLIE:** When France's gaunt General de Gaulle came to Washington last week it was exactly one year since he had marched into liberated Paris behind the might of U.S. arms. It was little more than 13 months since his last visit to the U.S., when he had repaid Franklin Roosevelt's cool reserve with a stiff hauteur of his own.

This time Charles de Gaulle was smiling, cordial, no longer unbending. His mission was obvious: to regain U.S. affection for France. At the airport he spoke in slow English:

"The first thing I want to say is thank you. We are in a period of confidence and friendship that will bind France and the United States together. Long live the United States of America."

A long, black car whisked the General off to the White House. He emerged with right hand outstretched, took a few long steps to where Harry Truman stood awaiting him. That night the red carpet of protocol was rolled out for a White House state dinner, after which Harry Truman and his guest talked together in the library until midnight.

After a night at the White House, the General began the long round of duties of a distinguished visitor. He went to Arlington National Cemetery, placed a wreath at the tomb of the Unknown Soldier. Everything seemed to be going fine. But that afternoon, President Truman dropped a bombshell. After his regular press conference, twelve French journalists remained to be presented. The President shook their hands, told them he thought it was high time that the French press began to give America a square deal.

If the remark bothered *le grand Charlie*, he did not show it. Next morning it was his turn. He met U.S. newsmen, smiled as a newsman brought up the President's remarks. Oh, yes, said Charlie, he could understand the U.S. President's being "struck" by some stories in France's newspapers. He, himself, had also been frequently "struck" by stories about him in the U.S. press.

ROUGH & HARSH: Harry Truman's abrupt termination of Lend-Lease reverberated around the world. Most nations took it philosophically, but Britain was hurt and worried. In the House of Commons, Prime Minister Clement Attlee, pale and plainly disquieted, officially broke the bad news, lamely admitted that Britain had not been prepared for it.

To Attlee's rescue went Loyal Oppositionist Winston Churchill who commented: "I cannot believe that this is the last word of the United States. I cannot believe that so great a country would proceed in such a rough and harsh manner."

Reaction in the U.S. was almost all in President Truman's favor. By week's end almost everyone realized that the President had not shut off U.S. aid to foreign countries. He had merely substituted one lending device for another. And he had notified the world that the U.S. would not be played for a sucker. The President had bolstered his own reputation as a hard-headed Missourian who could be trusted to handle money in a businesslike way.

SPEED: The big news in Washington and all across the land was the astonishing speed with which the U.S. was returning to the ways of peace. Wartime controls were lifted faster than the most hopeful had ever expected. Businessmen and contractors came to Washington expecting to stay weeks to tie up the loose ends of wartime business. Instead, they returned home in two or three days, their business completed.

The driving force behind this whirlwind was the plain man in the White House. He had passed word down the line that speed was the order of the day.

The President also:

¶ Put federal employes back on the 40-hour week.

¶ Urged Congress to continue Selective Service induction of men 18 to 25, cautioned it against a premature declaration of the end of the war.

¶ Displaced a model gun on his desk with a model plough.

UNCENSORED DOPE: Missouri-born Brigadier General Harry SEPT. 10 Vaughan, military aide to President Truman, is a large, uninhibited man, a veteran at draw poker. Genial and democratic to boot, Reserve Officer Vaughan is neither a finicky nor a formal dresser: in the White House he often does not bother to put on a blouse or cinch up his necktie.

Last week the Women's Auxiliary of the Alexandria (Va.)

Westminster Presbyterian Church—of which General Vaughan is an elder—were enchanted to discover that he was as excitingly frank as he was informal. They had invited him to speak, and by the time word of his speech got back to the capital, Washington wits cracked that they had now heard the uncensored dope on all topics of national interest.

General Vaughan compared his boss with President Roosevelt. "It's just like having a fancy dinner of caviar over a long period," he said. "But sometimes you like to get back to ham and eggs."

But the greater part of the General's talk was devoted to the Potsdam Conference.

"We were delayed the first day," said Historian Vaughan. "The story was that Churchill was a day late at Yalta and Stalin had to get even and be a day late at Potsdam.

"Churchill is a garrulous old gentleman and he would never say anything in less than 20 words where ten would do."

Then General Harry told about the terrible black-market prices in occupied Germany. As a happy illustration, he told how he had sold his $55 U.S. watch to a Russian officer for $500.

SEPT. 17 **OUT-DEALING THE NEW DEAL:** President Truman sent his first peacetime message to Congress. In 16,000 workaday words—the longest Presidential message since Theodore Roosevelt's 20,000-word document in 1901—he laid out his program for peace and prosperity.

There was little in it that the President had not recommended before. The news was: 1) the way he gathered all his eggs in one basket; and 2) the many respects in which he departed from his reputation as a man a little right of center and went over to Franklin Roosevelt's spot, a little left of center.

He again asked Congress for a "Full Employment" bill. Again he asked for a permanent Fair Employment Practices Committee. He bluntly called the 40¢ minimum-wage level "obsolete." And he demanded a multi-billion-dollar development and construction program.

Looking ahead, he saw that if the nation could deal with the problems of peace as boldly as it did with the problems of war, it could soon be off on the "greatest peacetime industrial activity we have ever seen."

The catchall message had a catchall reaction. New Dealers thought it great; the stock market jumped one to three points, reached the highest levels in eight years. Congressional Republicans, looking only on one side of the picture, thought they had something to crow about. Cried Minority Leader Joe Martin: "Not even President Roosevelt ever asked as much at one sitting. The scenery is new and there is a little better decoration, and he does dish it out a little easier. But it is just a plain case of out-New Dealing the New Deal."

HOME FOR THE WEEKEND: Harry Truman wanted to go SEPT. 24 home to Missouri for the weekend. So he and Bess Truman set out by plane. The Presidential C-54 lurched through stormy weather, sat down at Kansas City. Up the ramp of the "Sacred Cow" ran daughter Mary Margaret; her "Hi, Daddy!" rang out above the low roar of the engines.

Ten miles away, at Independence, Mayor Roger T. Sermon was waiting for them at the summer White House, 219 North Delaware Avenue. The night's poker game was all set up. Cook Vietta Garr had the corn in the kettle and the steaks on the fire.

That night there were enough guests at Mayor Sermon's house for two poker games. Harry Truman played until 1:30, enjoyed himself hugely. He was up at 6:30 next morning, ready for the 20-mile drive to Grandview to visit his 92-year-old mother.

Back in Kansas City he dropped in at the Men's Wear Shop owned by his ex-partner in haberdashery, Eddie Jacobson. He examined the stock expertly, bought 18 pairs of size 11 socks. To Eddie, who hadn't won a single pot in the poker game the night before, he chuckled: "I thought you'd need this sale, after what we did to you last night." Then, recalling the dark day in 1922 when they had gone bankrupt, he asked, "How's business, anyhow?"

"It's wonderful," said Eddie Jacobson, "but you know, there's one thing that's worrying me: it's this inflation."

"It worries me too," said the President. "But Eddie, I'm watching it all the time."

At Frank Spina's barbershop Harry Truman got his usual trim, reminded his old barber: "None of that fancy stuff. I don't want anything that smells." He got plain water. Next morning, instead of going to church ("it creates such a disturbance"), he stayed home and read the Sunday papers. Then he drove back to Grandview, and at the little airport said goodbye to his family. Reaching up to kiss him, his mother got in a final word: "You be good, but be game, too."

OCT. 8   **A SWELL OF UNREST:** The gale of war had blown itself out, and now a big swell was running: labor unrest. It crashed on every industrial shore in the nation, spread beyond the factories. In strike-stormy Detroit, cops clashed with labor-union men picketing a meeting of Rabble-Rouser Gerald L.K. Smith's followers, and men went down under blows of swinging nightsticks. High school children in New York City, Chicago and Gary, Ind., swirled out in a rash of protests, racial disputes and wholesale hooliganism.

    The pent-up economic pressures of peace had generated political pressures and had brought President Truman up against his first serious difference with Congress.

OCT. 22   **"THE LAST LADY":** Brown, bosomy Hazel Scott attained fame by changing Bach's stately counterpoint into boogie-woogie at Manhattan's Café Society Uptown. Last week Pianist Scott considerably enhanced her fame and earning power by not changing the stately D.A.R.

General Harry Vaughan is large,   Pianist Hazel Scott. The stately
genial, enchantingly frank. Page 31.   D.A.R. forbids her the use of its hall.

Solemnly and unanimously, the executive committee of the ancestor-worshiping Daughters of the American Revolution decided to keep its Constitution Hall for "white artists only." Miss Scott could not, as she had asked, give a concert there. Next day, a special messenger from 1600 Pennsylvania Avenue brought a letter to the office of Miss Scott's new husband, Congressman Adam Clayton Powell Jr. of Harlem.

In reply to Powell's demand for "action" against the D.A.R., President Truman said that he could not interfere with a "private enterprise." But, the President added testily, "one of the first steps taken by the Nazis when they came to power was to forbid the public appearance of artists and musicians whose religion or origin was unsatisfactory to the 'master race.'"

A few minutes later Powell received a telegram from the First Lady. Said she: "I deplore any action which denies artistic talent an opportunity to express itself because of prejudice against race or origin." But that afternoon Bess Truman attended a D.A.R. tea in her honor. Asked if she might be a guest at similar teas, later, the taciturn First Lady shrugged: "Why not?"

"From now on," trumpeted Congressman Powell, "Mrs. Truman is the Last Lady."

CHANGE OF PACE: Ever since Harry Truman said that it was NOV. 5 time for the U.S. people to cut out the foolishness and get back to work, official Washington had received persistent retorts from out in the country that Harry Truman might apply that maxim to himself. He had traveled widely since his own inauguration, and some of his junkets had obviously had less work than play in them.

This week the President suddenly canceled all trips scheduled for the next two months including a southern junket which would have included a football game. Official reason: pressure of business in Washington.

The President would not change his nature: he works hard, and when through with work he likes to relax. But he had apparently decided henceforth to clothe himself in a little more presidential dignity.

Hereafter, when he did go out again, Bess Truman would probably go with him.

NOV. 26 **LIFE WITH HARRY:** The President, confided White House Social Secretary Edith Helm last week, is a methodical domestic man. His methods:

¶ Up at 6 a.m. for a pre-dawn raid on a well-stocked refrigerator, installed for his convenience near the presidential bedroom on the third floor of the White House.

¶ Second breakfast with his wife and daughter at 8 a.m. (fruit, toast, bacon, milk and coffee); lunch (soup and salad) with his family; afternoon swim in the White House pool; then the long pull to 7 p.m. and the family dinner (steak and baked potatoes, if possible).

¶ Bedtime: 9 p.m.

HERE'S WHY: Baptist Harry Truman was all set to receive an honorary LL.D. degree from Baptist Baylor University, of Waco, Tex. But from the Texas Baptist General Convention in Fort Worth last week came 4,500 "nays." Said the chairman of the convention's Civic Righteousness Committee: "No Baptist school should confer a degree on a man who likes his poker and drinks his bourbon. I know that we all agree that no man—even the President of the United States —could be a good Baptist and drink his liquor."

But Baylor bethought itself, decided to give Harry Truman his degree anyhow.

DEC. 24 **MAN OF THE PEOPLE:** Although many a Congressman, laborite and editorial writer glowered balefully at him, Harry Truman's popularity with the U.S. public continued at a serene high. In a recent FORTUNE survey, 75.6% thought he was doing a good-to-excellent job on foreign policy; 58.9% liked his homework; 64.7% felt he knew how to handle Congress.

DEC. 31 **A POLICY IS BORN:** On the White House lawn, blanketed by the heaviest Washington snowfall in years, Harry Truman frolicked without topcoat, gleefully tossing snowballs. Then, back in his office, he tossed a snowball with a rock in it at General Motors and U.S. industry in general.

At the Labor Department, the heads of General Motors and the striking United Automobile Workers sat facing each other across a horseshoe-shaped table. The union's Walter Reuther insisted on a 30% raise unless "shown the arithmetic" to prove that such a raise would force higher auto prices. The company refused to lay the figures on the table.

Into the room hurtled the President's missile, wrapped in a mimeographed statement: "In appointing a fact-finding board in an industrial dispute where one of the questions at issue is wages, it is essential to a fulfillment of its duty that the board have the authority, whenever it deems it necessary, to examine the books of the employer in order to determine the ability of the employer to pay. In view of the public interest involved, it would be highly unfortunate if any party to a dispute should refuse to cooperate with a fact-finding board."

The President did not say that wages should be based entirely on ability to pay this was just one of the "relevant facts." But the doctrine of ability to pay might strengthen the union's demand for higher wages from General Motors. It might be used by unions to justify demands which would cut down the extra profits of efficient companies, might in turn be used by incompetent managements to justify substandard wages.

Whatever the President's pronouncement meant for the future, it had very definite results on the present. It undercut General Motors' contention that profits had nothing to do with the current wage negotiations. Hastily, General Motors decided to reopen negotiations with the union.

The Administration

The last domestic political fracas to engage President Roosevelt came three months before his death—just after he had started his fourth term in office. In the election year of 1944, he had rejected his previous running mate, Henry Wallace, whose advanced social and economic ideas had begun to make him a political liability, and had chosen instead Senator Truman to be Vice-Presidential candidate. Now President Roosevelt had to find something for Wallace to do.

PAYING THE DEBT: For weeks the rumors had raced: Jesse JAN. 29 Jones was going to get the ax. Last week he got it.

President Roosevelt has rarely fired anybody, but he swept aging Jesse Jones out as head of the Commerce Department, the RFC, and RFC's eight potent subsidiaries. The reason was purely political and Mr. Roosevelt made no bones about it. It was to give a job to lame-duck Vice President Henry Wallace.

Jesse Jones bowed out—since there was nothing else he could do—but not without having his say:

"I have had satisfaction in my Government service because I have had the confidence of the Congress, as well as your own. I have had that confidence because I have been faithful to the responsibilities that have been entrusted to me. For you to turn over all these assets and responsibilities to a man inexperienced in business and finance will, I believe, be hard for the business and financial world to understand."

The firing of Jesse Jones culminated the biggest undercover political battle which Washington has seen in many a year. From the very day of election, Franklin Roosevelt's biggest political debt was to Henry Wallace and the C.I.O.'s Political Action Committee, whose hero he is. Wallace could have what he wanted; what he wanted was Commerce and the lending agencies, with their titanic power in the U.S. economy. His party leader paid off.

FEB. 5 **THE FIGHT AGAINST WALLACE:** White-thatched Jesse Jones, the aging ex-Secretary of Commerce, stomped into the marble-walled Senate Caucus Room one day last week. Jesse was there, ostensibly, to testify on a bill to divorce the behemoth Reconstruction Finance Corp. from the Department of Commerce. But he, and everyone else, knew his prime purpose: it was to prove that Henry Wallace was not the man to handle the U.S. money. Jesse got to the point quickly:

"Certainly the RFC should not be placed under the supervision of any man willing to jeopardize the country's future with untried ideas and idealistic schemes. It is bigger than General Motors and General Electric and Montgomery Ward and everything else put together, and you don't hear much about it because it is being run by businessmen, by men who haven't any ideas about remaking the world."

Jesse Jones had painted Henry Wallace as many U.S. citizens still see him—a sincere but somewhat aimless dreamer who

Henry Wallace, fighting for a job,   *Jesse Jones, fired from the Cabinet,*
denies he is a "starry-eyed liberal."   *warns against idealistic dreamers.*

might be all right as an amiable philosopher but who should
be kept at least a mile away from a balance sheet.

Next day it was Henry Wallace's turn. He, too, got quickly
to what he believed to be the point:

"There are some who have suggested that this separation
of the lending functions from the Commerce Department is
desirable because of my alleged 'lack of experience.' This
talk does not fool me or the American public. It is not a question of my lack of experience. Rather it is a case of not liking
the experience I have."

Wallace then pointed out that "the real issue is whether or
not the powers of the RFC are to be used only to help big
business or whether these powers are also to be used to help
little business and to help carry out the President's commit-
ment of 60,000,000 jobs."

Thereupon, Henry Wallace launched into as clear, bristling
and forthright a political speech as he has ever made. He
talked of implementing the President's "Economic Bill of
Rights": of more jobs and more foreign trade, of increased
postwar production, of high wages and a guaranteed annual
wage, of safeguarding free enterprise for private industry, of
more houses and better roads, of public works and more
TVAs, of health insurance and expanded social security and
more education. All this he promised—and a reduction in

taxes and the national debt, too. It was a breathtaking vision, and the clear implication was that the huge lending powers of RFC could help to bring it all about.

FEB. 12 **VICTORY FOR WHOM?:** Henry Wallace, battling for a place in the Fourth Term sun, began his week with a speech in Manhattan. To a nationwide radio audience, Wallace lashed out at his opponents: "They are not fighting a starry-eyed liberal or mystic. They are fighting you, and millions like you to the third and fourth generations."

The Wallacemen now realized that they could never get Henry confirmed as a full successor to Jesse Jones, *i.e.,* both as Commerce Secretary and as dispenser of RFC's billions. They adopted a new tack: first pass Senator Walter George's "bill of divorcement" dividing the two jobs, then get Henry in as Commerce Secretary only.

In the end, this compromise proved so adroit that both sides could, and did, claim a victory. The Wallace opponents had blocked his way into the biggest lending agency on earth. But Henry Wallace, at 56, had won the hope of an effective sounding board within the Government.

MAY 28 **TVA'S TRIUMPH:** For decades the 42,000 square miles of the Valley of the Tennessee were ill-faring land. Floods devastated the lowlands and rains eroded the deforested hills. There was little industry. The malaria-ridden people were as impoverished as the soil. Like Aesop's fabled dog in the manger, Tennessee's paunchy, vituperative Senator Kenneth McKellar championed the land and the people; he wanted no improvements without patronage. When the vast experimental Tennessee Valley Authority was created in 1933 he set out to force the spoils system upon it.

He failed. Year after year TVA shunned politics, awarded jobs on a merit basis. Shaking with rage, Kenneth McKellar time & again rose in the Senate to denounce quiet, smooth-faced TVA Chairman David Eli Lilienthal, 45. This spring many a Washington politico believed that the 76-year-old spoilsman had TVA squarely in his sights at last. His enemy, David Lilienthal, faced reappointment for a nine-year term, and McKellar's influence in the Senate and the South could not be lightly considered by a fledgling President.

But time had worked for TVA. In twelve years it had become one of the wonders of the New World, and a pride of the South. And as the dams rose in the Tennessee Valley, the reputation of Dave Lilienthal rose with them. He fought attacks by power interests and partisan politicians; he ignored the advice of quacking liberals. TVA encouraged communities to form their own power districts. It never used its authority in attempts to compel acceptance.

This spring found the Tennessee Valley greener and richer than ever before. The river, which had once run brown with precious topsoil, was as clear as in Indian days—21 dams had harnessed and controlled the floods. TVA's electricity made aluminum for war, lighted houses and ran machinery for thousands who had read by coal-oil lamps. Since TVA's inception, incomes in the valley had risen 73%.

The South found this new possession too precious to be risked for the satisfaction of one man's anger. As McKellar moved in for the kill, his friends and his political supporters deserted him or stood in silence. Then President Truman reappointed Dave Lilienthal.

Last week, in one last flow of thin and bitter accusation, McKellar admitted defeat. The words were read by his fellow Senator from Tennessee, Tom Stewart: "Mr. Lilienthal is not entitled to credit for good work. He is personally and politically obnoxious, offensive and objectionable. We have therefore concluded simply to vote against his confirmation." That was the end of McKellar's opposition. This week, Dave Lilienthal's appointment was confirmed by the Senate.

SHAKE-UP: President Truman set out last week to mold his own administration and streamline Washington bureaucracy once & for all. Within 48 hours, he made three cabinet changes and asked Congress for permanent authority to untangle overlapping bureaus and agencies. JUNE 4

He rid himself of the three weakest members of the existing cabinet: Secretary of Agriculture Claude Wickard, Attorney General Francis Biddle, and Secretary of Labor Madam Frances Perkins. Into their places moved New Mexico's Congressman Clinton P. Anderson, 49; Texas' Tom Clark, 45; and Washington's onetime Senator Lewis B. Schwellenbach, 50. In one sweep, Harry Truman thus lowered the average age of cabinet members from 59 to 54; gave the cabinet a total of five members from west of the Mississippi; and put into important Government positions three double-dyed Democrats whose personal loyalty to him was unquestioned.

Of the new appointees, Clinton Presba Anderson had been most recently in the news. As chairman of a special House food investigating committee, he had roared about the country, blasting the ineptitude and red tape which had given the U.S. its greatest food shortage.

Next day he was summoned to lunch at the White House. Clint Anderson, who has sat in many a stud poker hand with Harry Truman, expected a friendly dressing down for going too far. Instead, the President said: "Clint, how would you like to be Secretary of Agriculture?" Said Anderson, later: "I almost swallowed my grapefruit."

The new Attorney General, Thomas Campbell Clark, came to Washington in 1937 with the blessing of Texas' Senator Tom Connally. He has a collection of 50 bow ties, an authentic cowboy Stetson, a broad grin, and a soft Southern drawl. [Tom Clark would later sit on the U.S. Supreme Court from 1949 to 1967.]

JULY 2 **NOBODY WANTS TO BE COP:** Herbert Hoover, who has had more experience than most men in feeding the hungry, spoke out again last week on the nation's food plight. The meat black market, said he, has taken over an astoundingly large part of the business of supplying civilians. It is now, he added, "an economic force that cannot be caught by a policeman."

Then he submitted a plan to solve the muddle. World War I Food Administrator Hoover recommended taking the price cop (OPA) off the beat, letting livestock growers, packers and retailers set up committees to police their own ceilings.

The Hoover plan put more heat under the U.S. public's rising temper over shortages. House Republicans, joined by about a dozen Democrats, squeezed through a "Hoover amendment" which would have sheared OPA of almost all its powers over food, handed them all to the Secretary of Agriculture.

One Congressman who argued strongly against the "Hoover amendment" was New Mexico's Clinton Anderson, who becomes Secretary of Agriculture and War Food Administrator next week. Said he: "I would not run from any responsibility, but I don't want to be a policeman."

Neither did anybody else. It was clear by now that the meat situation had got far beyond policing of markets, that apparently the only solution to black marketeering is a much larger supply of meat. Clint Anderson thought that by late fall there would be a sufficient, but not bountiful, supply of beef for civilians. Plentiful pork was at least a year away.

UNDERSTUDY: For the second time in nine months, the AUG. 27 State Department got a house cleaning. Secretary Stettinius had brought a whole new team with him last December. Now new Secretary Byrnes began to fire & hire.

The new Under Secretary, and Jimmy Byrnes' key man, was Dean Gooderham Acheson, 52, who had resigned as an Assistant Secretary just three days before. He had quit because he found it hard to live the life of a diplomat on $9,000 a year, was persuaded to come back to higher responsibilities —at just $1,000 a year more.

The son of an Episcopal Bishop of Connecticut, Acheson went to Groton and Yale (1915), was an ensign in World War I, took his law degree at Harvard. An honor graduate, he was snapped up by the late, great Supreme Court Justice Louis D. Brandeis as secretary, soon went on to a potent Washington law firm. A tall, tweedy, reserved man with a magnificently well-kept mustache, Dean Acheson looks like the average man's idea of the typical diplomat, elegant without being stuffy.

THE FIRST BIG TEST: After World War I, in the mirrored SEPT. 17 halls of Versailles, the world's statesmen, big & little, gathered to write what Woodrow Wilson hoped would be "open covenants openly arrived at." In the end, the covenants were not openly arrived at, and did not last.

This week, in London's century-old, bomb-scarred Lancaster House, the foreign ministers of the world's five great powers meet to begin writing the peace terms of World War II. To London with Secretary of State Jimmy Byrnes went his wife, Maude; his closest adviser, Benjamin V. Cohen, the middle-aged wonder boy of the New Deal; and a retinue of specialists. Another member of the party was Manhattan Lawyer John Foster Dulles, the most eminent Republican foreign-affairs expert.

There were some who still felt a little anxious about the U.S. being represented—and among all those experienced foreigners—by such a comparative neophyte. But Jimmy Byrnes had two great assets: 1) he was not only at Yalta, the key conference of World War II; he was there with pad & pencil in hand. His shorthand notes are still the best record— in the U.S., at least—of what went on at the Czar's Palace in the Crimea; and 2) in Jimmy Byrnes' favor is his thorough knowledge of the workings of the U.S. Government. He is one of the few men in history who has held high office in all its three branches. He has successively been Congressman (14 years), Senator (10 years), Supreme Court Justice (16 months), Economic Stabilizer (8 months), and War Mobilizer (22 months).

Byrnes is a thoroughgoing Irish extrovert. Common sense is his guide; compromise is his method. He has never made any money; his wants are few (he once described them as "two tailor-made suits a year, three meals a day, and a reasonable amount of good liquor"). He is without airs, without bluff, and without any talent or taste for high society. But he has a courtly, Southern manner, and intense ambition.

The Congress

JAN. 15   **THE 79TH SITS:** When it met for the first time last week, the Senate made its transition from old to new in less than an hour. It remained for newly elected Cowboy Glenn Taylor, the pride of Idaho, to supply the inevitable comic relief. Gathered with his wife & children on the Capitol steps, the wide-open Senator, banjo in hand, wailed his lament. Sample verse:

> *Oh, give me a home near the Capitol dome,*
> *With a yard where little children can play;*
> *Just one room or two, any old thing will do,*
> *Oh, we can't find a pla-ace to stay.*

A posse of Washington landlords offered to accommodate the Senator. (They were probably not aware that his family also owns a saxophone, clarinet, guitar, trombone and piano because they "like to sit around after supper and have a jam session.")

TO THE WORLD: On the floor of the U.S. Senate last week, APRIL 30 Texas' shaggy-maned Tom Connally, chairman of the Foreign Relations Committee, rose to speak. He was about to leave for the World Security conference at San Francisco. With Southern emotion, Tom Connally assured his fellow Senators that he and his seven colleagues on the U.S. delegation would do their utmost to bring back a document which would help preserve peace after World War II.

"We shall not be able perhaps to secure all that we desire," Tom Connally said. "We shall not be able to bring back perfection." Moved by the solemnity of the occasion and of his own words, Tom Connally sat down in tears.

Up rose Michigan's erect and greying Arthur Vandenberg, the Senate's other San Francisco delegate, who added: "I have no illusions that the San Francisco conference can chart the millennium. Please do not expect it of us. But I have faith that we may perfect this charter of peace and justice so that reasonable men of good will shall find in it so much good and so much emancipation for human hopes that all lesser doubts and disagreements may be resolved in its favor."

The Senators rose in a body and cheered him, as they had Tom Connally. They crossed the aisles and put their arms around the broad shoulders of the two delegates, wishing them well.

Now that Senator Vandenberg has become a world figure, the Vandenbergs' social life in Washington has changed radically. Invitations have come to them by the tens and twenties, and they have duly made the rounds of the embassies and the teas. Getting ready for San Francisco, Senator Vandenberg followed diplomatic custom and bought himself a black Homburg.

NEGATIVE TEST: Before the end of the Potsdam meeting, JULY 23 Harry Truman hoped to be able to tell Stalin and Churchill: the U.S. has kept faith, here is the signed pledge of our participation in world affairs. Last week the World Charter setting up the United Nations passed its first Senate examination—by the Foreign Relations Committee.

Carefully and objectively, white-suited Chairman Tom Connally and Senator Arthur Vandenberg explained the Charter would not abridge U.S. sovereignty; it would not impose some postwar schemes of disarmament upon the U.S. without U.S. approval; it would not, by itself, take away from Congress the right to declare war.

The hearings set off some fireworks but mostly from some dozen witnesses who saw international bogeymen lurking under the Charter bed.

The noisiest: Mrs. Agnes Waters ("National Blue Star Mothers of America"). Her line: the Charter would "set up a world government for the Soviets, make of this nation a feeding trough for the have-nots."

Among the other opponents:

¶ Buxom Mrs. Helen Virginia Somers, whose theory was that the Charter implements a plot to make the Duke of Windsor "king of the world." Qualified Mrs. Somers: "I know whereof I speak; I'm no crackpot."

¶ To Mrs. Grace Keefe ("Women's League for Political Education"), a mother of nine, the Charter was "an instrument insuring our perpetual involvement in all future wars."

¶ Snapped Mrs. Elsie F. Johnson: "This country is in the grip of a gigantic conspiracy."

After five days Chairman Connally called a halt on the hearings, called for a vote. Result: 21 to 1 for approval. California's Senator Hiram Johnson was the lone dissenter.

JULY 30 **OUT OF THE WOODS:** Congress last week approved the Bretton Woods monetary agreement. Thus was completed (except for President Truman's signature) the first long U.S. step toward participating in international agreements resulting from World War II.

Congress was clearly in step with the nation's march toward world cooperation. Even Ohio's Republican Senator Robert Alphonso Taft, who led a diehard fight against Senate approval, admitted that the country was now internationalist (but he termed it "pathological internationally").

Senator Taft fought vigorously and well for most of four

days. In the clinches he pulled several clichés ("we will just pour $6 billion down a rat hole"). But his infighting was good: he had carefully studied the involved Bretton Woods proposals, which many a Senator obviously had not. At times, Senator Taft had Administration proponents stuck on fine points of the agreement's $8.8 billion monetary fund and $9.1 billion international bank structures.

Then, one by one, the Senate majority crushed amendments that would have crippled or lessened U.S. participation. On the final vote, the count was 61 to 16 for approval. Next day the House, which had previously passed the bill by 345 to 18, roared its unanimous approval of the minor technical changes the Senate had made.

President Truman had what he wanted: an example of U.S. faith in world cooperation. The U.S. was the first of the 44 signing nations to approve the Bretton Woods pact.

"MY DEAR DAGO": Mississippi's Senator Theodore ("The AUG. 6 Man") Bilbo was off again. He had received many letters protesting his intemperate filibuster against the Fair Employment Practices Committee. Now he sat down to answer his mail.

To Miss Josephine Piccolo, a Brooklyn textile inspector, he wrote: "My dear Dago: (If I am mistaken in this please correct me.) Will you please keep your dirty proboscis out of the other 47 states, especially the dear old State of Mississippi?" He was really wound up when he replied to Leonard E. Golditch of New York, secretary of the National Committee to Combat Anti-Semitism. Cried "The Man": "If Jews of your type don't quit sponsoring and fraternizing with the negro race you are going to arouse so much opposition to all of you that they will get a very strong invitation to pack up and resettle in Palestine. There are just a few of you New York Jew 'kikes' socializing with the negroes for selfish and political reasons. You had better stop and think."

Said the New Orleans *Item:* "Truly there is no worse influence in high life than Senator Bilbo. He is a disgrace to Mississippi and to the nation."

"I OBJECT!": However history may judge him, Hiram Warren AUG. 13 Johnson was always in character. He was the last of the great isolationists. He was the "Billiken with a Bellyache," fighting as often for progress and reforms as for "the good old days." No person, cause or party ever fully controlled him. This obstinate independence cost him the Presidency of the U.S.

California remembers him best as one of its great reform governors. To win that office (in 1910) he smashed the grip which the Southern Pacific Railroad had long held on California politics. After his victory, his father, the railroad's attorney, refused to speak to him for ten years. Hi Johnson, the rebel, went on to establish workmen's compensation, woman suffrage, the initiative, referendum and recall.

In 1916 he won his U.S. Senate seat, but let California—and the Presidency—slip from Charles Evans Hughes to Woodrow Wilson, because the G.O.P. candidate had snubbed him in the campaign. Wilson found him no friend. Hiram harangued the Senate until U.S. adherence to the League of Nations was dead. In 1920, Johnson stubbornly ignored G.O.P. demands that he be Harding's running mate, later sulked when Coolidge succeeded to the White House. Unpredictable as ever, he supported Herbert Hoover in 1928, turned against him for Franklin Roosevelt in 1932, turned against Roosevelt in 1940 on the World Court fight and the Third Term. Four days after Pearl Harbor, when the bill authorizing the President to send troops overseas was up for debate, he pushed himself feebly to his feet on the Senate floor to croak: "I object."

Since that day, Hi Johnson, tired, sick and sore, had spent more of his time in his office or in hospitals, dreaming of the Presidency he never won. This week, as it must to all men, Death came in the 79th year to the California dissenter, one of the great independents of U.S. politics.

OCT. 8 **THE $200,000 DEAL:** The story of how Franklin Delano Roosevelt helped his son Elliott get a $200,000 loan, and then arranged for it to be settled at 2¢ on the dollar, was presented to Congress this week.

The testimony came out through a House Ways & Means Committee inquiry into a tax question: should the lender, John A. Hartford, president of the Great Atlantic & Pacific Tea Co., be permitted a $196,000 income-tax deduction for his loss on the loan? By a strict Democratic majority, the committee voted not to challenge the deduction.

Hartford had told how Elliott Roosevelt, struggling to finance his Texas State Network, Inc., a radio chain, came to him in 1939 and wanted to borrow the $200,000. He testified that Elliott came at the President's suggestion. To prove it to Hartford, Elliott got the President on the telephone. Testified Hartford: "I said 'Hello, Mr. President,' and I heard a familiar voice, a voice I had heard over the radio many times, say 'Hello, John'; and I told him that Elliott was in my apartment, and asked him what did he think about this $200,000 loan Elliott wanted to make in connection with the radio business, and the President said that he was entirely familiar with it, that it looked good and gave assurance to me that it was a sound business proposition and a fine thing. He said he would appreciate anything I could do for him.

"After the President was so enthusiastic about it, I felt that I was on the spot and I had to make a decision right then and there, and I did not want to do anything to incur the enmity of the President."

Three years later, when Elliott was off at war and wanted to settle up his tangled financial affairs at home, President Roosevelt got into the deal again, according to a Republican account, and sent the stalwart Texan Democrat, Jesse Jones, to settle the loan, on which no payments, either of interest or principal, had been made. Jones gave Hartford $4,000 and got back the Texas State Network stock that had been security for the loan.

The record, according to the Republican minority, showed that the loan was made at a time when Congress was considering a chain-store tax that would cost A. & P. $6,625,000 annually. And it was settled by Jesse Jones at a time when the ailing Texas State Network was beginning to flourish, with signs that the stock might some day be worth the full $200,000. As it turned out, the radio chain is now a prosperous company, with Elliott's ex-wife, Texas-bred Mrs. Ruth Googins Roosevelt Eidson, as its president. She and their children got all of his stock.

Elliott, an ex-brigadier general without a job, living in a friend's house in Beverly Hills with wife Faye Emerson, was preparing last week for a new venture—probably in radio again. He told a reporter: "If I fathered a flop in the Texas Network I would like to have another one like it right now."

NOV. 12 **FOR 1946:** The deepest surgery ever practiced on U.S. taxes—the slicing off of $5.9 billion—was completed without fuss or flowers. The taxpayer, though assured the operation had been a success, felt hardly better at all.

For businessmen, the 1946 tax cuts will provide $3,136,000,-000 of relief by eliminating all excess-profits taxes, by reducing corporation income-tax rates by 2 to 4%. But out of every dollar of profit over $50,000, business concerns will still pay the Government 38¢.

For individuals, the new bill eliminates all income taxes for 12,000,000 citizens who have been paying small amounts. It reduces total individual income-tax payments by $2,644,000,-000. But the 36,000,000 citizens who will still pay taxes will still pay vastly more than before the war. The 1946 scale, computed on net income after deductions:

Net Income	Single Person	Married Man, Two Children
$ 2,000	$ 285	none
3,000	484	$ 190
4,000	693	380
5,000	921	589
6,000	1,168	798
8,000	1,719	1,292
10,000	2,346	1,862
15,000	4,270	3,638
20,000	6,645	5,890
50,000	25,137	24,111

Wartime Living

JAN. 1 **THE PENALTIES:** Nazi tanks, crunching west through the mud and sleet of Luxembourg and Belgium last week [in the Battle of the Bulge; see page 88], gave the U.S. two separate setbacks: one on the Western front, one on the home front. For with the news of the German breakthrough, many U.S. preoccupations—even Christmas—seemed like luxuries. It was no time to scramble into a peacetime job, or to talk about manufacturing refrigerators.

Last week's communiqués were a resounding vindication

of those who had been denouncing over-optimism for three long years. With the bad war news justifying every move, Washington went to work fast and hard on civilians:

¶ War Mobilization Boss Jimmy Byrnes suddenly ordered all horse and dog tracks to shut up tight by January 3 and remain shut "until war conditions permit."

¶ The Office of Price Administration planned to ration most of the foods which had become point-free earlier this year: meat, canned vegetables, fats.

¶ OPA also warned that a revised shoe-rationing system is coming up, since there is not enough leather to let everyone have two new pairs of shoes in 1945.

¶ The War Production Board slashed the production of passenger car tires for the first quarter of 1945 by 1,650,000; informed ordinary drivers that they could: 1) try to find recaps next year or 2) get off the roads.

WARNING: Air raid wardens from Maine to Miami woke up. JAN. 22
Inactive for many months, they now had the word of burly Admiral Jonas H. Ingram, Commander in Chief of the Atlantic Fleet, that robomb attacks on the East Coast, similar to the V-bomb attacks on England, were not only "possible but probable" within the next month or two. Said Jonas Ingram:

"The next alert you get is likely to be the McCoy. It might knock out a high building or two. It might create a fire hazard. It would certainly cause casualties. It could not seriously affect the progress of the war. But think what it would mean to Dr. Goebbels."

Where could the robombs come from? Admiral Ingram replied: from submarine, long-range plane or surface ship.

COLD FACTS: To Middle Western cities which have gone FEB. 12
through the war in a nighttime blaze of neon lights, the brownout that went on last week was a shock. In Chicago, the usually bustling Loop was deserted. In Detroit, late shopping housewives complained that they could not find stores.

But no one had to be told why the lights had to go out: as civilians shivered in the coldest, snowiest, blowiest winter in years, the U.S. was smack up against a first-rate crisis in fuel. Blizzards and a manpower shortage had snarled up the overloaded railroads and disrupted fuel deliveries. And in a wide belt from Ohio to New England, many schools were closed and offices went on shortened weeks.

Householders in Columbus, Ohio were told to cut down on their baths, flush their toilets only once a day per person so that the huge Curtiss-Wright plant would have enough water. Reason: the severe cold had kept snow from melting normally, lowered water in reservoirs. Fuel oil was so near exhaustion in Manhattan that the Navy released 400,000 barrels to help tide civilians over. The Army chipped in with 5,000 tons of coal.

FEB. 26 **THEY THINK OF THE MOMENT:** How are the wives and sweethearts of U.S. servicemen meeting the cruel test of war? To touch more widely a story that can never be fully told, TIME correspondents in 30 U.S. cities surveyed their communities to see how U.S. women are living away from their men.

The results are generally reassuring. American women by & large are O.K. There has been no great moral collapse. There are some infidelities—on all levels of society. But mostly they are the tawdry cases of the Victory Girls—many of whom seem to have married.

U.S. women have changed. Hardly a woman under 40 has not seen new sections of America while visiting a husband, sweetheart or brother. They are more self-reliant. New work in factories and more work at home has given them new responsibilities, and they have met them.

But above all, U.S. women are lonely. Some hide it behind cheerfulness or a bright, hard face, but the loneliness is there. The women want their men to come home. With a unanimity which would startle oldtime feminists, they want to quit their jobs, settle down and have children. Three years of war, much of it spent in furnished rooms or with in-laws or in trailers or small hotels, has put a lonely light around the little white cottage.

In Atlanta, a young war wife, mother of a two-year-old daughter, said:

"I work half a day in a bank, while my in-laws take care of my daughter. Herb's letters are full of our little girl: 'How is she? Has she stopped wetting the bed? Does she talk about me?' I have to fill my letters with fake stories about her. I'm just living until the day Herb comes back. We used to gripe about our house: the roof leaked, we needed new screens, and all that. Well, just give me any old house now. Anything, anything."

In Boston, Mrs. William Walter Phelps Jr. laughed wryly at a letter and a picture from Captain Phelps. Like many another service wife, Mrs. Phelps doesn't know her husband well. She met him when her brother brought him home from Fort Monmouth. In his 30 months' absence, Mrs. Phelps' conception of her tall (6 ft. 3 1/2 in.) and handsome husband grew. The sweater she was knitting grew in proportion. When she got the picture of him, she saw what she had done: the sweater came halfway to his knees.

A MATTER OF CONSCIENCE: There was nothing so terrifying MARCH 5 about the newest pill: Jimmy Byrnes' midnight curfew on bars, nightclubs, theaters and other places of entertainment. In most U.S. cities bars close by 1 a.m. and most U.S. citizens go to bed betimes, anyhow. But many a U.S. citizen asked suspiciously which home-front ailment the curfew was designed to cure.

To thousands the official explanation—that the curfew was designed to save coal, manpower and transportation—was simply bunk. Mumbled a Chicago barfly: "Turn off the furnace and let us drink in our overcoats."

The only ordinary citizens who would really be inconvenienced were swing-shift workers. Many of them thought their lives were uncomfortable enough anyhow; there is something chronically annoying about working from 4 in the afternoon until midnight. Swing-shifters go after recreation in the small hours of the night, and in war-boom cities, dancehalls, bowling alleys, cinemas and skating rinks have swing-shift hour periods. Last week a Los Angeles aircraft local of the United Automobile Workers protested to Byrnes: "We seriously feel this order will retard production rather than speed it."

A Detroit bartender gave the new rule a name. "First we had the race tracks closed," he said. "Then we had the brownout and now we've got the Byrne-Out."

"FATHER, DEAR FATHER": While the nation grumbled rue- MARCH 12 fully at the midnight curfew, Judge Joseph E. Mayer of Des

Moines raised his voice in enthusiastic approval. The curfew, said the judge, was sure to cut down juvenile delinquency. Reason: parents will get home earlier.

MARCH 26 **NO STOPPING:** The Navy did not say who she was but it thought her letter typical of several received recently, and therefore made it public. Somewhere in the U.S. an American woman had written:

"Please, for God's sake, stop sending our finest youth to be murdered on places like Iwo Jima. It is too much for boys to stand. It is driving some mothers crazy. Why can't objectives be accomplished some other way? It is most inhuman and awful—stop, stop!"

Gravely and seriously, Navy Secretary James Vincent Forrestal, who had seen the first awful days of Iwo himself, sat down to reply:

"On Dec. 7, 1941, the Axis confronted us with a simple choice: fight or be overrun. There was then, and is now, no other possibility. Having chosen to fight, we have no final means of winning battles except through the valor of the Marine or Army soldier who, with rifle and grenades, storms enemy positions, takes them and holds them. There is no short cut or easy way. I wish there were."

Last week the nation learned just how many Marine soldiers, carrying rifles and grenades, had paid the price to take Iwo Jima: 4,189 dead, 441 missing, 15,308 wounded. This was higher than the number of Union casualties in any of the bloody battles of the Civil War except Gettysburg.

MAY 14 **"THANK GOD. . . .":** By noon on Monday almost every man, woman and child in the U.S. was sure the war in Europe was over. In Des Moines a housewife telephoned a newspaper: "Shall I go ahead and bake a pie for tomorrow?"

In Manhattan, the most effervescent U.S. city, the carnival sights and sounds bubbled spontaneously, then subsided, then fizzed again. For a while on Monday, torn paper and ticker tape by the ton fluttered from skyscrapers, and the streets turned white. Half a million people clotted Times Square, sober and undemonstrative, waiting for somebody to start the fun. Nobody did.

In New York harbor a police launch sped to investigate a

rumor that had swept through the Wall Street crowds: a German submarine had surfaced, flying a white flag. What the harbor police found: a Navy vessel, with the sailors' Monday wash out to dry. In Atlanta there were more people in the churches than at the Atlanta *v.* Little Rock ball game.

Tuesday was different. The country was at the radio. In Manhattan, as if someone had pulled a giant lever, the windows went up and paper tumbled in torrents, soon after the President's first words announcing Germany's official surrender were heard. For minutes, a diapason of booming whistles from the grey ships in the North River seemed to drown out everything. Then, as if they might burst unless they let it off, people began to shout.

But the undertone was sober and reflective. The churches were crowded early. Across the country the scene varied, but the theme was the same: "Thank God."

59% SOMBER: Into last week's chorus of heady news from Europe and hopeful words from San Francisco came a thin, somber note from U.S. public opinion. It came from a cross-section of adult civilians buttonholed by the University of Denver's National Opinion Research Center. The poll question: do you expect the U.S. to get in another war within the next 25 years?

Replied 36 of every 100 asked: yes. Another 23% thought there would be another war within 50 years. Only 20% felt in their bones that World War II was the last.

A WOMAN'S CHOICE: For four days Mrs. Helen Zuhars Goad MAY 21
MacDowell pondered a question that few women have ever had to decide: which of her two husbands did she want most?

Her dilemma stemmed from the fact that the Japanese had held her first husband, Army Air Forces Lieut. Harold Goad, a prisoner without notifying the U.S. He had been listed as missing in action for a year after his bomber exploded over Burma. Last fall, the War Department officially pronounced him dead, and two months later Mrs. Goad was married to Ensign Robert A. MacDowell, U.S.N.R. Then, a fortnight ago, she got numbing news—her first husband had been found alive and well in a Rangoon hospital.

Immediately she cabled: "Darling, I am so glad you are

Mrs. Helen Goad MacDowell must choose between two husbands: Ensign MacDowell (right) and Lieut. Goad, who is back from the dead.

alive; will see you soon. I love you with all my heart." But naturally she loved her second husband too. Since she had married him innocently, the law posed no problem—she was left to make her own choice. Last week she decided.

"My marriage to Mac was wonderful," she said, "but I know now that Harold is the one I love."

Said Lieut. Goad in Calcutta: "I am a lucky guy."

JUNE 25 **HAVE A CIGARET:** Most of the nation's smokers inhaled more easily last week. The cigaret shortage had definitely eased. In the East and South, druggists and tobacconists took the "Sorry" signs off their counters. In Miami, vending machines carried notices: "Yes, They're Back."

SEPT. 3 **THE LOVELY FUTURE:** The shape of things to come in the peacetime U.S. was still forming hazily, like ectoplasm at a spiritualists' meeting. But U.S. citizens, staring with a seance-sitter's skeptical fascination, began to nudge each other last week. Government and industry really seemed to be conjuring a facsimile of normal living.

After 43 months of drawing up blue laws for industry, the War Production Board giddily told startled U.S. manufacturers to make all the automobiles they wished. The same went for washing machines, ironers, pots & pans, electric razors, pottery, Kleenex, toys, radios, suits, dresses, storage batteries and photographic film. Few of these items would be available in any quantity before Christmas, but the words rolled on the tongue like bubble gum.

WANNA BUY A PIGEON?: Last week, Gimbels' Department SEPT. 24 Store announced a sale of Army DDT sprayers good for murdering anything from spiders to tsetse flies. From warehouses all over the U.S., $600,000,000 worth of war-hoarded Government goods were on their way to civilian stores.

The Army, Navy and other wartime purchasing agencies were brooding over at least $90 billion in leftovers. Included were 40,000 surplus homing pigeons (with little pigeons hatching every minute), thousands of dogs, mules and horses. The Surplus Property Board had actually sold a surplus chimpanzee, but it still had $50,000,000 worth of 60-inch searchlights, and ten million pounds of contraceptive jelly. Army-Navy boards in Rome and Paris were seeking purchasers for items as unrelated as kidney forceps and bangalore torpedoes. And who wanted a supply of Elizabeth Arden black face cream used by soldiers for night attacks?

VISTAS: Returning to peace, the U.S. was more like itself than NOV. 5 ever—in a world which would never again be remotely the same. Butter pats were served again in restaurants. Along the highways people were blowing out tires and bumping into each other again; the city traffic tieups were something awful. The fall's football games drew record crowds.

The great hit songs of the season were *Till the End of Time, On the Atchison, Topeka & the Santa Fe.* Best-selling novels were *The Black Rose* and *Forever Amber.* Young girls tried to look like Bacall with a dash of Hepburn.

A Navy doctor, soon to come home, wrote warning his wife rather sadly that he had gotten bald and heavy. She wrote back gently: "You will find that three years have done quite a bit to me, too."

HIGHWAY HARVEST: Alarmed by the amount of postwar DEC. 10 fender-bending, the National Safety Council released some grisly statistics:

October traffic deaths totaled 3,440, 53% more than for

the same month last year. The Council's advice to motorists: "Quit using worn-out automobiles as if you were on a *Kamikaze* mission."

DEC. 24 **HOUSING:** Every major U.S. city was jammed to its last trailer camp. More than a million families were doubling up; thousands of servicemen in search of a home were returning to the U.S. In Atlanta, 2,000 people answered an ad for a single apartment. In freezing Minneapolis, a man, his wife and baby spent seven nights in their automobile.

The housing muddle was no nearer a solution than it had been on V-J day. With Government controls removed, the bulk of available labor and materials was going into industrial building. Only 37,000 houses had even been started.

Last week President Truman asked Congress for price ceilings on both new and old houses, called for priorities which would channel 50% of U.S. building materials into the construction of houses costing $10,000 or less.

As winter deepened, the Senate voted unanimously to turn 75,000 units of war housing over to veterans and their families, remodel Government dormitories to house 11,000 more, find room for 14,000 in Army barracks. One thing was certain: the U.S. would be using makeshift housing for a long time. The country was short at least 4,660,000 dwellings, would have to build at top speed for ten years to catch up.

DEC. 31 **THIS SIDE OF PARADISE:** It would be the biggest, noisiest New Year's Eve in a long, long time. Manhattan's bars would stay open until dawn, U.S. roadhouses would be neon-lighted after dark years, and the stiff white shirt front would be back once more, a gleaming and irresistible target for females with an urge to write with lipstick.

Political Notes

MAY 7 **THE PEOPLE'S FRIEND:** After 28 years of protecting Jersey City from the consequences of low taxes, up-to-date schools, free speech, the C.I.O., and modern sewers, Mayor Frank Hague faced another election. With his old-fashioned starched collar tight above a chaste pearl stickpin, he went out to remind the people of his years of toil in their behalf. With revival-meeting fervor the Boss told his followers that he was still pure at heart: "Let them point to one blemish on my record as mayor of Jersey City!"

Liberation Candidate Paul E. Dougherty almost blew a gasket. Cried he: "On a salary of never more than $8,000 he can own a summer home worth $125,000, a home in Miami, an apartment, a hotel suite in New York! Perhaps the mayor does not consider it a blemish that children attend antiquated schools, that garbage disposal is 50 years behind the times."

Boss Hague disregarded such criticism for broader subjects less susceptible of factual proof. There was sin abroad. (Hague is against sin: he allows no prostitutes, burlesque shows or nightclubs in Jersey City.)

The mayor's claque applauded and sang. The mayor had a word for his Polish constituents: "I will stay in the fight until you get your relief, a free Poland with the same borders as before the war." To a meeting of Italians he pledged himself to do "everything possible to rebuild Italy."

But Boss Hague, whose registered voters have a way of remaining registered voters even after they are buried, spoke with a certain irritation about one trick perpetrated by his enemy Republican Governor Walter Edge: this year, for the first time, all Jersey City must use voting machines. [On election day, Jersey City would re-elect Boss Hague by a 3-to-1 majority.]

BRASS-KNUCKLE FIGHT: In New York City, for twelve years JUNE 25 and three elections, hen-shaped old Mayor Fiorello LaGuardia had ruled the political roost. He had been able to beat any & every combination of political bosses. Last month he had quipped: "I can run on a laundry ticket and beat these political bums any time." But the people had grown tired of his wham-handed whims, his snooping, his ranting. "The Hat" bowed out.

The minute he had, the bosses of all parties, sniffing the winds of power, put on brass-knuckle fights to pick their candidates. Democrats chose Brooklyn's District Attorney William O'Dwyer, onetime cop, hod carrier, onetime student for the priesthood, an ex-brigadier general, and the man who broke up Brooklyn's Murder, Inc.

Republican bosses, out of power so long that they could not find a dyed-in-the-wool GOPster, were confronted with a choice between two Democrats. They picked Judge Jonah J. Goldstein, one-time secretary to Al Smith.

AUG. 27 **JUST THE MAN:** California's Governor Earl Warren passed his magic wand over his political hat last week and surprised no one when he pulled out Joe Knowland's boy and named him U.S. Senator to succeed the late Hiram Johnson.

At 37, Major William Fife Knowland will be America's youngest Senator. Burly Earl Warren explained that Major Knowland, now with an Army historical section in Paris, was precisely the kind of man California's new Senator should be. The sharp-nosed Major was young, had been a G.I., had served six years in the state legislature, was married, had three children, had been a charity-drive organizer. Besides, the Major was a good Republican.

Most Californians smiled. Ever since the Major's father, Publisher Joseph Russell Knowland (Oakland *Tribune*), began backing Earl Warren more than a decade ago, it had been understood that if Earl became Governor, Joe's boy would get the next Senate vacancy.

SEPT. 24 **KENNEDY HITS THE TRAIL:** Joseph Patrick Kennedy, now 57 and with red hair greying, came out of self-imposed political exile last week and went back to work for his native state of Massachusetts.

At the behest of young, earnest Governor Maurice J. Tobin, Joe Kennedy had become chairman of a "special commission relative to establishing a state department of commerce." His job was to prepare legislation to rejuvenate Massachusetts' rapidly deteriorating industry.

Joe Kennedy had taken the job reluctantly. His last public service, as U.S. Ambassador to the Court of St. James's, had ended badly when he told newsmen that democracy was through in England. Then he had broken with his good friend Franklin Roosevelt and retired to write a book (still unfinished) to prove that he was right.

Joe Kennedy was not embittered; he is not a bitter man.

And he had had worse troubles: within two months last year, his eldest son, Joseph Jr., and his son-in-law, the Marquess of Hartington, had both been killed in action. He had tried to take his mind off his troubles; he had bought property in Manhattan and Albany, finally paid $17,000,000 for the Merchandise Mart in Chicago. Said Kennedy: "I thought I'd get a kick out of such trading, but I didn't."

But last week Joe Kennedy seemed to have his old zest again. In a midnight blue Chrysler, he rode like a Paul Revere through the textile, shoe and machinery-producing towns in Middlesex, Essex and Berkshire counties. In some 30 speeches he spread the alarm:

"I'm willing to come back to Massachusetts to live because this is where my heart is. But I don't expect to come back to stay until I think there has been a change for the better. During the next five years Massachusetts will have its last chance to keep itself out of the grave."

Cracked some critics: If Kennedy is so interested in the future of his state, why did he spend $17,000,000 for a building in Chicago? Joe Kennedy shot back, "Because the condition of real estate in Boston is scandalous and that of politics is worse."

HOW TO STEAL A SCENE: New York's mayorality campaign NOV. 12 was over before the election. The sure winner in the battle of personalities: 55-year-old, Erin-born Democratic and American Labor Party Candidate William O'Dwyer, who, like Tom Dewey, gained fame as a gang-busting district attorney.

But through it all, flashing the personality that had endeared him to New Yorkers even when they were weary of his clowning—fussy, dumpy, outgoing Mayor Fiorello H. LaGuardia never once lost the center spotlight he loves. On his Sunday radio program, the Mayor lectured New York housewives on the best way to cook a big turkey in a small oven: "The stern of the turkey, you know, the rear end—they call it the rudder here—is cut off about one inch."

On Friday night, following Governor Dewey's dignified, half-hour endorsement of Republican-Liberal-Fusion Candidate Jonah J. Goldstein, Fiorello LaGuardia had one of his most sparkling innings. "You know," he cackled, "we prepared the studio today to hear the Governor. We put tapes on the windows, we braced ourselves, we wore lead-glass goggles, ready for the atomic bomb. And all we heard was the snap of a wad of bubble gum."

As usual, Fiorello LaGuardia had enraged thousands of New Yorkers, tickled thousands, and fascinated thousands. But he had bored very few. Perhaps that was his secret, even more than his withering frankness and his relentless fight for honest government. Whatever it was, the people knew one thing for certain: after 12 years New York City was losing the best Mayor it had ever had.

William Knowland becomes a U.S. Senator, as planned. Page 59.   *New York's Mayor LaGuardia enrages and tickles many, bores few.*

NOV. 19 **THE BIG CITY VOTE:** Some 1,400 elections were held in the U.S. last week. The results in some half dozen mayoralty elections again demonstrated a prime fact of contemporary U.S. political life: Democrats, with the help of union labor, have a stranglehold on most of the big city vote.

In New York, Democrat Bill O'Dwyer ran up a record plurality (685,175) over Republican Jonah Goldstein, thus giving Governor Tom Dewey a kick in his political shins. In Boston, the ineffable James Michael Curley won out, even though he is under indictment for mail fraud. Pittsburgh was kept safely Democratic by the victory of short, greying David L. Lawrence. And Cleveland's colorless Democratic Mayor Thomas A. Burke was re-elected by a landslide.

Labor

In 1941, immediately after Pearl Harbor, President Roosevelt had secured a no-strike pledge from the nation's unions. With the exception of a coal miners' walkout and a threatened strike by railroad employes—both in 1943—the pledge was kept. Then, in 1945, as the war came to an end, labor unrest broke out across the country and nearly every major industry was plagued by strikes.

THE ARMY'S HERE AGAIN: In Chicago last week, Major General Joseph Wilson Byron politely stepped up to a Montgomery Ward & Co. receptionist, asked to see Ward's stubborn $100,000-a-year president Sewell Lee Avery. Over an inter-office phone, she conveyed General Byron's message. It was: the Army's here again. JAN. 8

A secretary led the General into Avery's paneled office. General Byron handed Avery President Roosevelt's order directing the U.S. Army to seize Ward's $302 million mail order and retail business for the second time in seven months. Franklin Roosèvelt also ordered Ward's to obey two War Labor Board directives: 1) to pay retroactive raises to 17% of Ward's 70,000 employes; 2) to sign a union contract guaranteeing maintenance of membership. Sputtered Sewell Avery, the New Deal's No. 1 industrial hairshirt: "Arbitrary. . . coercive. . . illegal."

Once again Sewell Avery refused to budge from his office. But this time, no one summoned G.I.s to carry Avery bodily out of his office, as they had in May 1944. General Byron left Avery at his desk, took for himself an adjoining office. For a day, while Signal Corps experts installed an Army switchboard, the General and his staff used a pay telephone down the hall.

Avery proudly told newsmen: "I am still running this place." But by week's end Avery had become an executive with no work to do. General Byron ran Montgomery Ward & Co.

AVERY'S "GREAT DAY": In Chicago, white-haired U.S. District Judge Philip Leo Sullivan turned from his lawbooks to FEB. 5

his dictionaries, solemnly pondered the meaning of two words—"production" and "distribution." Then, he handed the U.S. Government's labor policy a resounding judicial slap. President Roosevelt, he decided last week, had no power to seize the plants and facilities of Sewell Avery's Montgomery Ward & Co.

Unless reversed, the decision meant that under the War Labor Disputes Act the President may seize mines, plants or facilities only when they are equipped for the "manufacture, mining or production" of war-necessary materials. By Judge Sullivan's decision, the law does not cover businesses engaged solely in "distribution."

At the lush San Marcos Hotel in Chandler, Ariz., where he was resting, Avery called it "a great day for labor."

FEB. 19 **PETRILLO v. THE BOYS & GIRLS:** The boys & girls who study orchestra and composition each summer among the trees of the National Music Camp at Interlochen, Mich., pay no dues to the American Federation of Musicians. Hence they had every reason to expect trouble from A.F. of M.'s squat, owl-eyed Czar James Caesar Petrillo.

In July 1942 Petrillo ordered the cancellation of broadcasts by Interlochen's National High School Orchestra over the NBC chain. The boys & girls were displacing professional musicians, said Petrillo. Last week Little Caesar Petrillo tried to close up Interlochen altogether. He put it on the union's "unfair" list.

This meant that faculty members who teach there would forthwith be suspended from the union, could get no paying job anywhere in Petrillo's empire—which is the entire musical U.S.—until he lifted his ban.

Quick to defy Boss Petrillo was Dr. Joseph Edgar Maddy, president of the camp and professor of music at the University of Michigan. He said he would fight Petrillo in the courts, meanwhile would carry on the camp this summer with non-union teachers, if necessary. Musicians thought Dr. Maddy, member of the union himself for 35 years, a brave man. Among the great ones Petrillo has successfully defied is the President of the U.S., who was rebuffed by the czar last year when he publicly appealed to Little Caesar to lift his ban on making recordings.

A DIME FOR THE U.M.W.: The wind was warm enough last MARCH 12 week to melt the snow around the tipples of most of the nation's coal mines; there was a faint hint of spring in the air. Like a grey old bear ending his winter's hibernation, John Llewellyn Lewis lumbered from his den to negotiate with the nation's bituminous operators. Borrowing from Jimmy Petrillo's book (which provides that the union must receive a royalty on all phonograph records sold), he told the operators he wanted them to pay his union a royalty of 10¢ for every ton of soft coal mined in the U.S.

Three days before the negotiations began, Lewis filed formal notice of a labor dispute under the Smith-Connally Act —to which he referred as "that grotesque slave statute." [This act authorized the President to seize strike-bound plants and compelled unions to give 30 days' notice of a strike.] Thus he paved the way for a legal strike vote, and in so doing turned the act—passed by Congress in anger at the 1943 coal walkout—into a weapon for his own use.

Cried the Philadelphia *Record*, "John Lewis is brandishing a coal shovel over the heads of the American people again." But when he faced the operators and U.M.W. representatives in the ballroom of Washington's Shoreham Hotel last week, John Lewis spoke softly. With just the right note of threat and regret, he said he hoped that "the public and Government will not be inconvenienced through stoppage or loss of tonnage vital to our war program."

He discussed the royalty proposal with ironic innocence, as though he expected applause any minute from his squirming listeners. The royalty fund would enable the union to provide modern medical service, hospitalization, insurance, rehabilitation and—economic protection. Did not his listeners hope for the betterment, the protection, the comfort of their fellow men? He was certain that there could be no objection to this wholly charitable request.

The operators shuddered, went back to hotel rooms to plan a defense. After hurried scribbling they announced that Lewis' demands would add up to 65¢ a ton to the cost of coal. A union spokesman cried "80% wrong," and the soft coal battle was on. But John Lewis had the coal operators where he wanted them. The U.S. could not afford to lose one ton of desperately needed coal.

TROUBLE IN DETROIT: Industrial Detroit seethed with bitter squabbles. "Work stoppages" constantly interrupted production of direly needed war goods. Test drivers at the Chrysler tank arsenal threatened to strike because the proving grounds were dusty. When the company sprinkled them, the drivers threatened to strike because they were too wet.

Last week the ill feeling culminated in a grave work stoppage—a noisy, angry row which spread into the 13 Detroit war plants, sent over 35,000 Detroit workers into the streets. When the Chrysler Corp. fired eight gear cutters, 13,500 workers walked out. Production of tank transmissions, trucks, antiaircraft guns, engines for B-29 Superfortresses and rocket shells ground to a halt.

APRIL 9 **THIRTY-DAY TRUCE:** While big John Lewis and the soft coal operators jousted in a cloud of cigar smoke, the nation's soft coal miners went to the polls. They voted, under the Smith-Connally Act, on what John Lewis disdainfully called a trick question: "Do you wish to permit an interruption of war production in wartime as a result of this dispute?" Their answer: yes, 208,797; no, 25,158. John Lewis could now legally shut down the mines.

Then in stepped Secretary of Labor Frances Perkins as a mediator. In a new black grosgrain hat, a long black coat, a mink neckpiece and with a new sparkle in her eye, she appeared before the perspiring negotiators, suggested a compromise settlement. She almost got it. John Lewis accepted: the operators' spokesman, Charles O'Neill, balked.

After one session, photographers lined up Miss Perkins, O'Neill and Lewis, asked them to look pleasantly at one another. Lewis sternly gazed away from the other two, intoning: "Gentlemen, there will be no acting in this picture."

But at week's end there was no strike either. Although the old contract had expired and Lewis and the operators were hopelessly deadlocked, a shutdown was averted at the last minute. Both sides agreed to a War Labor Board order to continue under the old contract.

OCT. 8 **THE SEETHING TIDE:** Across the U.S., from Montauk Point to Malibu Beach, the tide of labor unrest seethed angrily. In oil, automobiles, coal, lumber, textiles and many another industry, there were strikes, shutdowns, and threats of strikes. At one time last week 420,000 workers were idle. And the first blows of violence rose ominously.

In Detroit, a wildcat strike at the Kelsey-Hayes Wheel Co. kept 50,000 Ford workers from their jobs. One night last week the United Automobile Workers' President R. J. Thomas personally begged and pleaded with the unruly strikers to go back to work. They drowned him out with boos.

By week's end, John L. Lewis and his United Mine Workers had moved into the show. A strike of foremen and supervisors had already closed 127 soft coal pits, throwing 53,546 out of work. John Lewis demanded that the operators come to Washington to talk it over; the operators balked. The miners' boss rumbled about "insolence," implied that a general strike of 450,000 miners might be called.

THE LION RELENTS: Leonine John Lewis, still king in the jungle OCT. 29 of U.S. collieries, made a regal gesture toward the nation and sent some 210,000 soft coal miners back to work after four weeks of idleness and a 13,000,000-ton loss of coal production. He simply told his United Mine Workers that demands for recognition of their foremen's union—basis of the strike —would be postponed to "a later, more appropriate date."

Actually John Lewis, having shown again that he can threaten the nation with cold homes and idle blast furnaces by a casual shake of his shaggy mane, was merely content to rest on his laurels for a while. The public interest coincided with his own because:

⁋ The strike was not too popular with U.M.W. rank-&-file, who are more interested now in pay than in organizing foremen.

⁋ Lewis had heard that President Truman was prepared to denounce him publicly for the strike, had decided to beat the White House to the draw.

FINISH FIGHT?: The glass transom was covered with card- DEC. 3 board. Outside the grey-enameled door stood three husky sergeants at arms. Newsmen lounged on the chintz-covered sofas, listening for sounds from behind the guarded door. Occasionally there were voices, strident and angry; then long stretches of muffled buzz-buzz. Finally there came a burst of applause and then, to the tune of the *Battle Hymn of the Republic*, a full-throated rendition of *Solidarity Forever!*:

> *They have taken untold millions that they never toiled to earn,*
> *But without our brain and muscle not a single wheel could turn;*
> *We can break their haughty power, gain our freedom when we learn*
> *That the union makes us strong.*

The newsmen knew what that meant: the first big postwar strike. For behind the door on the mezzanine of Detroit's Darlum Hotel, 200 representatives of the C.I.O.'s United Automobile Workers had voted to stop all production at giant General Motors Corp. the next morning. They seemed exhilarated by what they had done. Slapped on the back by a well-wisher, the U.A.W.'s tack-sharp Vice President Walter Reuther replied: "Just like old times, isn't it?"

Later, red-haired Reuther, scorning a hat but bundled up in overcoat and muffler, mounted a sound truck and went out to hearten the strikers. He reminded them that no strike benefits would be paid by the union, but in time there would be soup kitchens and the union would send a doctor to any member who needed him. "We will travel the road to the bitter end," he cried, "because we know we are right and are willing to fight for what is right."

As much as the strike of 175,000 men & women could be said to be the work of one man, it was the work of Reuther. As director of the U.A.W.'s General Motors division, he had planned it, and worked out the moves. He had called the strike even though the U.A.W. president, bumbling R. J. Thomas, thought it should be postponed.

It was not a strike for union recognition; it was not a strike against outrageous working conditions or starvation pay. It was a new kind of strike. What made it new was that Reuther had based his arguments on the sweeping effect a 30% increase in pay in the vast motor industry would have on the economy of the country; he said that better pay in the auto industry would step up wages everywhere, take the nation to higher production and abundance.

With the possible exception of John Lewis, Walter Reuther is the most resourceful labor leader on the U.S. scene. He is on the sunny side of middle age (38), above average in schooling (three years in Wayne University), a skilled phrase-maker. He has worked by hand at the trade he represents. He took out three years (1933-35) to work and study labor conditions in Germany, Russia, China and Japan.

His nimbleness in the verbal give & take of negotiations is famous. Sample (from the transcript of the G.M. negotiations):

Reuther: Nothing could be more asinine than to destroy G.M. and destroy the job opportunities with G.M. We want G.M. to be the most prosperous company in this industry.

Harry Anderson (of G.M.): God, what a change is coming over the union!

Reuther: There is no change. We are smarter.

TENSION & ACTION: As the second week of the General DEC. 10 Motors strike wore away, President Truman suddenly moved into the picture with intervention on his mind. With no advance notice, he sent a message to Congress proposing a plan to settle future strikes. He said he would apply it immediately —without the benefit of any law from Congress—to the General Motors strike.

The President's plan was based on the Railway Labor Disputes Act, which has worked successfully to stave off labor trouble on the railroads for 19 years. It called for the establishment of a fact-finding commission which would investigate any major strike on the President's orders. The commission would have power to subpoena all books and records; it would report directly to the President. For a 30-day cooling-off period, no strike could be called.

Putting his idea to work immediately, Harry Truman called on the General Motors strikers to go back to work, promised to follow up with appointment of some fact-finders.

OPEN BREAK?: For the first time in a dozen years, a big part DEC. 17 of organized labor was good and mad at The Man in the White House.

C.I.O. President Philip Murray nearly burned out the nation's radio tubes with his accumulated rancor. What did labor think of the President's new strike plan? Just this, said Phil Murray: "It is legislation that can have but a single purpose—the weakening of labor unions, the curtailment of the right of free men to refrain from working when they choose to do so. The C.I.O. shall mobilize its entire membership to defeat this specific measure and all similar attempts directed against labor."

Other C.I.O. leaders shouted amen. John Lewis called the Truman proposal "an evil, vile-smelling mess."

BACK AT THE TABLE: After 16 days of stalemate, General Motors Corp. and the C.I.O.'s United Automobile Workers' Union promptly sat down again at the collective bargaining table. The protagonists met in Pittsburgh, and also in Detroit. And the upshot was another stalemate.

DEC. 24 **STRONG WORDS:** As the G.M. strike entered its fifth week, the language grew more violent.

Walter Reuther to G.M.: "When a bunch of workers asks for their share you thumb your nose at them, tell them to go to hell, refuse to conciliate, refuse to bargain, refuse to negotiate, refuse to arbitrate. That is the way you do it. You are asking for a fight and, brother, you are going to get it, and if it is the last thing we do, brother, we are going to sweat this one out to the bitter end. The whole American labor movement is behind us. We are backed to the last goddam inch." [The strike was settled the following year after a presidential fact-finding board had recommended a wage increase.]

STEEL STRIKE: A sooty fog lay heavy over Pittsburgh. Smoke seeped into the steel and concrete canyons of the Golden Triangle, bringing the lights on early in the long rows of office windows. In the Roosevelt Hotel, the atmosphere matched the dismal day. The air grew thick with tobacco smoke, thick with angry words. The 175 top officers of the United Steelworkers, after meeting all day, came to a decision: the strike would start at 12:01 a.m., Jan. 14.

The Steelworkers might as well have announced that resumption of peacetime production must halt, for in the switchover from a wartime economy steel is the key. The Steelworkers, now the largest union in the U.S., have more than 800,000 members, contracts with 1,100 plants which make not only steel ingots but such more or less related products as nuts & bolts, thermometers, radiators, hardware, motors, refrigerators, kitchenware, paving bricks, caskets. More than 3,000,000 other U.S. workers depend on steel furnaces for the raw material which keeps them busy.

Characteristically, Steelworkers President Phil Murray said nothing about examining the steel company's books or debating the ins & outs of the profit system. He simply wanted a $2-a-day raise for his men, to keep their take-home pay around its $56-a-week wartime average. Despite Murray's advance notice that he would be happy to dicker, despite the steel companies' implied hint that they might be willing to raise wages if the Government would only let them raise prices, both sides girded furiously for battle. [The Steelworkers went on strike in January 1946, and the issue was settled the following month.]

Army & Navy

IT SHOULDN'T HAPPEN TO A DOG: Seaman First Class Leon JAN. 29 LeRoy, 18, had an emergency leave and a No. 3 priority. He was on his way to Antioch, Calif. to comfort his recently widowed mother. At Memphis Bluejacket LeRoy was told to get his gear off the plane: his No. 3 priority had been trumped by a No. 1, and a load of critical material was coming aboard. A Seabee and an Army technical sergeant, both on their way to ailing wives, had to get off too.

LeRoy's eyes popped and his temperature rose when he saw what was remaining aboard the plane. It was a huge crate occupying three-seats-worth of space in the transport. In it was a big (115 lbs.), tawny dog. On the crate was a No. 1 priority sticker and a label signifying that the beast within was the property of Colonel Elliott Roosevelt, the son of the President of the U.S.

LeRoy told a reporter, and the story was out. In England, where he had rejoined his A.A.F. photo-reconnaissance unit, Colonel Roosevelt was asked how come.

The dog was his, all right, he said. It was a pedigreed Eng-

The Elliott Roosevelts. Their mastiff bounces three passengers.   *Blaze Hero, a pedigreed dog with a No. 1 priority.*

ish bull mastiff named Blaze Hero, one of two he had bought in England and taken to the U.S. in a war-weary B-17. Before returning to duty, he had asked an A.T.C. friend to fly Blaze out to his wife, Cinemactress Faye Emerson, in Hollywood, if an empty plane happened to be going that way. That was all he knew about it.

Eleanor Roosevelt said she was shocked. A.T.C.'s Major General Harold L. George promised an investigation.

FEB. 26 **COURTHOUSE LEGEND:** Legends have begun to gather around starched Lieut. General John C. H. ("Courthouse") Lee, West Pointer, Army engineer, and boss of Army Service Forces in Europe. One story now going the rounds:

In a one-man campaign to get G.I.s to wear their helmets straight, Lee began stopping men in the street and asking: "Is my helmet on straight?" Told respectfully that it was, the General would crack back: "Well, yours isn't." This had the desired effect until Lee ran into one officer who answered: "No sir, your helmet isn't quite straight. Move it a little over this way—no, that way—no, that's wrong too." Word of the tactic got around; the General had to abandon his campaign.

MARCH 19 **WARRIOR'S MERCY:** Out of the flaming furnace of a crashed B-25 at a China base came the agonized screams of a dying,

20-year-old sergeant-gunner. Sickened airmen stood around the plane and listened, sobbing in helpless horror. They had tried rescue. As many as six had rushed in, had hauled and tugged, even tried to pull the sergeant loose from his legs, crushed and trapped behind the copilot's seat. They had failed, driven back by the consuming fire.

Suddenly a 31-year-old lieutenant colonel, veteran of 80 missions and ranking officer at the base, walked forward, lifted his heavy pistol and fired two shots. The screaming stopped.

Last week the Army told the tragic story and its aftermath. A general court-martial of seven colonels had tried the officer on a charge of voluntary manslaughter. For a half hour the court debated, then announced its verdict: since two-thirds had failed to vote for conviction, the officer stood acquitted.

MORE THAN A MILLION: By last week the U.S. counted its JUNE 11 World War II casualties in seven figures. Official Army & Navy reports listed 1,002,887 casualties.

More than 600,000 American men & women have been wounded. Some 60,000 are missing. More than 75,000 are still listed as prisoners of war. Almost a quarter of a million are dead. (World War I dead: 126,000.)

BILL, WILLIE & JOE: Willie was born, full-grown, during the JUNE 18 Italian campaign. He needed a shave and his clothes hung in weary folds on his weary frame. Even on his day of creation, his thick fingers were curved, as though from grasping a pick handle or an M-1 rifle. He did not smile then and he has never smiled since.

Willie was born into the 45th Infantry Division, where his creator, Private Bill Mauldin, also served. Willie had a side-kick, Joe. Together Willie and Joe slogged from Italy to Germany. For them, war was praying between artillery barrages; pitying the starved Italian children and the Italian women standing in the midst of their ruined homes. War was watching their friends die, one after the other, day after day after day. War was learning the ecstasy of wiggling a little finger just to see it move and know that you were still alive. War was hell.

Willie and Joe were combat infantrymen and citizen soldiers. Some brass hats have complained that Willie and Joe did the U.S. Army no credit. Well known is the story of General George Patton threatening to have *Stars & Stripes* banned from his Third Army as long as Mauldin's unkempt heroes appeared in it. Patton and Mauldin were told by Eisenhower's headquarters to discuss the matter. Said Mauldin after the conference: "I came out with all my hide on." *Stars & Stripes* continued to circulate in the Third Army. But last week in Denver, asked what he thought of the 23-year-old Mauldin's cartoons, Georgie Patton snorted: "I've seen only two of them and I thought they were lousy."

JULY 23 **MIDNIGHT MASSACRE:** One evening last week Private Clarence V. Bertucci, stationed at Salina, Utah, strolled out to the temporary camp at Main Street's east end, where 250 German prisoners of war slept.

A cooling breeze rustled through the tents and the dusty town. At midnight Private Bertucci climbed a tower, relieved the guard. Below him lay the silent tent-city whose occupants, next morning, would be in the fields, thinning beets.

A .30-caliber machine gun pointed into the sky. Private Bertucci picked up a belt of cartridges, carefully threaded it into the gun. He had never been in action, but he knew how to work a machine gun. He lowered the muzzle and, aiming carefully, pressed the trigger. Methodically he swept the 43 tents, from left to right and back again. Screams and strangled shouts came from the tents.

As the Army buried eight prisoners at Fort Douglas last week, and treated 20 more for wounds, Army psychiatrists examined Private Bertucci. His own calm explanation: he had hated Germans, so he had killed Germans.

JULY 30 **HURRY HOME:** On one day 31,445 soldiers arrived in New York on seven ships from Europe; the huge *Queen Elizabeth* brought an entire division.

Last week the Army Air Forces gave out some eye-popping statistics of history's biggest air passenger movement: in a 72-day period, 125,370 military personnel had been flown from the European and Mediterranean theaters to the U.S. By this week 532,258 shouting, cheering G.I.s had arrived back home in the States.

A gaping hole in the north side of the Empire State Building marks the spot where a bomber struck, 79 stories up. Wreckage was found five blocks away.

IN THE CLOUDS: Flying down from Bedford, Mass., Lieut. AUG. 6 Colonel William Franklin Smith Jr., D.F.C., Air Medal and *Croix de Guerre*, found LaGuardia Field all right. After he had let his two-engined B-25 bomber down under a 900-ft. ceiling he radioed for permission to go on to Newark. La-Guardia approved, warned him of low visibility (about two miles), concluded, "We're unable to see the top of the Empire State Building."

"Roger," said West Pointer Smith and headed across New York City barely under the thick cloud layer.

In Manhattan, a few minutes before 10 a.m., workers in the midtown towers heard a plane close by—very close. It thundered past the stark, stone structures of Rockefeller Center and barely missed a 60-floor building at Fifth Avenue and 42nd Street. Then the craft, southbound, pulled up into the cloud.

On the 75th floor of the Empire State Building a man heard the throbbing motors, turned quickly to the window. Coming straight at him out of the fog was a twin-engined bomber. In the next instant there happened what many a Manhattanite had often predicted and feared. The ten-ton airplane, flying at an estimated speed of 225 m.p.h., crashed head-on into the north side of the Empire State Building at the level of the 78th and 79th floors.

The bomber gored through the thick steel and stone of the building as if they were papier-mâché. Then, in a flash of flame, the gasoline tanks exploded. Bright fire gushed from the 18-ft. wound in the structure's side. Red gasoline ran into elevator shafts and exploded. Parts of the plane sheared elevator cables, and one elevator fell. One of the plane's engines crashed into an elevator shaft, screeched 79 floors, fell on the elevator cab, carried it down to wreckage in the basement. The other engine and other heavy parts ripped through seven inner walls, then tore a hole in the south side of the building. On the streets, 913 feet below the crash area, bits of wings, hunks of metal and stone fell as far as five blocks away.

In the instant of the crash, 13 persons were dead. Among them: Colonel Smith, his crew chief and a Navy bluejacket who had hitchhiked a ride from Bedford. Most of the others were girls and women employed by the National Catholic Welfare Conference, which has offices on the 79th floor. The injured were counted at 26.

Bad as it was, New York had been spared worse. The crash came on a summer Saturday; in the building were only about 1,500 people. On a normal week day there would have been 15,000 office workers, perhaps several thousand visitors.

DRAFT DODGERS: The FBI has cleaned up almost half a million draft-evasion cases in the five years since Selective Service became a law. This week it announced some results: 12,559 men were sentenced to prison terms; fines of more than a million dollars were imposed. Some FBI adventures:

¶ By aircraft and snowshoe, agents pursued two draft dodgers in Alaska, caught them at the base of Mt. McKinley.

¶ One 200-lb. fugitive from Selective Service tried to skip across an ice floe, fell in. Pursuing FBI men fished him out.

¶ Another vowed he was on his way to his draft board when he heard about the food shortage, patriotically went to milking cows instead.

¶ Declaimed one delinquent: "Danged if I'm going to fight in any war I didn't start."

AUG. 27 **TURNABOUT:** Off the Canal Zone the voice on the bull-horn of the transport *General Harry Taylor* blared: "Now hear this! Watch the shadow of the ship." Then the *Taylor*'s skipper, Captain Leonard B. Jaudon, added: "As it turns toward New York." More than 3,000 soldiers let out a cheer that shook the ship from bow to stern. The war was really over and they had been diverted from the Pacific.

BACK FROM THE GRAVE: Year after year they had vanished SEPT. 10 into Japan like wanderers sucked into the mud of a fever swamp—the men of Hong Kong, of Bataan and Wake, men of the ships sunk at sea, the planes shot down in combat. Last week they were found—those who were still alive.

U.S. planes swooped over Jap prison stockades to drop food and supplies. U.S. trucks and cars wheeled into prison compounds to pick up bony, half-naked men. Aboard U.S. transports and hospital ships they were bathed, fed, clothed, given medical treatment. Then, like men awakened from nightmares, they talked.

Almost all suffered from malnutrition. Few had ever received Red Cross packages; their guards, almost to a man, had engaged in graft which cut prison fare to watery soups, half-spoiled vegetables and chalky gruels. They had been beaten and kicked, forced to bow, to obey endless rules. Husky guards took pride in breaking jaws and eardrums in an effort to make prisoners divulge information. There were also more refined methods: metal bits were fastened into soldiers' mouths with thread which gradually drew tighter & tighter; match slivers were thrust under men's fingernails, and jagged ends of bamboo twisted against their faces. The fate of prisoners who fell sick was hardly better. Many a man who was sent to the dirt-floored buildings of Shinagawa, lone hospital for 8,000 prisoners near Tokyo, simply went to his death. When the hospital's crematorium was bombed to rubble, prisoners were forced to cremate the dead on spits over an open fire.

Thanks to the Jap trick of not reporting many a prisoner, there was the cheering word that men long believed dead had survived. Three hundred men of the cruiser *Houston*, unreported for the three-and-a-half years since their ship was sunk in Sunda Strait, were discovered alive in Thailand. Also found alive was the Marine air ace, Major Gregory ("Pappy") Boyington, last seen on Jan. 3, 1944, over Rabaul with Jap fighters on his tail. At the time, Pappy Boyington was believed dead. But he had flipped his plane, jumped out and landed in the sea, with a broken ankle and riddled with machine-gun slugs. A Jap submarine had picked him up.

The Japs knew Boyington well. He had taunted them over his radio as he roared in for kills and they gave him special treatment. Last week he told about it: "The first ten days were the hardest. They wouldn't let anybody help me. They would make me walk on my bad leg, and shove me with a rifle butt to make sure I did. After ten days I was getting pretty ripe—I don't know how they stood the smell. Finally they let a doctor wash me.

"Then I was taken to Ofuna. I got slugged in the jaw about every day, mostly for not being polite. To get to the toilet you had to ask the guard's permission politely, then thank him politely for the favor when you came back. If you were having dysentery, as most of us did at times, it meant a hell of a lot of politeness day & night."

OCT. 15   **HOW IT WAS DONE:** General of the Army George Catlett Marshall this week delivered to the nation his "Biennial Report to the Secretary of War." In it he told how the war had been won.

The long report was the story of disaster narrowly averted, when the security of the nation rested dangerously in hands not hers. Said George Marshall: "The refusal of the British and Russian peoples to accept what appeared to be inevitable defeat was the great factor in the salvage of our civilization."

The other great factor: "Failure of the enemy to make the most of the situation." The German High Command—almost incredibly—had no overall strategic plan. Wrangling between Hitler and his generals, lack of coordination between the Axis powers had wrecked what might have been a conquest of the world. Japan's strategic plan, its climax an invasion of the Aleutians, bombardment of the U.S. Northwest and seizure of critical areas, had "initially failed when she missed the opportunity of landing troops on Hawaii." George Marshall made it crystal clear that the U.S. had had much good luck in the war before it had much good management. When Hitler first massed his forces, the U.S., "in terms of available strength, was not even a third rate military power." The next time such a thing happened, Marshall indicated, *almost* too late would be *too* late.

END OF AN ARMY: As rapidly as it could, the U.S. was strip- OCT. 22
ping away its military strength. Pushed by Congressmen and
public demand ("Get the boys home and out of the service"),
the Army had already discharged more than 1,000,000 men
and would soon be tearing itself down at the rate of 1,000,000
a month. By March 15, the world's greatest air force (2,385,-
000 in 1944) will be down to 165,000.

HISTORIC TABLE: Through the Panama Canal last week
steamed 48 ships of the U.S. fleet carrying 57,000 veterans of
the Pacific war—and one historic metal table.

The table was an ordinary folding mess table. On the September morning, in Tokyo Bay, when Japan's representatives
were due aboard the *Missouri* to surrender, somebody discovered at the last minute that there was no table on hand
big enough for the signing. A table from the enlisted men's
mess was carted topside and set up on the *Missouri*'s teak-
planked veranda deck. The ceremony over, the table was
taken back to the mess where it belonged. A dozen men had
eaten spaghetti at it before the ship's officers shouted,
"Where's the table?" They retrieved the now historic object
and stowed it reverently away in an officer's room to await
shipment home as a souvenir of history.

ONE-YARD LINE: In the battle now going over possible NOV. 26
merger of the separate armed services, the Navy's position
finally became clear last week: what the Navy is fighting
against primarily is an independent Air Force.

Navy Secretary Forrestal has indicated that a compromise
could be reached on unification of command. But on creation
of an air department coequal with War and Navy—"I am
not yet prepared to agree." Why not? Fleet Admiral Chester
Nimitz bluntly answered that question: the Navy "either
gradually or at once would become a secondary service."

In spite of everything the war taught—the devastation of
Germany and Japan by the Air Forces and the delivery of the
atom bombs—the Navy's high brass still talks of air power
as an inseparable adjunct of sea power (comparable, say, to
the submarine force) and some admirals will fight to the end
any threat to the old, traditional prestige of the surface ship.
They were fighting desperately last week, somewhere near

their one-yard line. The Army, all out for merger, had kept the ball. Said General of the Army Dwight Eisenhower: "Unless we have unity of direction in Washington through the years of peace that lie ahead we may enter another Pearl Harbor."

DEC. 24 **FISHWIVES:** The merger argument reached a shrill, fishwifely pitch last week. Fleet Admiral Ernest King used his final report to labor his contention that unity of command in Washington would have done nothing to shorten the war.

Navymen presented colored charts which purported to show how superior was the Navy's plan to the Army plan for out-&-out service merger. Navy Secretary Forrestal added the ill-tempered charge that the Army had "muzzled" its officers, forbidding them to express their views frankly. War Secretary Patterson ridiculed the charge, and called the Navy charts a "fancy brochure."

DEC. 31 **THREE-IN-ONE:** Referring to the merger brawl between Army & Navy brass hats, Harry Truman had said that they would all be in the same boat when he sent up a message. Last week, the President launched his boat, and sure enough they were all in it—but it flew the Army's flag. Ex-Artilleryman Harry Truman's plan:

¶ One Department of National Defense, headed by a single Secretary.

¶ Three "coordinated branches" for land, sea and air (the Navy to retain the Marine Corps and its aviation).

¶ A chief of staff of the entire Department (an Armyman, a Navyman and an Airman, in turn); a commander for each service.

¶ A permanent staff composed of these four military chiefs, serving as advisers to the Secretary and the President.

The President's plan shocked the Navy into silence, shocked the Navy's good friend, Congressman Carl Vinson, into frenzied cries that it smacked "of the Kaiser, of Hitler and of Japanese militarism."

By what line of reasoning had Harry Truman arrived at his conclusions? In the message to Congress the President explained: "We should have integrated strategic plans and a unified military program and budget."

Pearl Harbor Report

A few weeks after the surprise attack on Pearl Harbor, the two senior Army and Navy officers there were relieved of their commands and went into retirement. Investigations continued into why the U.S. military had been caught off-guard, but most of the testimony was withheld from the public for reasons of military security. In 1945, as the fighting reached an end, Congress began the first open inquiry into the disaster, and testimony was made public.

WHO WAS TO BLAME?: For almost a year the official Army SEPT. 10 & Navy reports on Pearl Harbor had lain under cover, marked "Secret." Last week, President Truman made them public. Congressmen shouted that it was a "whitewash" or that it was incomplete. Harry Truman said that it proved everyone was to blame.

Two men had already been adjudged as derelict in their duties: Lieut. General Walter C. Short, Commander of the Army's Hawaiian Department, and Rear Admiral Husband E. Kimmel, Commander in Chief of the Pacific Fleet on the day the Japs attacked. New light shed by the reports did nothing to brighten their records; it cast them, indeed, into darker shadow.

The reports for the first time gave eye-popping details of the Jap attack. On Nov. 27-28, a Jap task force, carefully and particularly trained for its mission, set sail from Tankan Bay in northern Japan and headed east, in radio silence. Its orders were to sink any vessel it should meet, even Japanese; nothing must be left to a chance betrayal of its course. Like sitting ducks in Pearl Harbor were eight of the battleships of the U.S. Pacific Fleet, in a condition of only partial readiness. This the Japs knew; they were well supplied with every detail of intelligence about their target.

Kimmel had enough information, according to the Navy's report, to make him aware of the need to take extraordinary measures. His preparations were little more than routine. On Dec. 2, when Kimmel's Fleet Intelligence officer told him he had suddenly lost track of four Jap carriers (which they were checking on by radio), Kimmel was not alarmed.

The Army's report recounted a tragic, sometimes ludicrous story of doodling and unawareness. When General Short arrived in Hawaii in February to take command, the nation's outpost was woefully deficient. Hawaii needed aircraft, artillery, searchlights, more airfields for dispersion of planes, aircraft warning systems.

On Dec. 7, a handful of radar stations were in operation. But only a handful of men knew how to run them. One man who did, Pfc. Joseph L. Lockard, was sitting at one on that fateful Sunday morning and spotted a large formation of planes. He notified Air Forces Lieut. Kermit Tyler, sole officer at the Information Center. Tyler thought Lockard's planes were probably a flight of B-17s, due to arrive from the West Coast.

General Short's greatest concern was not the possibility of an attack from the sea but of sabotage by Japanese on the island and he decided that an anti-sabotage alert was enough. This was the position in which the Jap carrier planes found him, with his planes parked wing-to-wing on the airstrips and his guards on the *qui vive* for saboteurs.

There was a "Joint Defense Plan" and an "Air Agreement" by which Army & Navy would divide responsibilities, come the attack. But neither was in operation on Dec. 7. The Navy failed to inform Short that it had sunk a Jap submarine in outer Pearl Harbor at about 6:30 a.m. on Dec. 7—a sure sign that attack was imminent.

NOV. 26 **IN HISTORY:** The most interesting evidence in the latest Pearl Harbor hearings came from a 253-page printed booklet introduced as "Exhibit I." This was a complete dossier of coded Japanese messages intercepted by U.S. Army and Navy Intelligence between July 1, 1941 and Pearl Harbor Day. It showed conclusively that official Washington was intimately aware, long before Dec. 7, 1941, of the warlike intentions of the Jap Government.

On Nov. 22, Tokyo had cabled to Ambassador Nomura and Special Ambassador Kurusu in Washington: "There are reasons why we want to settle Japanese-American relations by the 25th. After that things are automatically going to happen."

Testimony developed at the hearing, from captured documents, indicated that the attack on Pearl Harbor was conceived by Admiral Yamamoto as far back as January 1941. The actual date for the attack (Dec. 8, Japanese time) had been fixed by Nov. 7.

How far things had gone was illustrated by a telephone conversation on Nov. 27 between Kurusu and Kumaicho Yamamoto, head of the American section of the Jap Foreign Office. The two men used a voice code in which "Miss Umeko" referred to Secretary of State Cordell Hull and "Miss Kimiko" to President Roosevelt. The term "matrimonial question" meant the negotiations in Washington, and talk of childbirth meant that a crisis was at hand. All this was clear to the U.S. agents who had tapped the wires; the U.S. had all the Jap signal codes. This was what the agents heard:

Yamamoto: How did the matrimonial question go today?

Kurusu: There wasn't much that was different from what Miss Umeko said yesterday. Does it seem as if a child will be born?

Yamamoto (in a very definite tone): Yes, the birth of the child seems imminent. It seems as if it will be a strong, healthy boy.

On Dec. 1, the messages showed, the Jap Embassy received instructions on how to destroy its codes and other confidential material. On Dec. 2, Washington intercepted a message from Canton to Tokyo: "If hostilities are to begin, we are all prepared."

Patently official Washington had known that the outbreak of war was just a matter of days. Army Intelligence even intercepted a garbled message from Tokyo to Bangkok which said: "X-Day is the 8th and the day on which the notice is to be given is the 7th."

THEY CALLED IT INTELLIGENCE: To the stand went balding, DEC. 10 bumbling Major General Sherman Miles, wearer of four rows of ribbons, Assistant Chief of Staff for Military Intelligence in 1941. Into the record went a long series of Japanese code messages intercepted before Dec. 7. Most significant: instructions sent by Tokyo on Sept. 24, ordering a spy in Honolulu to report on the ships at anchor in Pearl Harbor.

Other intercepted messages, sent between Nov. 24 and Dec. 6, were even more revealing. Tokyo was asking for detailed information on ship movements and schedules, for any reports of barrage balloons over the harbor. The Honolulu spy was reporting that there appeared to be no aerial reconnaissance, that "opportunity is still left for a surprise attack." But these messages were not decoded in time. The Signal Corps' "Magic" project, which held the secret of the Jap code, was short of men and facilities.

Other facts disclosed by Miles:

¶ Jap messages decoded by "Magic" were seen by only a few top brass hats, were not always shown to the President, were not sent to commanders in the field at all. (The Army & Navy were afraid the Japs might learn their secret.)

¶ Neither Army nor Navy Intelligence placed any credence in a report from Tokyo by Ambassador Joseph Grew, in January 1941, that the Peruvian Minister had learned "from many sources, including a Japanese source" that the Japs planned to open the war with a sneak attack on Pearl Harbor. (Intelligence officers somehow figured out that no Jap in a position to know would be so stupid as to say.)

DEC. 17 **MAGIC WAS THE WORD FOR IT:** U.S. citizens discovered last week that perhaps their most potent secret weapon of World War II was not the atom bomb—but a harmless little machine which cryptographers painstakingly constructed in a hidden room at Fort Washington.

With this machine, built after years of trial & error and deduction, cryptographers had duplicated the decoding devices used in Tokyo. Testimony before the Pearl Harbor Committee had already shown that the machine—known in Army code as "Magic"—was in use long before Dec. 7, 1941, had given ample warning of the Japs' sneak attack. So priceless a possession was Magic that the U.S. high command lived in constant fear that the Japs would discover the secret, change their code machinery, force U.S. cryptographers to start anew.

General Marshall had a long series of bad moments after U.S. flyers, showing a suspicious amount of foresight, shot down Admiral Yamamoto's plane at Bougainville in 1943. And once a decoder was caught in Boston trying to sell the secret. The worst scare of all came during the 1944 presidential campaign, when George Marshall heard that Thomas E. Dewey knew the secret and might refer to it in speeches in order to cast dôubt on President Roosevelt's role before Pearl Harbor. [General Marshall wrote a top secret letter to Governor Dewey begging him not to divulge the information for fear that the Japanese would change their code and thus end the U.S.'s access to priceless military intelligence. Dewey remained silent, and the Japanese never did learn that the U.S. had cracked their codes and was intercepting and deciphering Japanese messages.]

ADMIRAL v. ADMIRAL: After 30 days of testimony and bick- DEC. 31 ering, the Congressional Pearl Harbor Investigating Committee last week got back to the man in the middle of the mess: Rear Admiral Husband E. Kimmel, commander of the Pacific Fleet on the fatal day.

Twangy, caustic Admiral Richmond Kelly Turner—in 1941 chief of the Navy war plans division—testified that he had thought, as early as July 1941, that war was inevitable. He not only thought that Hawaii was a "probable" target, but also that the attack would come by air. He was just as positive that Admiral Kimmel had been prepared for "just such an attack." Admiral Turner testified that he had given him "perfectly specific and entirely clear" orders in a warning message on Nov. 27; nothing else should have been necessary. Cracked Pennsylvania's Democratic Rep. John Murphy: "I have never seen a Monday morning quarterback who ever lost a game."

Heroes

24-STAR GENERAL: New England had rarely seen anything like JUNE 18 it. But, after all, the world has rarely seen anything like General George Smith Patton Jr. Last week, when he came home from the wars, 750,000 people jammed the 20-mile parade route into Boston to see and cheer the conquering hero. Georgie Patton did not disappoint them.

He stepped down onto U.S. soil agleam with 24 stars, variously placed, all glittering: four on his shiny steel helmet, four on each shoulder loop, four on each collar tab, and four on the black butt of the automatic pistol at his hip. He wore two rings on his left hand, one on his right. His hair was

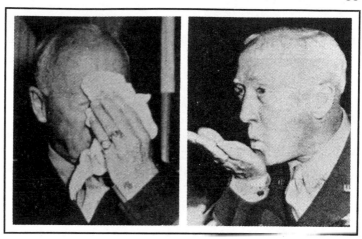

General George S. Patton Jr., a star-spangled, gun-toting hero, responds to a Boston welcome with tears and kisses.

white, his face lined. But he was still erect and turkey-cock as ever. Governor Maurice J. Tobin compared Patton to Washington, Sheridan, Grant, Forrest and Stonewall Jackson.

That night, at a state dinner, the General blew kisses, beamed happily at his wife. But as he rose to speak—still wearing his pistol—tears rolled down his cheeks and his high, thin voice grew almost inaudible. He sat down after less than five minutes, put a big handkerchief to his face. Then he lighted a big cigar. Said his son, West Point Cadet George Smith Patton IV: "Same old Pop."

JULY 2 **HOME TO ABILENE:** The U.S. last week got its first good look at Ike Eisenhower, top hero of the war. The U.S. liked what it saw—a modest man, natural in everything he did; a kindly, common-sense man; a warrior who remembered that he was a citizen; a son of the Middle West, unspoiled by fame.

He arrived at Washington's crowd-fringed National Airport, tanned, smiling, taller and more youthful-looking than the crowd had expected. As cheers and applause went up, he caught sight of his wife, Mamie, ran down the steps and kissed her with unabashed fervor. A million men, women & children were jammed along the capital's wide avenues, as the General passed on a triumphal tour unparalleled in U.S. history. He stood in his car, grinning as though at old friends.

Next day New York welcomed him with a tumult which dwarfed the memory of receptions for Charles Lindbergh and Admiral Byrd.

Then he boarded his special five-starred plane (the *Sunflower*) for Kansas City. When it landed he stood stiffly at attention as a band played *The General's March.* The moment the last note sounded, he hurried toward his 83-year-old mother, Mrs. Ida Eisenhower, and gave her a hug which lifted her off the ground. There was yet another parade, another speech, another reception. Then the Eisenhowers got aboard a train for the trip to Abilene, Kansas. As he stepped down in his old home town (pop. 5,757) he called, "Boy, I'm glad to be back here!"

In the week's celebration, many a verbal bouquet was thrown at General Ike. Not the least was the frequent call: "Our next President." But Ike replied: "There's no use denying that I'll fly to the moon because I couldn't if I wanted to. The same goes for politics."

PATTON LEGEND (CONT'D.): No other U.S. general has got OCT. 15 himself in so much hot water or made so many legends in the war as flamboyant George S. Patton Jr. Last week, as he was banished to the command of a phantom Fifteenth Army, he landed in the middle of another. The background:

In March 1945 the 4th Armored Division of Patton's Third Army rested, out of breath, on a bridgehead along the river Main. Some 50 miles northeast, near the town of Hammelburg, was a *stalag* filled with Allied prisoners of war. Hammelburg was in the path of General Alexander Patch's Seventh Army, but slashing Georgie Patton decided to take matters into his own hands. He ordered a task force of the 4th Division to deliver the prisoners.

The man who got the assignment was tall, quiet Captain Abraham Baum. His task force: 301 men, 53 armored vehicles. Apparently convinced that the whole 4th Division was driving through, the Germans rushed in men and weapons, counterattacked Baum's little force with tanks. Baum was wounded and captured. His force was wiped out and all but seven of his men were captured or killed. Ten days later, Hammelburg was duly overrun by Patch's Seventh Army.

Why did Patton order such a desperate undertaking? One

of the prisoners at Hammelburg was Patton's son-in-law, Lieut. Colonel John K. Waters, who was badly wounded in the fracas. Patton, denying that he even knew Waters was there, said that his motive was concern for all Allied prisoners. Some men wondered if Patton should not have shown more concern for his own soldiers.

DEC. 31 **DEATH & THE GENERAL:** In the Station Hospital in Heidelberg General George Smith Patton Jr. was fighting for his life. His neck had been broken in an auto accident when he was on his way to a German field to shoot pheasants. He fought with the same tenacity with which he had fought his enemies. He was mending so well that medics took off the elaborate traction apparatus and put their 60-year-old patient in a plaster cast. There was talk of flying him home. Then a respiratory infection set in. Last week—twelve days after his accident—George Patton died in his sleep. Thus ended the career, but not the legend, of the most spectacular, most controversial U.S. field general in World War II.

Twice George ("Old Blood & Guts") Patton had been stripped of his command. The first time was after a public furor in the U.S. over his slapping and abusing a shell-shocked soldier in a Sicilian hospital. For the old war horse, that was a bitter period. One day he borrowed Mark Clark's Packard, and in this conspicuous vehicle rode recklessly up to the front lines toward Cassino. When he could ride no farther he got out and walked, erect, though mortar shells were bursting all around. More than once, Patton had said that he wanted to die on the battlefield.

The second time he lost a command was last October, when "Ike" Eisenhower yanked him out of the Third Army command after Patton had belittled the differences between Nazis and anti-Nazis. He got the Fifteenth, a paper Army doing paper work.

A cavalryman by training and by temperament, George Patton was the medieval man on horseback—in mechanized armor. Even before his country was at war, he wanted to joust with Nazi Erwin Rommel—each contestant in a tank. "The two armies could watch," said he. "I'd shoot at him, he'd shoot at me. If I killed him, I'd be the champ. If he killed me—well, he won't."

(WORLD BATTLEFRONTS)

The year saw the end of the war both in Europe and the Pacific. In Europe, U.S. troops beat back the enemy's last massive counterattack in the "Battle of the Bulge," after which Allied armies moved into the enemy heartland on all fronts. In the Pacific, as Allied forces closed in on Japan, the final assault was made unnecessary by the dropping of two atomic bombs.

Western Front

BODY BLOW: The initial impact of the German offensive in JAN. 1 the Ardennes had been stunning. Much more so was the size of the breakthrough, the continuing torrent of Nazi power poured through the gaps, the speed of the German spearheads.

At first everything was wild confusion. Germans suddenly appeared over the crest of hills and shot up towns. They overran rear-area supply points, pounced upon U.S. artillerymen before they could get to their guns. U.S. generals found their command posts the centers of battles, hastily armed cooks, clerks, medics, runners.

Field Marshal Gerd von Rundstedt's skillful breakthrough had the first great element of success: surprise. He had struck the thinnest sector of the American line. He had cleverly begun with light attacks, concealing his intentions, playing upon the Americans' underestimation of his strength. Then, savagely, the full force of the German blow was unleashed and sent the Americans reeling like a boxer who has taken a terrific punch to the solar plexus.

TO OUR GREATEST VICTORY: Last week the eyes of the U.S. turned with fear and questioning on General Dwight D.

Eisenhower as he faced the gravest setback of his career. But Eisenhower refused to admit that a battle was lost while it was still being fought. He proclaimed to his troops:

"The enemy is making his supreme effort to break out of the desperate plight into which you forced him by your brilliant victories of the summer and fall.

"He is fighting savagely to take back all that you have won, and is using every treacherous trick to deceive and kill you.

"He is gambling everything, but in the face of your proven bravery and fortitude, he will completely fail.

"Let everyone hold before him a single thought—to destroy the enemy. United in this determination and with unshakable faith in the cause for which we fight, we will, with God's help, go forward to our greatest victory."

The size and scope of the Nazi thrust into the Bulge made it imperative for Allied forces to keep the breakthrough point as narrow as possible, thus making it more difficult for the Germans to push enough supplies and reinforcements through the bottleneck to keep their offensive rolling. As a result of this strategy, the holding of two positions became enormously important to the Allies. One was the town of Malmédy, to the north of the German penetration. The other was the village of Bastogne to the south. The Allies managed to hold on to both positions, and the attacking German troops were so effectively contained that most of them were eventually killed or captured.

JAN. 8 **THE GENERAL SAID "NUTS!":** Bastogne suddenly became important. If the German offensive were to be slowed in its thrust it would have to be done there, where the Liège-Arlon highway meets six other roads. To Bastogne hurried parts of two U.S. armored divisions of Lieut. General George S. Patton's Third Army. In speeding trucks came almost the full strength of the 101st Airborne Division, the "Screaming Eagle" paratroops and glidermen. The U.S. command had given one order: hold Bastogne at all costs.

On a perimeter about two miles out of the town the Americans set up a line of foxholes, manned by the 101st's paratroopers. Just outside the town was a last-gasp inner defense circle, manned largely by stragglers. Slight, salty Brigadier General Anthony Clement McAuliffe, the 101st's acting commander, called them his "Team Snafu." Inside the town was a reserve force of tanks and tank destroyers, to dash out against a major enemy attack. "Tony" McAuliffe called this force his "Fire Brigade."

The Germans probed at all the entrances to Bastogne. Wherever the Germans poked there were Americans. The Germans kept on wheeling around the town, soon had it surrounded, a little island fortress in a swirling sea of gunfire. On the first night one of the worst things that could befall an island of besieged happened to Bastogne: the Germans captured its complete surgical unit. Bastogne's wounded would have to get along without amputations, without fracture splints, without skilled care at all.

Shells poured in from all sides. Some 3,000 civilians huddled in cellars with the wounded. By Friday Bastogne was a wrecked town, its outskirts littered with dead. There had been at least four fighting Germans to every American. The dead were probably in the same ratio. The Germans became sick of "crazy Americans," and tried a surrender offer. Through the lines came an enemy envoy carrying a white sheet. He delivered an ultimatum: two hours for the Americans to decide upon surrender. The alternative: "annihilation by artillery." General McAuliffe did not hesitate. He had heard the wounded beg him, "Don't give up on account of us, General." He sat at a debris-littered desk, printed his reply with formal military courtesy: "To the German Commander—*NUTS!*—the American Commander." So there would be no misinterpretation, an officer translated for the blindfolded German envoy: "It means the same as 'Go to Hell.'"

Christmas was the turning point. As darkness fell the next day, a sentry spotted several U.S. Sherman tanks rolling down a ridge from the south. Out of the leading Sherman's turret popped a bandaged head. The man with the bandage and the big shiner on his right eye yelled the proper password. He was Lieut. Colonel Creighton ("Abe") Abrams, commanding the 4th Armored Division's rescue spearhead.

"DEAR ME, COME, COME": To Field Marshal Sir Bernard JAN. 15 Law Montgomery last week went Supreme Commander "Ike"

Eisenhower's praises. The doughty little Briton had acted swiftly to bring U.S., British and Canadian Armies to bear on Rundstedt's north flank. In Washington, President Roosevelt explained that the switch in command from U.S. General Omar Bradley to Montgomery was made necessary when the German thrust split U.S. forces.

"Monty" was in fine fettle. At his headquarters he received the press for his first conference in several months. Monty had something to say—in fact, a rambling hour's worth. Excerpts:

"When Rundstedt put in his hard blow and parted the American Army, it was automatic that the battle area must be untidy. Therefore, the first thing I did was to busy myself in getting the battle area tidy—getting it sorted out. I collected here and there, pulled in divisions and formed an army corps under that very fine American General Collins [Major General J. Lawton Collins].

"It took a knock. I said 'Dear me, this can't go on. It's being swallowed up in the battle.' I managed to form the corps again. Once more pressure was such that it began to disappear. I said, 'Come, come,' and formed it again."

What had turned the trick?

"The good fighting qualities of the American soldier. I take my hat off to such men. I salute the brave fighting men of America—I never want to fight alongside better soldiers. I have tried to feel that I am almost an American soldier myself."

FEB. 12 **A NEW PHASE:** American divisions had hammered the bulge flat. Now a new phase was opening up. Along a 40-mile front east of the Ardennes some ten U.S. divisions were clawing their way through the saw-toothed tank traps, over the concrete pillboxes of the Siegfried Line. The snow that had blinded them during the German breakthrough, the ice that had immobilized their trucks turned into deep slush and mud through which they slid and slithered.

MARCH 19 **OVER THE RHINE AT REMAGEN:** When Major General John W. Leonard heard of the U.S. capture of Cologne, he gave an open order to his 9th Armored Division: keep going; if you reach the river try to establish a crossing and hold it.

On the morning of March 7, dark, handsome, Missouri-born Brigadier General William M. Hoge got the order. Getting across rivers was one of his specialties. His Distinguished Service Cross testified to his part in bridging the Meuse under fire in World War I's decisive offensive. General Hoge's outfit was to come up to the Rhine near Remagen.

At first General Hoge's men met spotty opposition, then almost none. By late afternoon they sighted Remagen through a break in the hills. The double-tracked railroad bridge across it still stood, but that was hardly worth remarking: the Germans usually waited until the last moment to destroy all bridges. The U.S. spearhead force sped down the slope to the bridge entry. There was a flurry of shooting. A German gun was knocked out, some German soldiers killed. Then, warily, some of the Yanks ran onto the bridge. There was an explosion. A guard had touched off one of the charges. But it did little damage.

Soon the Americans were swarming over the bridge. They cut and jerked out wires leading to dynamite charges. Gingerly they detached detonators, lifted boxes of explosives from the piers. Suddenly Hoge's men realized that they had forced a fantastic break in the fortunes of war. They had seized a Rhine bridge intact. It was a moment for history.

TRAIN-BUSTER: To his mates of the 365th "Hell Hawk" group of Thunderbolt pilots, 22-year-old Lieut. Edward Syszmanski is "The Mad Polack of Brooklyn," in recognition of his fanatic artistry at ground-level train-busting. The Syszmanski technique: "I come in from the back of a train, aiming at the third car from the engine. I watch the bullets creep up toward the locomotive, and my plane is usually about 25 feet above the cars before I get enough shots into the boiler. Some of the locos blow up a few feet and settle back on the tracks as if heaving a big sigh. Others just puke steam—I only claim them as damaged." The Mad Polack's record in three days of mediocre strafing weather: 13 locos blown up, four steamspewers, one enemy tree branch captured (and brought home in his engine cowling).

THE STAR HALFBACK: Last week SHAEF correspondents APRIL 9 were telling another anecdote about unpredictable Lieut. General George S. Patton Jr. An Allied officer had asked Supreme

Commander Dwight Eisenhower where in Germany Patton might be. "Ike's" reply: "Hell, I don't know. I haven't heard from him for three hours."

George Patton was sitting in his headquarters van, his high-polished cavalry boots cocked on the glass top of his desk, his long-fingered hands relaxed in his lap. He listened now & then over his command radio to battle reports. Willie, the General's white bull terrier, snuffed sleepily on the rug.

Patton had reason for calm and happy reflection. He was having the time of his action-choked, 40-year career. Some of Patton's men were fighting less than 180 miles from Berlin. The Germans seemed to be scattering before his attacks. They had reason to fear him. The Germans had always put more men and guns opposite Patton's outfits. Now there were fewer German men and guns. And now Patton was playing his favorite role. He was the swift, slashing halfback of Coach Eisenhower's team.

George Smith Patton Jr. is fast becoming a legend. The U.S. public, always more interested in the ballcarrier than in the blockers who open a hole for him, liked Patton's flourishes, his flamboyance, his victories. And in slim, big-chested Patton, hero-worshiping Americans had a candidate to fit the mass idea of what a Hero General should be—the colorful swashbuckler, the wild-riding charger, the hell-for-leather Man of Action, above all the Winner.

George Patton, General, is a dazzling mixture. The oldest field commander of any Allied army in Europe (he will be 60 next Armistice Day), Patton is still tigerish in action. On the field he can rawhide a private or a lesser general with a flow of profanity that is perhaps the richest in all the hard-swearing U.S. armies. A moment later he can be gently lifting a wounded man from a tank, calming him with soothing words. Patton the General is also Patton the Actor. Showmanship is instinctive in him. And he fits his act to his audience's mood. Example: his greeting to a Negro battalion arriving at his battlefront—"I don't give a damn what color you are so long as you get out there and kill those sonsofbitches in the green suits."

No other U.S. Army in Europe has higher unit pride. Third Army men do not call Patton "Old Blood & Guts" (that nickname came from such fervid advice to trainees as: "Rip their belly buttons; spill their guts around"). To his own men Patton is "The Old Man" or "The Big Guy"—and they say it respectfully. A favorite story with his officers is how the General stopped the rain after the Rundstedt breakout last December. Rundstedt's offensive was blessed by soupy days at its start. No planes flew. Tankmen, called on to drive 80 miles in a night, could not find the enemy in the endless drizzle. By the third day Patton called in one of his chaplains. The reported conversation:

Patton: I want a prayer to stop this rain. If we got a couple of clear days we could get in there and kill a couple of hundred thousand of those krauts.

Chaplain: Well, sir, it's not exactly in the realm of theology to pray for something that would help to kill fellow men.

Patton: What the hell are you—a theologian or an officer of the U.S. Third Army? I want that prayer.

The General got his prayer; it was printed on thousands of small cards with Patton's Christmas greeting on the reverse side. On the fifth day of rain it was distributed to the troops. On the sixth day the sun shone.

DISINTEGRATION: It was a week of almost incredible military APRIL 16 events. In six days at least 25,000 Germans had been killed or wounded. These were the casualties of a *Wehrmacht* falling swiftly apart. All of Germany, from Hamburg to Vienna, from the Oder to the Ysselmeer, was one gigantic pocket.

MORE BRIDGES: The exact number was censorable. But last week the Allies had nine more bridges over the Rhine than the Germans themselves had a year ago. The first new railway bridge, at Wesel, was built in two hours less than ten days.

NEWS IN THE NIGHT: Eisenhower, Bradley and Patton had APRIL 23 put in a busy day. They had inspected a horrid concentration camp at Ohrdruf, visited a salt mine with its hoard of Nazi gold and art, traveled several hundred miles by plane and Jeep. When they returned to General Patton's headquarters they were tired—and a little sick from the things they had seen. They dined, then sat in a big, sparsely furnished room, talking against the steady roar of supply trucks passing outside. Around midnight they went to bed. Eisenhower and

Bradley took two bedrooms upstairs. Patton's heavy boots clattered down the front steps and out to the caravan where he slept.

General Patton undressed and was about to get into bed when he noticed that his watch had stopped. He turned on his radio, spun the dial to BBC and an instant later heard a voice say with emotion: "We regret to announce that the President of the United States has died." A precise man, the General waited exactly two minutes to get the time. Then he set his watch at 12:15, put on a bathrobe and slippers, and walked back to the house.

General Bradley had just fallen asleep when the light woke him. Bradley and Patton went into Eisenhower's room and the three men talked for more than an hour. Sometimes it was hard for them to hear each other because the trucks still roared by outside. That was how the news of the Commander in Chief's death came to the commanders of his armies in Germany.

MAY 7 **"HELLO, TOVARISH!":** In the early days of last week the small German town of Torgau was almost deserted. Soviet Marshal Konev's artillery had battered it from across the Elbe. Two infantry and one armored divisions of the U.S. First Army had pulled up along a narrow tributary. One morning a patrol from the U.S. 69th Division, sent out to direct surrendering German soldiers to the rear, rolled beyond its officially prescribed radius of action and found itself in Torgau. This patrol consisted of four Yanks in a Jeep—Second Lieutenant William D. Robertson and three enlisted men.

The Russians on the other side of the Elbe sent up colored flares, the prearranged signal to designate friendly forces. Robertson had no flares. He took a bedsheet from a house, broke into a pharmacy, found mercurochrome and blue ink, made a crude representation of a U.S. flag and waved it from the tower of an ancient castle. The Russians, who had been tricked by Germans waving U.S. flags, sent over a few antitank shells.

Then Robertson decided on bold action. He and his men strode confidently out in the open, toward a German-blown bridge whose twisted girders offered a precarious footway across the river. The Russians decided that only Americans would do such a thing and two Russian officers scrambled out from the eastern end. In the center, only a few feet over the swift-running water, the men of Eisenhower and the men of Stalin met. Robertson slapped a Russian leg and cried: "Hello, *Tovarish!* Put it there!"

The great meeting, so long awaited, was real at last. Moscow fired its maximum salute of 24 salvos from 324 guns; Joseph Stalin, Winston Churchill and Harry Truman issued resounding statements. A Red Army lieutenant, rising in the midst of a joyful hubbub, said:

"My dear, quiet please. Today is the most happy day of our life, just as Stalingrad was the unhappiest when we thought there was nothing to do for our country but die. But now, my dear, we have the most crazy of our life. You must pardon I don't speak the right English, but we are very happy so we drink a toast. Long live Roosevelt!" A comrade whispered Harry Truman's name; the speaker looked at him blankly and went on: "Long live Roosevelt! Long live Stalin! Long live our two great armies!"

Eastern Front

During the winter and spring of 1945, the advance of the Russian armies from the East was just as rapid as the American and British thrust from the West. Early in January the Russians had reached the outskirts of Budapest. It would take them four months to cover the 400-odd miles to Berlin.

CITY IN TORMENT: All week long a cloud—part frost, part JAN. 15 smoke, part dust—hung over the agony of Budapest. As the battle neared its 15th day, the Russians had won more than 1,900 of the 4,500 blocks of buildings in the city. Landmarks of one of the most beautiful capitals in Europe were crumbling under artillery and mortar fire.

The German defenders had the advantage of fighting from old houses with thick stone walls. Antitank guns were hidden in gateways and cellar windows. Entrances, street intersections, bridges were all mined. The Russians concentrated on taking corner buildings, setting up a sweeping fire along the streets and leapfrogging to another corner building.

In cellars not used as forts, Budapest's civilians huddled, dying by hundreds. The dead did not stink. They froze hard as stone and in the morning they were wrapped in eerie shrouds of frost.

JAN. 29 **HUNGARY SWITCHES:** Hungary, last of Germany's military satellites, changed sides in the war last week. In Moscow Marshal Klimenti Voroshilov granted an armistice to the Hungarian Provisional National Government. By its terms Hungary agreed to: 1) furnish eight divisions to fight against Germany; 2) pay reparations of $300,000,000 (in goods); 3) renounce the territorial spoils of her six-year cruise aboard Adolf Hitler's pirate ship.

APRIL 16 **VIENNA'S TURN:** Last week came old Vienna's turn on the Nazi torture rack. The Germans had willed that the city of 2,000,000 Austrians should die—slowly, to gain a little more time for Naziism. But this week it seemed that the Red Army would foil that murder by swift conquest.

The Germans had not yet solved the Red Army's technique of taking bastioned cities by complex, encircling attacks. As they had at Budapest, two big Soviet armies struck swiftly at the sides of Vienna. Cossack horsemen slashed into the eastern approaches after crossing the Morava River. From a flotilla of small boats on the Danube, Red raiders leapfrogged ashore at night to attack from the rear. Infantrymen infiltrated the Vienna Woods to the west, slammed over the main roads, then cut swiftly to the Danube, north of the city. Vienna was almost surrounded. Then the Russians burst through, by this week were battling in the parks and palace grounds in the center of the city.

APRIL 30 **DOOM & TRIUMPH:** Though every Berliner must have known in his heart that the mammoth march of Red Army power could not be stopped, thousands of Berliners, men and boys, ill-clothed, ill-weaponed, even hundreds of women, went to the fields and forests at the edges of the city to man the trenches, pillboxes, antitank ditches and enormous numbers of antiaircraft, dug-in tanks and machine guns.

Then, from the wall of smoke on the close horizon, broke the first bolts of doom. Russian shells and rockets showered, then poured. After them came the Red Army tanks. Thus, in a 70-mile arc of flame and steel, had the soldiers of Red Marshal Georgi K. Zhukov come up to the outskirts of the Nazi capital. In five days they had fought through five defense belts, smashing down a great concentration of enemy tanks in what may have been the war's biggest battle of armor.

The millions of Berliners who could not fight milled in panic. They fought each other to get on the last trains to anywhere. They massed in the air-raid shelters, choked the *Untergrundbahn* platforms and tracks. Stunned, they huddled wherever they could find shelter and waited for the end.

ON MOSCOW TIME: Berlin's end came 16 days after the armies MAY 14 of Marshals Zhukov and Konev lunged for the Nazi capital, twelve days after they reached its streets. The date was May 2 and the time was 3 p.m.—Moscow time.

It had almost ended sooner. In the gloomy dawn of May Day a German colonel bearing a huge white flag appeared at a ruined side street held by the Russians. "Will the Soviet Command receive emissaries to discuss negotiations?" he asked. Red Army Major Belousov agreed and walked with the Germans toward their lines. A shot cracked out. Belousov dropped with a Nazi sniper's bullet through his head.

The raging Russians answered with the greatest artillery barrage they had yet loosed on the capital, continuing without letup through the day, the night and the next morning. Then the German commander—Nazi Artillery General Kurt Webling—came himself with a white flag, and did his surrendering within the Soviet lines.

The Berlin that surrendered was the pounded corpse of a city. Wrote a Soviet correspondent: "Ruins, craters, smashed guns, tramcars riddled with holes, half-demolished trenches, heaps of spent cartridge shells, fresh graves, corpses still awaiting burial, masses of white flags, crowds of glum and hungry inhabitants lie before our eyes. The Tiergarten is burning. The Reichstag is smoking. Hitler's Berlin residence is also burning. The windows are blocked with heaps of books, and machine guns stick out between them."

By week's end a Berlin edition of *Pravda* appeared.

Victory in Europe

The actual capitulation of the German armies was a confused and piecemeal operation. The first large-scale surrender was made to Britain's Field Marshal Montgomery in northern Germany on May 4. Three days later General Jodl unconditionally surrendered the entire German military force to General Eisenhower. But Stalin insisted that formal ratification should follow in Berlin. Accordingly, a third acknowledgment of defeat was signed in the presence of General Zhukov at his field headquarters near Berlin on May 9.

MAY 14 **AT LAST:** Like a long-deferred spring, victory in Europe came at last—in its own sweet time. For most people, the war in Europe ended—not when they heard the hoarse voice of the radio, nor when they saw paper blizzards falling between skyscrapers, nor when they ate their first food in freedom—but slowly, silently, by degrees, somewhere in each man's heart.

MONTY'S MOMENT: Like a householder who took his visitors for tradesmen, Field Marshal Sir Bernard Law Montgomery stood in the door of his motor van and demanded icily: "What do you want?"

Facing him, beside a copse of silvery birches on the bleak, rolling moorland of northern Germany stood four German officers, the Commander in Chief of the German Navy, the Chief of Staff of the *Wehrmacht* command in the north, and two members of their staffs. It was up to General Admiral Hans Georg von Friedeberg to reply. Grey-faced and grim, that scion of a long line of Prussian officers asked permission to surrender three German armies—not those facing Montgomery to the north but those facing the Russians to the east.

Said Montgomery, "No. Certainly not. Go surrender to the Soviet commander."

The Germans, still hoping to surrender to Britain and the U.S. but not to the Russians, still hoping to split the Allies and pose as undefeated opponents of Bolshevism, had another tricky proposal: an agreed retreat before a slow advance of the Allied forces, permitting the Nazis to carry on the fight against the Russians.

Monty refused even to discuss such terms. With the ultimate gesture of military scorn, he took them into his tent and showed them where they stood—on his own battle operations map. Then he sent them off.

An hour later Von Friedeberg came back, red-eyed. He had been weeping. Monty made his take-it-or-leave-it offer; unconditional surrender of all the forces facing his armies in Germany, Denmark and The Netherlands. "If you do not agree to the surrender, then I will go on with the war and I will be delighted to do so." Friedeberg agreed to return next day with a decision.

Late in the grey, gusty afternoon of the next day, word reached Montgomery of Friedeberg's return. He let the Germans wait—ten minutes, 20 minutes. Then, still deliberate, he walked to his van and sent for Friedeberg. The German commander came, puffing a cigaret to its finger-burning end. A few moments later he emerged, his shoulders drooping. With the others he walked quickly to a brown tent with two of its sides rolled up. They sat stiffly at a plain trestle table covered with a grey blanket. On it was an inkwell with a plain, wooden pen, the kind a post office provides.

Monty let them sit another ten minutes while he dressed for the occasion. A lieutenant colonel recited in German the terms of surrender: unconditional. The wooden-faced Germans signed. At 18:25 hours (6:25 p.m.) Field Marshal Montgomery signed the paper, accepting.

The next day at Monty's headquarters the gunners of the 160th Heavy Antiaircraft Regiment, veterans of many a blitz night, fired 21 salvos from 24 guns. Their long-barreled guns shouted victory into a bombless sky.

HOW IT ENDED: The final unconditional surrender of all German forces was signed in a humble trade school of once-conquered, now liberated France. In that plain red building in Reims, Supreme Commander Eisenhower had established advanced headquarters. To it came the German negotiators, headed by Colonel General Alfred Jodl, last chief of staff of the dissolving German Army, and General Admiral Hans Georg von Friedeberg, last commander in chief of the dissolved German Navy.

Eisenhower himself did not receive them. They did their

talking to his chief of staff, brilliant Lieut. General Walter Bedell Smith, and officers of the Russian, British and French armed services. The final discussions went on through the afternoon and evening: there were endless technical details to be set down, mainly to guarantee the orderly transmission of surrender instructions throughout the shattered German military machine. Finally, at 2:41 a.m. on May 7, at a long wooden table, in the bare, map-walled "war room," the surrender was signed.

Then, and only then, were the German envoys escorted down the hall to meet General Eisenhower. Sternly he put the question: did they fully understand the terms they had signed? Would Germany carry them out? They answered yes.

At the signing, Jodl had spoken the last words for Germany. Ramrod-stiff, in a voice that choked and almost broke he said:

"With this signature the German people and the German armed forces are, for better or worse, delivered into the victors' hands. In this war, which has lasted more than five years, both have achieved and suffered more than perhaps any other people in the world. In this hour I can only express the hope that the victors will treat them with generosity."

For Germany the war had ended, not with a bang but a whimper.

War in the Pacific

By 1945 the Allies were closing in on Japan in a series of bold island leaps. They had taken the Solomons, New Guinea, the Gilberts, Marshalls and Marianas. Now they had ahead of them the final liberation of the Philippines; the remaining threat of a battered but still dangerous Japanese Navy and Air Force; and the problem of capturing Iwo Jima and Okinawa to use as staging bases before launching the attack on Japan itself.

FEB. 12 **"VEEKTORY! MABUHAY!":** Last week, as U.S. mechanized cavalrymen battered through a Japanese road barrier and roared into Manila from the east, neither Manila nor her liberators were garbed for a gala. The city was drab and dirty after the Japanese occupation. The incoming soldiers were dust-caked and sweat-streaked. But next morning, as the sun mounted, the miracle of freedom restored called forth a rush of popular emotion that was louder than the music of bands, gayer than whipping banners.

Suddenly Manila's unkempt streets swarmed with men, women & children, shouting "Veektory!" and *"Mabuhay!"* —Tagalog for "Hurrah!" The Filipinos pressed gifts on their deliverers. A small boy darted out to hand a precious egg to one startled American. One gaunt, toothless, ragged woman had nothing to give. But she hobbled out to catch and kiss the hand of an embarrassed colonel. She sobbed: "God bless you, sir! God bless all the Americans!"

BURNING CITY: The Japanese "fadeback" from Manila FEB. 19 proved to be illusory. Early in December, a month before the landings at Lingayen Gulf, the Japs had installed demolition charges in large buildings. Flimsy warehouses had been stocked with drums of gasoline. Forty-eight hours after U.S. forces entered northern Manila, Jap demolition engineers pressed the buttons. Electrically connected charges went off in series. The main business district began to burn. There was no water pressure to fight the fires. Fanned by a stiff wind from the Bay, the flames drove part of Ohio's 37th Division back from the Pasig River. All night the city was wreathed in fire.

At the approaches to the dock area, the Japs really showed what they could do. Any position with heavy stone walls was turned into a strong point. Churches suited the Japs perfectly. One churchyard fortress had to be burned out with artillery, mortar fire and flame-throwers. The Japs had 5-in. naval guns on the second and third floors of the Philippine General Hospital. But this week, the U.S. cavalry and infantry had joined and the enemy was being "compressed into extinction."

MacARTHUR'S BACK!: On the north side of Manila, where U.S. troops were still hunting out Jap snipers, a command car whisked across the city limits, pulled up near a command post. Within a few minutes the word had gone down to the lowest ranks: "It's MacArthur!"

Douglas MacArthur had lost no time getting back to the capital he had evacuated on Christmas Eve 1941, after declaring it an open city to save it from destruction by the Japs. He made a swift inspection of the areas his troops had already taken. His next stop was a hospital where some of the rescued veterans of Bataan and Corregidor were lodged. "These are my own men and I am one of them," he said. "I owe them a lot. I promised I would return, and I'm long overdue."

Down through a double line of cots the General strode, pausing at bedside after bedside. Down the gaunt faces ran the unashamed tears of fighting men—now the wasted victims of malnutrition and dysentery. Said MacArthur: "I'm going to give you all the medical attention you need. And then you're going home."

Then the General inspected Santo Tomás University, where 3,700 had endured Japanese imprisonment for three years. Occasional shells from Jap artillery still fell in the compound. While gaunt and sickly survivors cheered from the windows ("He's back!"), the General strode inside. He poked through jammed corridors and rooms, grimly inspected the ravages of slow starvation. As General MacArthur left Santo Tomás, maimed veterans hobbled toward him to salute, and some to touch his uniform.

FEB. 26 **HELL'S ACRE:** Little Iwo Jima, covering only eight square miles, lay almost exactly halfway between Guam and Tokyo. From its airfields enemy planes had attacked B-29s and their fields at Saipan; its radar station had tattled to Tokyo whenever B-29s were on the way. The Japs knew how vital it was to U.S. forces to capture Iwo. They knew what a blow its loss would be to the defense of Japan. So they packed Iwo with 10,000 to 15,000 men, with heavy coastal guns, well-sited antiaircraft guns, machine-gun nests hewn out of the rock.

For 72 days Iwo had been bombed without surcease. But air attack left Iwo unchastened and unsoftened. When a bombardment group of the Fifth Fleet arrived to give it the Navy's full treatment with big guns, Iwo was still spitting fire.

For three solid days it took the worst that the Navy could give it, and it gave back. On the fourth day new battleships added their 16-in. salvos to the big-gun chorus; carriers sent

The Marines raise the flag atop Iwo Jima's Mt. Suribachi, in the most widely reprinted photograph of World War II (see page 236).

in more planes. Iwo absorbed more than 7,000 tons of shells plus untold tons of bombs—a record for a Pacific island.

Then it was D-day—Feb. 19. Dawn broke clear on a calm sea black with ships: 800 craft under Vice Admiral Richmond Kelly Turner, hard-driving conqueror of Guadalcanal, Tarawa, Kwajalein and Saipan. With Turner on the bridge of his command ship was Lieut. General Holland M. ("Howlin' Mad") Smith, boss of the Fleet Marine Force.

When the first landing craft nosed into Futatsune Beach, the opposition pulled back from the beach, but from the heights of Suribachi in the southwest, and a series of hills in the northeast, the Japanese poured enfilading fire into the attackers. Said Howlin' Mad Smith: "Our men are spread all over hell's acre out there, and most of those guns are in caves. They come out and fire five or six rounds and then go back into hiding."

Finally, U.S. tanks clattered up the rocky hillsides, the flash of their guns alternating with the dragon's breath of flame-throwers. The beachhead was secure along a 4,500-yd. front. But many a marine had passed from hell's acre to God's acre.

REUNION: In Manila General Douglas MacArthur found an old friend, looking fit and ready despite years of servitude under the interloping Japs: the General's Rolls-Royce.

MARCH 5   **SOME MARINES WEPT:** On Iwo Jima last week at least 40,000 marines fought to the death with 20,000 entrenched Japanese. As the 28th Regiment took Suribachi Volcano and the U.S. flag was raised over this highest point on the island [see page 236], some marines wept openly.

MARCH 19   **AUTUMN LEAVES:** A dream came true last week for U.S. Army aviators: they got their chance to loose avalanches of fire bombs on Tokyo and Nagoya, and they proved that, properly kindled, Japanese cities will burn like autumn leaves.

APRIL 9   **LONG STEP NEARER:** Less than two weeks after the end of the Iwo Jima battle the U.S. Navy had assembled the greatest invasion armada ever to operate in the Pacific: 1,400 ships and up to 100,000 soldiers and marines. When it was all ready, they poured this power into Japan's front yard. The main objective: poverty-stricken, malaria-ridden, snake-infested Okinawa. Once firmly established on Okinawa, Americans could move up the 370 miles to Kyushu, Japan's southernmost main island.

At 8:30 on Easter Sunday morning, the Okinawa invasion was launched. Jap opposition on the beach was almost nonexistent. Some men marched a mile without hearing a shot. But there was little serious expectation that the rest of Okinawa would come cheap. The island was too important a strategical prize for that. If it were lost, said the Tokyo newspaper *Yomiuri-Hocki,* Japan would have "no hope of turning the course of the war."

DIVINE TEMPESTS: Last week Fleet Admiral Chester W. Nim- APRIL 23
itz reported "desperate, suicidal" Japanese air attacks on U.S.
ships near Okinawa by a "special attack corps." Thus the
Pacific fleet boss lifted secrecy from an enemy tactic that had
been a tabooed topic and a source of endless scuttlebutt since
the Leyte campaign.

The Admiral's communiqué told the U.S. public what the
U.S. press had dutifully refrained from telling: that the Japanese have organized a suicide corps of flyers whose mission
is to crash-dive their explosives-laden aircraft into ships; that
this *Kamikaze* (Divine Tempest) Corps has damaged some
major U.S. fleet units and sunk some smaller ships.

Contrary to rumor, the *Kamikaze* Corps is not made up
entirely of specially recruited personnel with only enough
flight training to carry out one fatal mission. Many attacks
are at night; it takes skilled pilots to attack a target in the
dark. There is also no confirmation of widespread Navy rumors that the pilots are chained to the controls. Several have
chosen not to be "divine tempests," and have been fished out
of their planes after ditching them in the sea.

CIGARS & BOMBS: Major General Curtis E. ("Ironpants") MAY 21
LeMay has lately become known as "The Cigar." He usually
has one clenched in his teeth (it helps to cover a slight facial
paralysis, the result of an old wound), and the boys of his 21st
Bomber Command, in sincerest flattery, have also become
cigar puffers. Last week their stogies stuck up at a cocky angle.

In the two biggest and most destructive attacks so far
launched, The Cigar sent more than 900 B-29s against Japan.
Not one of the big bombers was lost. Next day, LeMay relaxed somewhat, sending a smaller force (100 to 150 B-29s).
That day again all the Superforts got back.

Then The Cigar wound up and really let the Japs have it.
The war's greatest B-29 fleet—"well over 500" Superforts—
poured a searing load of 3,300 tons of fire bombs on Nagoya,
third city of the Japanese Empire and home of the main Mit-
subishi aircraft factories. Two bombers were lost.

TO THE DEATH: The biggest and fiercest battle in the post-V-E
world was in progress last week in Okinawa. U.S. troops were
advancing in the old-fashioned, inescapable way, one foot at

a time, against the kind of savage, rat-in-a-hole defense that only the Japanese can offer. Total U.S. casualties on Okinawa have reached 23,188, of whom 3,877 are dead and 2,611 missing. "We will take our time," said Lieut. General Simon Bolivar Buckner Jr., "and kill the Japanese gradually."

MAY 28 **AND THEN THERE WAS ONE:** There were 50 marines on top of Okinawa's Sugar Loaf Hill. They had been ordered to hold the position all night, at any cost. By dawn 46 of them had been killed or wounded by Japanese hand grenades. Then, into the foxhole where the remaining four huddled, the Japs dropped a white phosphorus shell, burning three men to death. The last survivor crawled down to an aid station.

JUNE 11 **TWILIGHT IN TOKYO:** At his headquarters on a Guam hilltop, General LeMay added up the results of three months' massive B-29 attacks on Tokyo:

¶ 51.3 sq. mi. of Tokyo (46% of the built-up area) had been burned or bombed to ashes.

¶ 4,500,000 people who had lived in the area were now homeless.

¶ 50 Superforts had been lost—one per sq. mi. of devastation.

¶ "We have destroyed all the target areas we have set out to destroy."

JUNE 18 **SERGEANT BROWN GOES TO TOWN:** For Technical Sergeant William L. Brown of De Witt, Ark., it all began in New Guinea, where the 32nd Division commander badly needed a Jap prisoner to question, and promised a furlough as payment. Brown scurried off into the bush, brought back a live Jap, spent his leave in Australia and got married there.

When the division moved to Luzon, there were new terms: for every live Jap, one case of beer and a three-day pass to Manila. Sergeant Brown took a prisoner in a cave by persuading him to discard his hara-kiri grenade and come out. Then Brown picked up his beer and went to Manila.

Twenty-four hours after his return, Brown ran into a Jap officer who went after him with his saber. The Sergeant wrestled him down, took the saber as a souvenir, again collected his beer and went back to Manila.

Two days after his return he copped one live prisoner with a flying tackle, turned him over to a second soldier to hold, then chased a second Jap, who promptly sat down and pulled out a hara-kiri grenade. Thoughtfully, Sergeant Brown stopped, took out a cigaret and lit it. The Jap's face brightened. Brown replaced his .45 in its holster, walked up to the Jap and offered him a cigaret. The Jap put down his grenade for a moment to accept the gift and Brown went to Manila again.

KNOTTY PROBLEM: In his high, airy office in Manila, with the glare of summer sun cut down by Venetian blinds, General of the Army Douglas MacArthur conferred with General Joseph W. Stilwell. The commander of all Army forces in the Pacific and the commander of all the Army's ground forces had a knotty problem to resolve: how to deploy more than 3,500,000 men for the final onslaught against Japan.

Not even these two able strategists could know precisely what sort of campaign they must prepare for. Japan supposedly had 1,750,000 men under arms, ready to defend the homeland. Would they fight to the same bitter end as the 85,000 on Okinawa? Would they exact the same toll, of one U.S. soldier killed for every ten Japanese? Must the U.S. prepare for at least 175,000 killed—twice as many as in the European Theater of Operations?

CLARENCE: For ten days on Okinawa the 96th Division had JUNE 25 stood stymied before Hen Hill, a knobby 450-ft. crag just northeast of Shuri. Two battalions had taken turns charging up; both had failed—with heavy casualties.

Then one of the battalions, its ranks refilled with battle-green replacements, tried again. Once again a hail of Jap fire pinned the troops to the ground. But this time one soldier just kept walking and throwing hand grenades at every Jap he saw.

He was Pfc. Clarence B. Craft, a sandy-haired 23-year-old from Santa Ana, Calif., eight months in the Army and brand-new to combat.

Veterans who watched said it was unbelievable, the sort of thing that could happen only once in a war. Craft reached the top and stood against the skyline directing the grenade-throwing of the troops below. Two other replacements crawled up to give him covering fire. Others formed a chain to pass him hand grenades.

Craft went along the crest, hurling grenades into foxholes and trenches. Japs popped up to fire at him; Craft pitched a hand grenade first. Japs tried to charge him with bayonets and spears. Craft shot them with his M-1 rifle. The whole thing took about 15 minutes. When the rest of the unit reached the hilltop, they counted 58 dead Japs.

Said Clarence Craft's mother when she heard the news at her home in Missouri: "He's the most accurate thrower I ever saw. Why, I've seen that boy kill fish in a stream throwing rocks at them."

Said the New York *Times:* "Great must be the rejoicing among all the Clarences of this world."

JULY 2 **END ON OKINAWA:** The last-ditch Japanese defenders were split into pockets and Fleet Admiral Nimitz announced that organized resistance had ended. To the Japanese, the cost of defeat on Okinawa was staggering. They had lost (by preliminary count) 98,564 men killed and 4,500 captured. For the U.S., with 6,990 Americans dead or missing and 29,598 wounded, it was indeed the bloodiest campaign of the Central and Western Pacific.

JULY 16 **HOW IT STARTED:** According to Radio Tokyo, the *Kamikaze* Corps began its "death-defying, body-crashing" tactics last Oct. 15, when Vice Admiral Masabumi Arima flew his plane into a U.S. aircraft carrier, lest "the traditional spirit of the Japanese Navy be spoiled." Thereafter, Radio Tokyo daily intoned the names of "hero gods," and Japanese journalists interviewed little boys whose ambition was to grow up and become suicide pilots. Not until April did the U.S. Navy relax censorship to permit mention of enemy suicide air tactics. Since then the Navy has admitted that 19 ships have been hit by suicide planes, including the carriers *Bunker Hill* and *Saratoga*. Radio Tokyo says all Jap pilots now are suicidal.

AUG. 6 **OBSTETRICIAN:** Hunting snipers on Luzon, Paratrooper Sergeant John L. Sweet found a Filipino woman in distress. He rolled up his sleeves, heated some water, sent a native boy for help, delivered triplets.

"MY GOD!": The run was short and straight. At 9:15 a.m. Major AUG. 20
Thomas Ferebee pressed the toggle and the single bomb was
away. Colonel Paul Warfield Tibbets, the pilot, took back the
controls and ten pairs of eyes strained at the plexiglass windows as Tibbets turned the plane broadside to Hiroshima. It
took less than 60 seconds. Then the brilliant morning sun-
light was slashed by a more brilliant white flash. It was so
strong that the crew of the Superfortress *Enola Gay* felt a
"visual shock," although all wore sun glasses.

The first atomic bomb had been dropped. A few seconds
after the flash, the shock wave from the blast reached the
Enola Gay, several miles away, and rocked it like a giant burst
of flak. From the men who had rung up the curtain on a new
era in history burst nothing more original than an awed
"My God!"

Hiroshima had once harbored 344,000 people, thousands
more in the adjacent quartermaster depot. A Jap corporal was
in a hotel and put his head out the window when he heard the
drone of engines overhead. "I looked up," he said in a
Tokyo radio interview, "and simultaneously a lightning-like
flash covered the whole sky, blinding my eyes. Unconsciously,
I dived for cover and a torn quilt miraculously was blown
over me, which I hugged to myself for dear life.

"Several minutes later I was outside. All around, I found

*Hiroshima, after the bomb. "A lightning-like flash covered the whole sky.
All green vegetables perished."*

dead and wounded. Some were bloated and scorched—such an awesome sight, their legs and bodies stripped of clothes and burned with a huge blister. All green vegetation, from grasses to trees, perished in that period."

Hiroshima was covered with a giant, mushrooming cloud of smoke and dust. When reconnaissance photographs were at last obtained, they showed 4.1 square miles—60% of the city's built-up area—destroyed by fire and blast. There was no crater in which the blast effect would have been largely wasted; the bomb had exploded well above ground. How many tens of thousands of Hiroshima's people had perished was not yet known. [The final toll was 71,000 dead or missing and 68,000 injured.]

Three days later, the Superfort *Great Artiste* was out on a similar mission. Major Charles W. Sweeney had a rough trip to Japan in bad weather; his primary target, Kokura, was socked in. Over the second-choice target, Nagasaki, he had just enough gas left for one run. It was begun on instruments, and then there was a hole in the clouds so that the bombardier, Captain Kermit K. Beahan, was able to bomb visually. This bomb was more powerful than the one dropped on Hiroshima; in ways that could not be revealed [the use of plutonium instead of uranium and an improved detonating system made it explode more efficiently] it was also so much of an improvement that the first bomb was already obsolete. It exploded on or near the ground, blasted a ghastly crater. It destroyed only one square mile of the Kyushu seaport, but spokesmen said that it had been more devastating than the first. [The bomb killed 35,000 people, injured 60,000.]

AUG. 27 **THE SURRENDER:** The task of occupation was without precedent. The U.S. and her Allies simply were not ready for sudden victory. Never before had any power or alliance of powers been confronted with so great a victory without invasion. Beaten to her knees by air power and sea power, Japan still had 2,500,000 or more undefeated troops on her own soil.

To enter and occupy such a country, the Allies had need of a man with great experience, great gifts and well-nigh infinite wisdom. Weeks before the actual problem arose, they had chosen General of the Army Douglas MacArthur.

This week, in Manila, members of MacArthur's staff received, with icy dignity, the first envoys of surrendered Japan. There were still irksome details to be settled and irritating delays to be overcome, but soon the first occupiers of Japan would go ashore in strength, from combat-loaded attack transports, under the great guns of the fleet and with clouds of carrier aircraft standing by—just in case.

FINAL DETAILS: When the Japanese envoys who went to Manila to prepare for the surrender insisted that MacArthur spell everything out twice for "clarification," MacArthur curtly cut them off: "The directive from this headquarters is clear and explicit and is to be complied with without further delay." When the Japs at last decided to get on with it, MacArthur rubbed the salt of Bataan into their wounds, insisting they use the word Bataan as their planes' radio call.

In Manila, the Japs were quartered at the damaged but serviceable Rosaria Apartments. Supper was sent over from a nearby officers' mess. Lieut. General Torashiro Kawabe showed a huge roll of U.S. money, sent an American orderly out for six cartons of U.S. cigarets. Then the envoys were whisked to the hastily repaired City Hall where MacArthur and his staff have their headquarters.

Kawabe bowed low to stone-faced Lieut. General Richard K. Sutherland. MacArthur's chief of staff quickly led the six ranking members of the delegation to a conference with four other staff generals and Rear Admiral Forrest P. Sherman. For five strained hours, the victors extracted information about harbors and airfields around Tokyo, which Allied forces would need for their entry.

The Japs had five hours to sleep (on Army cots), and in mid-morning Kawabe was handed 24 or 25 pages of detailed orders. By lunchtime the Japs were on their way back to Tokyo.

Said MacArthur, in a statement such as only he can write: "In my capacity as Supreme Commander for the Allied Powers I shall soon proceed to Japan with accompanying forces composed of ground, naval and air elements. Subject to weather that will permit landings, it is anticipated that the instrument of surrender will be signed within ten days. It is my earnest hope that pending the formal surrender, armistice conditions may prevail on every front and that a bloodless surrender may be effectuated."

Missouri's Harry Truman had asked that the final surrender be signed aboard the Third Fleet flagship, the 45,000-ton battleship *Missouri.*

SEPT. 3   **FOR THE AGES:** MacArthur spent his last days in Manila putting the finishing touches to the great performance in which he would play the leading part. The Supreme Commander painstakingly wrote and rewrote the short speech he would deliver (and practiced it aloud). He was writing for the ages.

SEPT. 10   **THE LAST BEACHHEAD:** A brisk south wind was scattering tiny white clouds across the blue sky above Atsugi airfield when the first U.S. troops landed. Witnessing the scene, a Japanese reporter said it made his eyes smart: "So much emotion packed into a single moment."

There was emotion, too, but of a different sort, in the hearts of the 11th Airborne Division as they dropped down on Atsugi, of the 4th Marines as they plunged ashore at Yokosuka, heavily laden with battle gear that was to be useless. This was the last beachhead, and they hit it standing up. There was no fight left in the enemy.

As Douglas MacArthur stepped from his transport plane *Bataan* his sternly sculptured features relaxed in an easy smile. The austere man who used to forget faces called first names, clasped hands, and complimented the military band. Later he dined with his junior officers; he had not done so since Dec. 7, 1941.

The invasion proceeded with machine-like precision. Transport planes floated down on the airstrips at four-minute intervals. U.S. and British battleships, cruisers and destroyers marched in stately file into Tokyo Bay. It was almost too smooth. Said a dry Britisher, watching a general and a few marines raise the U.S. flag over Yokosuka's naval base: "Now he'll declare the bazaar open."

As the Americans entered Tokyo, Japanese children laughed and waved. Their parents closed their doors or hid in the corrugated iron shacks that sheltered the bombed-out. Nubile Japanese girls scampered for cover as U.S. troops approached. And civilians in the streets of Tokyo—the men wearing ran-

dom bits of army uniform—stared at the invaders with un-
concealed hostility. Humility was not conspicuous. Correspondents asked a Harvard-educated Foreign Office spokesman if Japan would ever again attempt world conquest.
The spokesman gazed out of his window overlooking the
city's devastation. Then he answered: "We are paying a very
great price for our attempt. However, if your treatment is too
severe, the Japanese will react."

Jap propaganda, by stressing the atomic bomb, likened defeat to a natural calamity. Said Premier Prince Higashi-Kuni:
"The cause of our defeat was the sudden collapse of our
fighting strength." Japanese seemed eager to accept this explanation. Perhaps they would never realize that, before the
atomic bomb was dropped, their navy & merchant marine
had been sunk, their air force whipped, their army outclassed.
War guilt they seemed to feel not at all.

But for the happy, peaceful moment, the victors were content to survey the inscrutable vanquished and to be glad the
Japs had had sense enough to quit. One G.I. looked from a
plane at the tumbled hills and mountains of Honshu's spine
and said: "Am I glad I don't have to fight over this country—
just like Okinawa."

". . . PEACE BE NOW RESTORED": On the decks of the giant
U.S. battleship *Missouri* the brief, fevered course of Japan as
a great power came to a quiet end.

TIME Correspondent Theodore H. White cabled:

"The veranda deck of the slate-grey battleship shone with
the color of red-striped Russians, red-ribboned Britons, olive-
drab Chinese, and row upon row of khaki-clad American
admirals and generals.

"The Japanese had been piped aboard four minutes before
MacArthur made his appearance. The first aboard was the
silk-hatted Japanese Foreign Minister Mamoru Shigemitsu,
limping on his wooden leg, leaning on his cane and clutch-
ing at the ship's ropes as he pulled himself up the stairway.
The second was the dour, solemn-faced Chief of the Imperial
General Staff, Yoshijiro Umezu—his chest covered with ribbons and hung with gold braid, his eyes blank and unseeing.

"MacArthur stepped out from a cabin, stood stiffly erect
and began reading with all the mellifluous, sonorous qualities

On the "Missouri," Japanese General Umezu signs the surrender document in the presence of General MacArthur and khaki-clad Allies.

of his magnificent voice. The only sign of his emotion was the trembling of the hands in which he held his paper.

"As he closed the introductory remarks he half turned and faced the Japs with a piercing stare and said: 'I announce it my firm purpose to insure that the terms of surrender are fully, promptly and faithfully complied with.'

"Shigemitsu, doffing his silk hat and peeling a yellow glove from his right hand, limped forward to sign the document and was assisted to a chair. With a blank, expressionless face he composed himself and signed. Umezu followed. He slowly drew off his white gloves and, without sitting, bent his stocky body forward and affixed the authority of the Japanese Army to the acknowledgment of total defeat.

"At precisely 9:08 MacArthur stepped forward, removed a handful of fountain pens from his pocket. He started his signature, then handed the first pen to the gaunt soldier standing by his left shoulder. General Jonathan Wainwright saluted stiffly, accepted the pen, and stepped back.

"MacArthur hesitated a moment after the final signature. Then he stepped forward and said slowly: 'Let us pray that peace be now restored to the world and that God will preserve it always.'

"He lifted his eyes from the script, faced the Japanese, and declared: 'These proceedings are closed.'"

ATOMIC AGE

President Truman's decision to use the atomic bomb against Japan not only revolutionized warfare but ushered in an awesome new era of science and technology. To help explain the origins and significance of the new weapon, TIME *created a temporary new department.*

BRUTAL CHALLENGE: The atomic bomb was something more AUG. 13 than an instrument to shape 1945's history. It also represented a brutal challenge to the world to keep the peace. The scientists had created, and had successfully applied, a weapon which might wipe out with a few strokes any nation's power to resist an enemy.

The story of the atomic bomb had been the greatest and the best-kept secret of the war. It began in 1941 when the British set a board of experts to work. It had its drama: one winter day in 1942, British and Norwegian volunteer commandos raided a point in Norway, found a heavy-water plant where the Germans were working on the process. U.S. scientists, too, had been at work smashing the atom. They now found the Germans had been ahead of them. The race of the laboratories began.

The fact that the U.S. now has the bomb (and presumably the only facilities for producing it) was in part a result of Britain's trust of this nation. As they did with radar, Britain, Canada and the U.S. pooled their knowledge of splitting the atom, pooled their atomic scientists. Three vast plants were built: at Oak Ridge, Tenn., at Pasco, Wash., and at Los Alamos, N.M.

In the War Department, the super-secret program was referred to as the "Manhattan Project." It had top priority on materiel and Army specialists. But few, if any, of the 65,000 who at one time worked on materials, handled blueprints, and expedited the job, ever knew what the "Manhattan Project" was. Not until this week did they know the end results of their labors. The cost was tremendous, but it was worth it. Said Harry Truman: "We have spent $2 billion on the greatest scientific gamble in history—and won."

THE FINAL TEST: In an old ranch house on the New Mexican desert near Alamogordo, a company of jittery men watched Cornell Physicist Robert Bacher assemble the first atomic bomb. At one point a vital part jammed. The scientists gasped but were coolly reassured by Bacher. When all was ready the expedition waited.

Thunder & lightning rumbled and flashed in the early morning of July 16 when the final test was to be made. The bomb was carefully mounted on a steel tower hung with instruments to record the effects of the explosion. Over five miles away, the scientists lay flat, listening breathlessly to the time signals announced over the radio: "Minus 15 minutes, minus 14 minutes, minus 13 minutes." At "minus 45 seconds" a robot mechanism took over the controls and the watchers lived the tensest seconds of their lives.

Suddenly there was a tremendous sustained roar. In Albuquerque, 120 miles away, the sky blazed noonday-bright. The scientists close at hand looked up in time to see a huge, multicolored pillar of cloud surging up over 40,000 feet in the sky. But where the steel tower stood, there was only a crater. The tower had completely vaporized.

AUG. 20 **FEARFUL RESPONSIBILITIES:** The greatest and most terrible of wars ended this week in the echoes of an enormous event —an event so much more enormous that, relative to it, the war itself shrank to minor significance. More fearful responsibilities, more crucial liabilities rested on the victors even than on the vanquished. With the controlled splitting of the atom, humanity was brought inescapably into a new age in which all thoughts and things were split—and far from controlled.

The sudden achievement of victory was a mercy, to the Japanese no less than to the United Nations; but mercy born of a ruthless force beyond anything in human chronicle. The rational mind had put into the hands of common man the fire and force of the sun itself.

HOW THE BOMB WAS BUILT: Behind the blackout curtains, physicists had gotten their work orders. A few, horrified by what was planned, refused the summons. But most went to work, knowing that discovery could not be stopped, that the U.S. and its scientific allies must make it first. Many hoped that they would fail.

Last week the War Department told the story of their success. Professor H. D. Smyth, chairman of Princeton's physics department, who wrote the report, could not tell it all. But what he could tell made the most fantastic and meaningful story to come out of the war.

The U.S. entered the atom race in the fall of 1939 when Franklin Roosevelt appointed an informal "Advisory Committee on Uranium." It was a small project until the Nazi *Panzers* roared across France. Then on Oct. 11, 1941, nearly two months before Pearl Harbor, President Roosevelt wrote to Winston Churchill, offering British nuclear physicists a plan to work in the U.S. Churchill accepted. The U.S. and Britain were partners.

The centers of "The Manhattan Engineer District" were full of G-men. The District's couriers were Army officers, briefcases chained to their wrists. From dozens of universities and industrial plants physicists, chemists and mathematicians vanished into thin air; the Manhattan District had snatched them. Like an ever-growing snowball the Manhattan District rolled around the nation, picking up men, money ($2,000,000,000), mountains of materials, trainloads of equipment. It enlisted famed corporations—Eastman, Dupont, Union Carbide and others. Under the cover name of "The Metallurgical Laboratory," some of the most important discoveries were made at the University of Chicago directed by famed Dr. Arthur Holly Compton. His leading associate: Italian-born Dr. Enrico Fermi, whom many consider the world's foremost nuclear physicist.

To carry out some of the complicated technical processes involved in preparing some of the fissionable materials needed for the bomb, vast plants were constructed in a sparsely inhabited region at Oak Ridge, Tenn., and a brand new city (called "Dogpatch") sprang up around them. Here, amid oceans of mud and battlefield confusion, the scientists produced the supply of U-235 which would detonate the bomb.

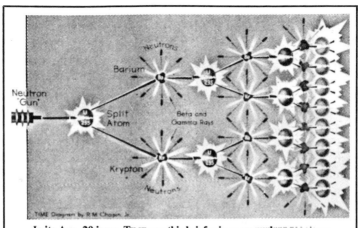

In its Aug, 20 issue, TIME ran this brief primer on nuclear reaction:
When a piece of paper is ignited with a match, the paper particles first heated set others on fire; these in turn ignite others, and so on. The same sort of chain reaction must be started for a successful atomic explosion. In this diagram the "match" at left is a neutron source. (A common source of neutrons is radium mixed with beryllium.) When these neutrons bombard a particle of uranium 235, the uranium nucleus splits into barium and krypton atoms which are highly unstable and artificially radioactive. They throw off gamma and beta radiation and finally, in an effort to lose mass, spout their own neutrons. Under proper conditions these neutrons will touch off other uranium nuclei. In a tiny fraction of a second, the chain reaction will run through a good-sized sample of uranium containing trillions of atoms, and the result will be a cataclysmic blast.

Then, to produce the supply of plutonium which would act as an alternate nuclear explosive, an even more dramatic effort took place. On a squash court under the stands of the University of Chicago's football field, a strange apparatus took form. It was the world's first chain reaction "pile"—graphite bricks with lumps of uranium embedded in their corners. If it worked according to Dr. Fermi's theories, it would produce the first chain reaction ever set up on earth.

With care, and great trepidation, the physicists laid the bricks. They knew they were deep in unknown territory; anything might happen. Nearby, students passed on their way to classes. By theory, the chain reaction should start spontaneously when nearly all the bricks were laid. Then it could be stopped short of a disastrous explosion by inserting strips of cadmium to break the chain.

But far below the "critical size" of the theory, the instruments gave an alarm. The reaction was starting to cook. Luckily, the cadmium strips had been inserted at "retard" position. Slowed down by their influence, the reaction was easily stopped. "This," commented Dr. Smyth dryly, "was fortunate."

This momentous experiment marked the beginning of the Atomic Age. Long before the queasy process had been reduced to an orderly procedure, a gigantic, full-sized plutonium plant had been started at Hanford on the desert near Yakima, Wash.

The original pile at Chicago had been a ticklish business, but the giant piles at Hanford were studies in unexplored dangers. Theory warned that as soon as they started working they would generate floods of deadly radiation and produce unknown radioactive elements, most of them fiendishly poisonous. These effects could conceivably be so powerful and so long-lasting that no living thing could approach a pile which had once been in operation.

Accordingly, elaborate devices were developed for operating the piles by remote control from behind thick protective shields.

Even so, the deadly unknowns escaped. The cooling water was radioactive. It had to be impounded and exhausted of radioactivity before going back to the river. Rigid precautions guarded the health of the workers. They all carried small electroscopes or bits of photographic film for nightly tests to show the amount of radiation to which each had been exposed. A gadget called "Sneezy" measured radioactive dust in the air. Clothing was carefully checked. Devices rang an alarm when a radioactive worker came near.

Besides plutonium, the Hanford plant produced two frightening by-product effects. The water which cooled the piles carried off enough energy, derived from the chain reaction, to heat the Columbia River appreciably. The second by-product was pure horror. In the ordinary operation of a large-scale pile, calculated Dr. Smyth, enough radioactive poisons could be produced every day to make "large areas uninhabitable."

While the mighty plants were being built, another team of physicists, led by Professor J. R. Oppenheimer of the Uni-

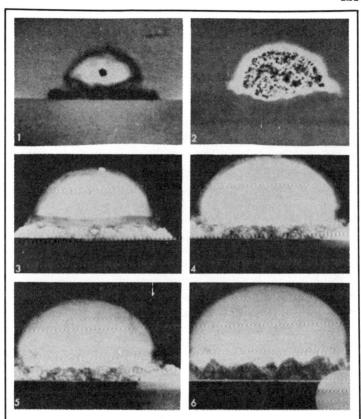

THE FIRST ATOMIC BOMB BLAST

Taken by an automatic movie camera six miles away, these pictures show in split-second intervals the explosion of the first atomic bomb, at Alamogordo, New M. on July 16. The explosion of the test charge left a crater a quarter-mile wide lined with melted rock and sand. The flash lit up every crevasse and ridge of a nearby mountain range and was immediately followed by a red wall of flame. Then a huge, multicolored cloud of fire, smoke and dust billowed up 40,000 ft., turning swiftly from ball to mushroom shape. It was lit from within by the lightning-like flashes of two supplementary explosions.

versity of California, gathered at Los Alamos, New Mexico. Their job was to design, assemble and test the atomic bomb itself. The pile constructors had struggled to keep their brain child from blowing up. The bomb men had the more deadly mission of finally blowing up theirs at the time and place that war demanded.

NOW IT CAN BE TOLD: He had the story of his, or any news- SEPT. 17
man's life—but he couldn't write it. There he was, sitting
in a B-29 bomber, with arc-welder's glasses to protect his
eyes from the glare, watching the atomic bomb bore down
on Nagasaki. But able, sad-faced Journalist William L. Laurence's lips were sealed.

Last week, at last, the Army released Laurence's account
of the Nagasaki raid. Thirty days after it happened it was
still top page-one news in the New York *Times*, and in many
another paper.

Wrote Timesman Laurence, "A giant ball of fire rose as
though from the bowels of the earth. Then a pillar of purple
fire, 10,000 feet high, shooting skyward. At one stage it
assumed the form of a giant square totem pole, with its base
about three miles long. Its bottom was brown, its center was
amber, its top white. Then, just when it appeared as though
the thing had settled down, there came shooting out of the
top a giant mushroom that increased the height of the pillar
to a total of 45,000 feet. The mushroom top was even more
alive than the pillar, sizzling upward, a thousand Old Faithful geysers rolled into one."

DOWN TO CASES: President Harry S. Truman finally got OCT. 15
down to cases: "Scientific opinion appears to be practically
unanimous that the essential theoretical knowledge upon
which the discovery is based is already widely known. There
is also substantial agreement that foreign research can
come abreast of our own present theoretical knowledge in
time."

That paragraph changed everything. It meant that the President of the U.S. had taken the whole atomic bomb discus-
sion out of the unreal context of "Shall we share the secret of
the bomb with the Russians, or shall we keep it?" The secret
about the secret was that there was no lasting secret.

BETTER THAN DYNAMITE?: In ignorance the world played OCT. 22
with the awful atom. From Newport, Ark., a farmer wrote a
letter to the nonexistent "Atomic Bomb Co." of Oak Ridge,
Tenn.: "I have some stumps in my field that I should like to
blow out. Have you got any atomic bombs the right size for
the job? If you have let me know by return mail, and let me

know how much they cost. I think I should like them better than dynamite."

OCT. 29 **"TERRIBLY MORE TERRIBLE":** One of his colleagues described Dr. J. Robert Oppenheimer, head of the Los Alamos branch of the atomic bomb's Manhattan Project, as "the smartest of the lot." Last week, just before he resigned to go back to teaching physics, tough-minded, 41-year-old Dr. Oppenheimer made some startling statements.

A Senator asked him if it were true that one raid on U.S. cities could kill 40 million Americans. Said Oppenheimer: "I am afraid it is." A newspaperman asked him whether the atomic bomb had any significant limitations. Said he: "The limitations lie in the fact that you don't want to be on the receiving end. If you ask, 'Can we make them more terrible?' the answer is yes. If you ask: 'Can we make a lot of them?' the answer is yes. If you ask: 'Can we make them terribly more terrible?' the answer is probably." [Returning to academic life after the war, Oppenheimer also served as chairman of the advisory committee to the Atomic Energy Commission. In 1954 he was stripped of his security clearances because of alleged association with Communists. In 1963 he was presented the Enrico Fermi Award for his "leadership of the atomic energy program during critical years." He died in 1967.]

NOV. 12 **IN A LOCKED ROOM:** Kenneth McKellar, President of the U.S. Senate, last week temporarily yielded his chair, stepped down to the floor and informed his astonished colleagues that he had solved the problem of the bomb. Outlaw it, said the gentleman from Tennessee.

Snapped Colorado's Edwin C. Johnson: "If it is possible to outlaw the bomb, why not go the whole step and outlaw war?"

Four Oak Ridge, Tenn. scientists warned that the U.S. edge in atomic bomb production is unimportant. Said they: "It is as though two men who don't trust each other sit face to face in a locked room, each pointing a loaded machine gun at the other. It makes no difference that one man's gun is a later model, or that he has 1,000 cartridges to the other's 100. Whoever shoots first wins."

FOREIGN NEWS

Great Britain

With victory assured in Europe, the government scheduled the nation's first general election in ten years. Prime Minister Churchill, who had led the British through five years of crisis, offered to continue as leader of a coalition. But the opposition Labor Party refused the offer and campaigned vigorously against Churchill on a platform calling for immediate social reforms.

THE 2,000TH DAY: While yellow crocuses bloomed in Hyde MARCH 5 Park, Britain counted up one day last week and found that it had been at war for 2,000 days & nights—2,000 days & nights of invasion threats, blitz, robombs, immense suffering, gnawing discomfort and imperturbable defiance of near defeat. For most of those 2,000 days Britons had stared into the hollow eyes of disaster and death; it had not occurred to them to wince. Now the unseasonably warm winds brought not only the scents of thawing soil and growing things, but the sense of long deferred victory.

There was no special celebration. But Britons attended to sundry matters:

¶ The House of Commons passed a bill making rear lights compulsory on bicycles (in 2,000 nights of war more people had been killed by traffic on country roads than by bombs or V-weapons).

¶ The London *Times* noted "an invasion of robins" from the Continent and pointed out that European robins are quite distinct (smaller red breasts, whiter underparts) from British robins.

WIN WITH WINNIE: The scene was the annual conference of MARCH 26 the Conservative Party in London. At noon on the second day of the conference Winston Churchill made his entrance with the grandeur of royalty. The 2,000 delegates waved agenda sheets in well-bred excitement, burst into a politely modulated *For He's a Jolly Good Fellow.* Rosy-cheeked and beaming, in tail coat and striped trousers, "Winnie" waved back.

Then he launched into his speech. It was one of Churchill's best: a masterly mixture of lofty patriotism and adroit politics. Well brushed, well tailored old metaphors ("We held aloft the flaming torch of freedom when all around the night was black as jet") clothed his sturdy Tory form. By the time he reached his glowing peroration, the Tory leader had shown how he proposed to win the election.

It sounded like a foolproof formula: "We have to finish the war. We have to bring the men home. We have to get our dear country on the move again and into its full swing of natural health and life." The Conservatives would promise no "easy, cheap-jack Utopia of airy phrases or windy platitudes." Nevertheless, for Britons in & out of uniform, weary of restriction and regulation, the Party offered "a large release from the necessary bonds and controls which war conditions have imposed."

APRIL 16 **WHAT TO DO WITH 'ITLER:** Lord Beaverbrook's *Evening Standard,* beating the circulation drum, had a bright idea: a prize of one pound sterling for each answer printed and a grand prize of five pounds for the best answer to "What to do with Hitler?" Some 9,000 tried their hand. Some suggestions:

¶ Exhibit Hitler—preferably in a cage, with the public paying a fee for looking; spitting privileges extra.

¶ "Let Hitler live with my in-laws for a month."

MAY 7 **GOODBYE TO ALL THAT:** The blackout was officially ended in Britain last week. For most Britons the best thing about the lightup was that they could at last take down their blackout curtains. For 2,061 nights they had been one of the biggest minor nuisances Britons had had to struggle with. Now the curtains were being converted into black clothes and funeral coverings. Said a housewife: "With the curtains gone, I feel I've got no clothes on."

JUNE 4 **FATEFUL ELECTION:** Preparing for the fateful general election, the Labor Party held a conference at Blackpool that ended with a series of verbal thunderclaps. The mood of British labor, echoing Europe's mood of social change, was grimly set by Aneurin Bevan, leftist M.P.: "Britain is an island bedded on coal and surrounded by fish; only an organizing genius could produce a coal shortage and a fish shortage simultaneously. We want the complete extinction of the Tory Party and 25 years of Labor government."

For its prospective Prime Minister, the Labor Party picked amiable, colorless Clement Attlee.

BUYING BINGE: Wedgies will be widely worn in London this JUNE 11 season (there is a two-inch limit on high heels). This was important news to London women who, heedless of the warning that they must make their present ration coupons last until September, were wearing out shoes faster than ever last week in their biggest shopping spree since 1942. So dense were the shopping swarms that it took 20 minutes to move a few blocks on busy Oxford Street.

Part of the shopping battalions concentrated on the pet shops. Since the V-2s stopped, there has been a big boom in dogs, cats and birds. Siamese cats are favorites. Last week pet shops were deluged with orders for unborn kittens.

BOOS & BALLOTS: The baby-kissing, like the political name- JULY 16 calling, pursued Britain's 23,000,000 voters almost up to the moment they stepped into polling booths last week. Seldom had a rowdedow campaign ended in such eleventh-hour fireworks.

Prime Minister Winston Churchill, 70, wound up his campaign at Walthamstow Stadium, one of Britain's biggest dog-racing tracks. Well-primed rowdies howled, booed and shouted: "We want Attlee!" Said Churchill: "In a free country like ours. . . ." Boos blitzed him out.

Then the Prime Minister peeled off his political jacket and jabbed at his enemies. Some of the jabs: "I want to talk about London's wonderful war record—would you like to boo that?" "You ask for my policy? I'll tell you—it is to beat Japan first. Another two minutes will be allowed for booing, if you'd like."

Next day Churchill was nearly hurt. On Tooting Bec Common, Michael Gloor Le Pelley, 17, tossed a lit firecracker at the Prime Minister's face. Momentarily staggered, Churchill told police "not to hurt the little fool."

AUG. 6 **THE WINNERS:** It was the biggest electoral upset in British history. When Britain's sealed ballot boxes were broken open for the count last week, it was found that the Labor Party, under the leadership of Clement R. Attlee, had defeated the Conservative Party. Labor's astonishing majority—195 seats —was so sweeping as to constitute a mandate.

WHO IS ATTLEE?: Sincere, sensitive and shy, Major Clement Richard Attlee is a colorless, self-effacing, somewhat chilly little man who walks with a shuffle, talks without rhetorical tricks. At the Big Three Conference he looked, critics said, like Winston Churchill's butler. But there is a good mind behind his glistening bald pate.

"Clem" Attlee is a Labor politician by act of will rather than by birthright. The son of a Tory lawyer, he seemed headed for a profitable law practice, was a Conservative. Then fate stepped in. The young barrister was invited to visit London's East End slums. Attlee went—in a white tie, top hat and tails. His appearance nearly caused a revolt of the masses. In the scrimmage he lost his topper and gained a black eye. He also acquired an interest in social problems. Soon young Attlee became secretary of a pioneer social settlement, took to lecturing at the London School of Economics. The ragged denizens of London's vast Limehouse slums came to know his tweed jacket and his fuming pipe (he is almost never without it). He acquired a firsthand knowledge of working-class misery and labor problems.

The cockney stevedores of Limehouse were grateful. They launched Attlee on his Parliamentary career (1922). Since then his seat has been one of the safest in England. In the first Labor Government (1924), Attlee was Under Secretary for War, presently filled a variety of other Cabinet posts. Impatient left-wing Labor comrades found him a fine target for their barbs: "His speeches win warmer applause before being heard than after." They liked to point out that Attlee has only one platform gesture—he raises his right arm and scratches his head just above his left ear.

But his neutral coloration also advanced his career in the

Labor Party's factional feuds. Attlee is above all a homebody. He spends most of his leisure time at his Middlesex home, puttering in the garden, tending his chickens or doing carpentry. He has torn down and rebuilt his chicken coop four times, is still dissatisfied with it.

THE LOSER: To London flew Prime Minister Winston Churchill, to give King George VI a first-hand report of the Big Three meeting. Then he waited for the election count. Next evening, when defeat was sure, he went back to Buckingham Palace to resign and hand over to the King the seals of office. His Majesty offered him the Order of the Garter. Churchill refused the dignity. An hour later he issued a statement:

"I have laid down the charge which was placed upon me in darker times. I regret that I have not been permitted to finish the work against Japan. It only remains for me to express to the British people, for whom I have acted in these perilous years, my profound gratitude for the unflinching and unswerving support which they have given me during my task and for the many expressions of kindness which they have shown toward their servant."

In defeat, there was one thing no one could take from Winston Churchill: seldom had so many owed so much to one man.

REPERCUSSION: In Manhattan this week Plummer's, importers of fine English china, hastily announced a bargain—their entire stock of Winston Churchill Toby jugs.

SOCIALIST ERA: Socialism inaugurated its reign with regal AUG. 27 pomp. By historic chance, V-J day came on the day the new Labor-dominated Parliament opened. In one burst Britons were hailing victory, the Crown and Socialism.

In the newly painted crimson-&-gold state coach, Their Majesties smiled and bowed toward the tumult as they rode from Buckingham Palace to Westminster. Precisely at 11 a.m. the King and Queen entered and seated themselves on the newly gilded thrones. In a clear voice, with his stutter scarcely noticeable, the King read the Speech from the Throne. Written and revised by Prime Minister Attlee, it proclaimed in the King's name the first steps in the Socialist future Labor has charted for Britain. In 20 unhurried minutes, the King announced plans for the nationalization of the coal mines, the extension of social insurance, the establishment of a national health service. The Socialist era had officially begun.

One unpleasantness that the British endured throughout the war was the nightly radio broadcast from Berlin by "Lord Haw-Haw," a defector from England named William Joyce. In May, Joyce was picked up by the British in Germany and returned to England for trial.

OCT. 1 **A ROPE FOR HAW-HAW**: In a small, oak paneled room of London's Old Bailey, the chief criminal court in England, William Joyce strode to the dock, bowed jerkily to the red-robed presiding justice, Sir Frederick Tucker, and sat down in a straight-backed chair. The charge against him was treason: that he had "adhered to the King's enemies" by broadcasting propaganda from Germany.

Joyce based his defense upon his origins. He was born on April 24, 1906, in Brooklyn, N.Y. When he was two, William's parents took him to England. At 17 he was already a Fascist. He joined Sir Oswald Mosley's Fascist group. Whenever he needed credentials of any sort, he claimed British citizenship.

When he fled to Germany, just before World War II, Paul Joseph Goebbels' propaganda machine paid him $75 a month. Adolf Hitler bestowed on him the War Merit Cross, First Class. According to his own statement, he became a naturalized German citizen. The British nicknamed him "Lord Haw-Haw" and they laughed at him. But they never forgot his taunts at Britain.

Faced by the evidence that Joyce was not British, the presiding justice threw out the first two counts of the indictment. But there was a third count: that Joyce behaved as a traitor in Germany between Sept. 18, 1939 and July 2, 1940, when his British passport expired. The prosecution argued that during this period, since he enjoyed the protection of a British passport, he owed allegiance to the British Crown.

The jury of ten men and two women retired to consider this point. In 25 minutes they returned a verdict: guilty. A figure in black came to stand beside the presiding justice. Mr. Justice Tucker sentenced William Joyce to be hanged by the neck until he was dead. Then the man in black, a chaplain, intoned "Amen." William Joyce was whisked away to await the noose at the famous Hammersmith prison, Wormwood Scrubs.

BATTLE OF THE BULGE: The fact was not pretty, but hundreds of DEC. 10 thousands of young British women had to face it. In their years of work in war factories and the services they had become bigger in the wrong places—hands, feet, and hips.

The average British girl of 25 now wears gloves and shoes at least one size larger than did the British girl who was 25 in 1939. Around the hips she is a 38, two inches broader than her older sister was six years ago. Dress designers have rallied to fight the battle of the bulge—with greatly exaggerated squaring of shoulders, nipped-in waists, flaring skirts. Typical London fashion ad last week: "for the more awkward figure."

France

TECHNOLOGY LESSON: In things that count, the French are a JAN. 29 very practical people. They watched with detached wonder when the U.S. Army laid a gasoline pipeline from the Normandy beachhead to Paris. Then an idea galvanized them into action: if gas can flow through a six-inch pipe, why not wine? Last week Frenchmen laid their own pipeline. Across the practically bridgeless Loire River it will bring wine from southern France to break a drought that has been desiccating Paris and northern France.

DEFINITION: From Paris last week came a new definition of a collaborationist: "Anybody who collaborated more than you did."

"I, ALONE. . .": General Charles de Gaulle sent word to the MARCH 26 fuming, frustrated Consultative Assembly: gladly would he confer with them about his Ministers. Into his presence trooped some three dozen leaders of France's advisory parliament.

Politely the General listened. He had heard their complaints before. His Justice Minister, François de Menthon, was too reluctant in purging collaborationists. His Food Minister Paul Ramadier was too slow in allaying hunger.

The General gave the impression of laughing a little inside. "You are not elected," he replied. "And neither am I. Therefore we must do our best and just try to get along until popular suffrage has decided for us all. Until universal suffrage shall be operating, I, alone, am responsible before the country."

The Assembly went back to talking in a vacuum. What else could they do in the face of the General's integrity, prestige and stubborness?

APRIL 9 **THE LIGHTS GO ON AGAIN:** For the first time in five years, street lights gleamed along the Champs Elysées and floodlights bathed the Arc de Triomphe. On Easter night 2,300,000 Parisians marveled anew at their City of Light.

JULY 23 **PROGRESS:** On the eve of Bastille Day the French Government made a revolutionary announcement: the guillotine, like military conscription, one of the fruits of the French Revolution, is about to be done away with. Henceforth condemned Frenchmen will not have to lie down and bare their necks to the falling knife; they may, as soon as transportation and the French electric-power shortage permit, sit down in a shiny new, U.S.-made electric chair.

One of the first moves taken by the government of France after the war was to put on trial the thousands of citizens who had collaborated with the Nazis. Chief among the defendants were Marshal Henri Pétain, the elderly chief of state of the Vichy government who was accused of betraying France's interests, and Premier Pierre Laval, who had turned over to German labor camps more than a million French prisoners.

JULY 30 **CAPACITY:** The President of France's High Court of Justice pondered a broad question: how wide are the average newspaper correspondent's buttocks? The answer was crucial, for it was desired to cram as many reporters as possible into seats at the collaboration trial of Marshal Henri Philippe Pétain, which opens this week in Paris. At last an allowance of 20 inches was decided upon—a figure which should seat 40 French and 40 foreign newsmen.

"WE ALWAYS LOSE": After 90 days of sanctuary, Pierre Laval AUG. 13 was "formally invited" by the hard-pressed Spanish Government to leave Spain. At Barcelona the haggard refugee and his wife boarded the same plane that had flown them in. A few hours later they came down on a U.S. Army airfield in Austria. Rumor said that Traitor Laval had vainly offered his pilots one million francs if they would head for Portugal. U.S. officers promptly turned Laval over to the French, who flew him to Paris.

Next day he was whisked to court as a witness in the treason trial of Marshal Henri Philippe Pétain. The testimony of another figure from France's dingy past had prepared the way for him. To the crowded courtroom the Marshal's lawyers had summoned their star witness: ailing, emaciated General Maxime Weygand, 78, commander in chief of the French Army when it surrendered to the Germans in 1940.

Hotly the General denied the charge that Pétain had "plotted" France's defeat in order to seize personal power. If Pétain had erred, said Weygand, it was the fault of "his evil genius," Vichy's Chief of Government Pierre Laval.

The jury demanded to hear testimony from Pierre Laval. After shuffling into court, Laval sought to identify himself and Pétain as partners in collaboration and to define collaboration as a double game to fool the Germans and insure French survival. (Hoots of derision from the jury.) Shouted Laval: "Who in his right mind would have thought otherwise than that Germany would win the war?" (The hoots swelled into a roar.) Screamed Laval: "I am not a Nazi. I am not a Fascist. I hate war—even when we win, and we always lose."

DISHONOR BUT NOT DEATH: The old man was awakened at AUG. 27 4 a.m. He sleepily rose from his prison cot, donned his seven-star uniform, shuffled into the hushed courtroom. Nonagenarian Marshal Henri Philippe Pétain sat nervously at first, then fell into a half-doze. For 20 minutes Presiding Judge Pierre

Mongibeaux intoned judgment. The verdict: guilty of intelligence with the enemy. Sentence: national dishonor and death. Recommendation: in view of the condemned's age, the death sentence should not be carried out.

Two days after the old man's condemnation, the Ministry of Justice announced: "General de Gaulle has commuted the death sentence to perpetual imprisonment." Pétain would be transferred to Sainte Marguerite Island off the Riviera. There he would have sun and warmth. His wife, freed of all charges, would join him. But he could not have his seven stars back, nor his honor.

SEPT. 3 **DEFENSE IN DEPTH:** Between six and seven million unexploded German land mines are still hidden in the fertile fields and sandy beaches of Normandy and Brittany. Since D-day an average of 200 people, including many children, have been killed each month by German mines.

Last week Frenchmen got a grim report of progress in dealing with them. By last month's end, only one-tenth had been removed (partly by German prisoners of war trained by U.S. sappers). The dangerous job would not be finished before 1947.

OCT. 15 **DEVIL'S ADVOCATE:** Last week Pierre Laval came to judgment. With him came none of the dreadful pity, the sense of terrible duty that had been in every Frenchman's heart during the trial, death sentence and commutation to life imprisonment, of old Marshal Henri Pétain. The elimination of Pierre Laval, a necessary chore, might have been a satisfying vengeance. He made it a shameful farce.

Bawled Laval at the start: "I am a patriot and I will prove it!" Up jumped the Judge, the prosecutor, all 24 jurors to shout him down. Having robbed the Court of its dignity, Laval smirked. His lawyers walked out, protesting that they had had no time to prepare. Laval pleaded humbly for a delay. It was refused; he slammed his briefcase down on a table.

"Well, then, condemn me now!" he yelled. The enraged Judge bellowed at the guards. Pierre Laval, thrice Premier of France, was hauled away to his cell. He was brought back the next day, on the promise of good behavior. The third day he was expelled again, after exchanging loud insults with

Judge & jury. By week's end he was boycotting the Court and defying the Judge to bring him back by force. But with or without him, his trial would not last very long.

WITHOUT HONOR: Pierre Laval spent his last days in sack- OCT. 22 cloth in the death row of the Fresnes prison. He wrote farewell letters to his family, his lawyers. He chain-smoked. General de Gaulle refused every request for a new or re-opened trial; the grotesquerie of the first one had revolted all France.

Laval turned philosopher. To a fellow prisoner going to death he said: "*Ne t'en fais pas:* it lasts only a few seconds. It's like being killed in a bus accident on the Place de l'Opéra."

For Laval, death was indeed like a very messy bus accident. He was lying on his cot as officials approached the cell to take him. Before they could reach him, he slipped a poison capsule into his mouth, rolled writhing to the floor. For two hours prison doctors labored over the prostrate *Auvergnat* with emetics and stomach pumps. The firing squad waited. At length two men escorted him to the stake. A hearse stood by, a coffin rested on the ground.

Tied to the stake, Laval stood facing the rifle points. "*Vive la France,*" he cried. The volley sent a chilly stir through the prison building. Slowly Laval sank to his knees. An officer fired a final bullet into his ear. Pierre Laval's death, like his life, had brought no honor to France.

LA QUATRIÈME REPUBLIQUE: The Fourth Republic was OCT. 29 born. Some 24,000,000 Frenchmen and Frenchwomen trooped to their country's first free election since 1936. By a resounding majority they chose a Constituent Assembly, ordered it to frame a new Constitution, approved a strong executive interim government.

By her vote France gave a solid mandate to middle-way socialism. Of 596 seats in the new Assembly, the Socialists and the moderate Popular Republicans, who form France's biggest political bloc, held 60%. By voting for a strong executive, the electorate showed its support of Provisional President Charles de Gaulle, who stands above all factions, a politician without a party. No other personality rivals him in prestige and authority. He is as arbitrary, difficult, downright contrary as ever. But to most Frenchmen he is still The Symbol,

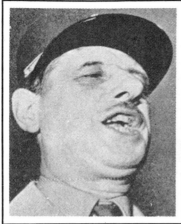 

General Charles de Gaulle tells critics,   *Pierre Laval is saved from poison so*
"I alone am responsible." Page 131.   *he can be shot at the stake.*

the man who saved France's honor. Said an electrician, "We still have France, thanks to De Gaulle, and we are alive, thanks to the Allies."

NOV. 19 **"LES FEMMES–POUF!":** Greying, pompous, misogynous Monsieur Jules has been official barber to French parliamentarians for upwards of two decades. Last month, when he heard that women would sit for the first time in a French National Assembly, Jules resigned. *"Les femmes,"* he sputtered. *"Pouf!"*

NOV. 26 **DEADLOCK & GROG:** *Le grand Charlie* had doffed his uniform and his general's stars, donned dark blue mufti and become simple M. de Gaulle. Having resigned as Provisional President, he retired to a villa in suburban Neuilly. There he waited for the new Constituent Assembly to call him back to duty. When the call came, only one of the Assemblymen did not vote to have M. de Gaulle serve as President of the Government until the constitution of the Fourth Republic is drafted.

While tactful Mme. de Gaulle served hot grog for journalists waiting outside the villa in the chill autumn weather, her husband talked on & on with party notables. All the talk and the grog could not put together a coalition government on the President's terms. M. de Gaulle was up hard against Communist insistence that theirs, as the party which polled the most votes (5,000,000), should name its own man for one of the three key posts: Foreign Affairs, War, Interior. De Gaulle refused to put a Communist in any of these posts, but offered them other places in the Cabinet.

In the deadlock M. de Gaulle carried the issue to the public: "I did not believe it possible to confide to the Communists many of the levers that control foreign policy: the diplomacy that expresses it, the army that sustains it, and the police that protect it."

This week the Assembly met in a tense atmosphere made more tense by heavily armed guards surrounding their chamber, quickly reached a decision, voted down the Communists, 400-to-163, and directed M. de Gaulle to continue his efforts to form a coalition government. [De Gaulle got his way. He kept the three important ministries out of Communist hands, gave them instead three less sensitive ones—Industrial Production, Labor and National Economy.]

THE NEEDLE: On the eve of the Big Three meeting at Moscow, DEC. 24 the uninvited Big Fourth somewhat grandly—and frostily— proclaimed a policy of her own. Said President Charles de Gaulle in a broadcast to his nation:

"In the world as it is today, there are two very great powers and we lie exactly between them. Our vital interests command us to follow a policy of friendship, to the East and to the West, with our eyes open and our hands free. We know that our equilibrium is identified with the equilibrium of peace, and we are fully decided not to abandon it, in the certainty that our attitude will finally determine the equilibrium of the needle for the good of all."

Germany

THE FÜHRER'S VOICE: In a London studio, correspondents JAN. 15 listened intently to a recording of Adolf Hitler's New Year's speech. They were sleuthing in sound, trying to unravel a mystery that had the British press agog: was this New Year's orator really Adolf Hitler?

In long passages the voice flowed on, as if it were weak and being nursed along: "The National Socialist State—our 2,000-year-old civilization—can neither be replaced by Bolshevism nor by democratic-plutocratic ideology. This nation and its leading men are unshakable in their will and unswerving in their fanatical determination to fight this war to a successful conclusion."

The peroration, though not as full-throated as in the past, had the high hypnotic timbre:

"I am at present speaking less frequently, not because I do not want to speak but because my work leaves little time for speeches. I have not been sleeping. I promise solemnly to the Almighty that the hour will strike when victory will come to the Greater German Reich."

This was the old shrill cry; it was unmistakably Hitler.

FEB. 12 **THE MAN WHO CAN'T SURRENDER:** Terror came on the cold, wet wind with the sound of Russian guns. Panic came on the heels of the milling, stumbling horde of refugees. Berlin, at last, was a battle zone. Berlin had not been captured by a foreign invader since 1806—and there was no battle then. Headed by their mayor, the citizens came out and welcomed Napoleon's troops with open arms.

Last week the citizens were part of the Army. Women rode on the antiaircraft guns pulling out for the Oder front. The radio spewed an endless stream of threats to traitors, cowards, shirkers, defeatists. All Army "stragglers" and all males over 13 were ordered to report for duty. The defense of the city was laid out. Even the zoo was fortified. Streetcars stopped running. Food cards were stretched for an extra week and the potato ration was cut.

Yet the panic and the terror seemed somehow to be kept in bounds. Berlin and the rest of uninvaded Germany were carrying on the fight, under the inexorable hand of Heinrich Himmler. Clearly or dimly, most Germans realized that Himmler was the new master of the Third Reich. Last October, Himmler himself had told how Germany would be defended: "Every village, every house, every farm, every ditch, every forest and every bush."

As Adolf Hitler's longtime chief butcher, torturer and slavemaster, Heinrich Himmler is the archetype of the top

Nazi who cannot surrender. Now while keeping Hitler as the Führer symbol, Himmler does the dictator's job of maintaining Germany at war. Around himself and his henchmen he has formed the last granite-hard core of German resistance. Himmler is the creator and chief of the SS (the *Schutzstaffel,* or black-uniformed "Elite Guard"), as well as the infamous secret police, the Gestapo. He is also Reich Minister of the Interior, and Reich Minister of Home Defense.

In contrast to some Nazis who have been addicts of drink, drugs, homosexuality or women, Himmler seems almost normal. He does not appear to delight in brutality for its own sake. He simply uses terror with absolute cold-bloodedness and efficiency as his main professional tool. The fact that he has kept ten to twelve million foreign slaves at work in Germany is a testimonial to his police ability. His continued personal rise in the last five years shows his aptness for political intrigue.

Himmler's present role is crucial. For as Germans begin to see absolutely no hope of winning, more & more of them, not so sunk in guilt as the Nazi malefactors, will want to cry quits. There will be only one way to keep them in line: terror.

ADOLF HITLER'S LAST HOURS: In Berchtesgaden, last week, MAY 21 Gerhard Herrgesell, stenographer to Germany's Supreme Headquarters Staff, told TIME Correspondent Percy Knauth the story of the last recorded conferences which the Supreme Command held in a little bomb-proof room deep in the earth under the Berlin Chancellery.

Said Herrgesell: "The decisive briefing which determined the fate of all of us began at 3 o'clock on the afternoon of April 22 and lasted until nearly 8 o'clock that evening. At this briefing Adolf Hitler declared that he wanted to die in Berlin. He repeated this 10 or 20 times in various phrases. He would say: 'I will fall here' or 'I will fall before the Chancellery' or 'I must die here in Berlin.' He reasoned that the cause was irretrievably lost, in complete contrast to his previous attitude, which had always been: 'We will fight to the last tip of the German Reich.'

"Hitler himself was generally composed. Every time he really began to get angry or excited he would quickly get himself under control again. His face was flushed and red, however, and he paced the floor almost constantly, walking back & forth, sometimes smacking his fist into his hand. But of all the participants at all the conferences, the Führer was generally the one who kept his nerves best under control.

"The really decisive conference took place in late afternoon. It lasted only about 15 minutes. Present were Hitler, his personal representative, Martin Bormann, Field Marshal Wilhelm Keitel and Colonel General Alfred Jodl. All others were sent away except two stenographers.

"Hitler again expressed his determination to stay in Berlin, and said he wanted to die there. Keitel, Jodl and Bormann all came out strongly against Hitler. Jodl declared very firmly that he, personally, would not stay in Berlin; he thought it was a mousetrap, and his job was to lead the troops.

"The Führer was by now rather vague and uncertain, giving no direct orders, apparently preoccupied with the prospect of his own imminent death. Jodl interjected that

Adolf Hitler inspects a Germany in ruins. In his last hours he gives no orders, repeats over and over: "I must die here in Berlin."

Germany still had some armies capable of action. Perhaps, said Jodl, these armies could change the course of events around Berlin. Hitler evidenced little interest. He shrugged his shoulders and said: 'You do whatever you want.'

"During all this time, artillery fire on the Chancellery was increasing and even deep down in the cellar we could feel concussions shaking the building. The conference finally broke up in indecision. My fellow stenographer and I were ordered to leave Berlin with our stenographic reports. That was the last plane and we were the last people to leave Berlin."

PHASE ONE: A clear explanation of U.S. procedure in Germany came last week from General Eisenhower's No. 1 deputy for the occupation, tough-minded Lieut. General Lucius Du Bignon Clay. Said he: MAY 28

"Our first objective is to smash whatever remaining power Germany may have with which to develop a future war potential, to drive the Nazis out of power and keep them out. War criminals will pay for their crimes with their lives and their liberties, their sweat and blood. That is the first objective of military government in Germany. When that has been accomplished we will begin to worry about long-range policies and long-range treatment of Germany."

TOWARD CONTROL: In six hours and 45 minutes it was all over. U.S. General Eisenhower, British Field Marshal Montgomery and French General Delattre de Tassigny had landed at Tempelhof, met Soviet Marshal Zhukov and signed the papers. The four-power Allied Control Council was now in formal existence. JUNE 18

THE MISSING BRIDEGROOM: Marshal Zhukov told Allied correspondents visiting Berlin that 1) Hitler married his blonde companion, Eva Braun, two days before Berlin fell; 2) no identifiable trace of Hitler had been found. [Later investigations confirmed that Hitler had shot himself and that his corpse was set on fire in the Chancellery garden. No trace of his remains were ever discovered.]

THE UNDEFEATED: At last the victors met the German people. Not the Nazi Party, not the horror-masters of Buchenwald JUNE 25 and Dachau, not the General Staff and the *Wehrmacht,* but the people, from whom all the evil and the vigor sprang.

The German people were surprisingly well dressed and healthy. Thanks to the Nazi policy of looting Europe of food, the children were sturdy. Nearly all of the Germans were full of resentments. Most of all, they resented the bombing of their homes and cities. The Americans, they felt, had gone far beyond the evident necessities of war.

They had other grievances. After all, Nazi rationing had worked to the very last, and there had been some food for every German. Now, in many places, there was little or none. In a thousand ways, the defeat had added personal inconveniences to the general ruin. The Germans did not like it.

From themselves, if not from the conquerors, the Germans hid their guilt. Among British Tommies and American G.I.s, the most commonplace wisecrack was: "There are no German Nazis." Only those committed by some public record owned any allegiance, past or present, to the vanished party.

Thousands of Germans had been driven to the horror camps, forced to look at the barely living and to bury the bare dead. Many more had been made to view the evil truth in pictures, on billboards and in movie houses. Most of the German audiences shuddered, some of them wept. Practically all of them said: "*They* did it!"

IT WAS HIS FAULT: Captive Hermann Göring told U.S. interrogators: "In your aerial warfare you had a great ally—the Führer." Göring implied that Germany would have won if the air war had been left to him, said that his *Luftwaffe* had developed a marvelous jet fighter "that was to sweep Allied bombers from the skies." Hitler rejected it.

SEPT. 24 **IF. . .:** When Neville Chamberlain flew to Berchtesgaden to placate Adolf Hitler in September 1938, he upset the plans of top-ranking German officers. They were getting ready to arrest Hitler. This astounding statement was made in London last week during the interrogation of stocky, taciturn Colonel General Franz Halder. Chief of the German General Staff from 1938 to 1942, Halder planned the campaigns against Poland, Norway, the Lowlands, France, the opening attack on Russia. He told his interrogators that in 1938 the *Wehr-*

macht had only 21 divisions, including two *Panzer* divisions. The Czechs had 45 well-trained divisions behind a fortified belt. The German prospect, said Halder, was "nothing less than catastrophic."

Accordingly, the conspirators determined to overthrow Hitler and expose his reckless gambling to the German people. "The commander in chief, von Brauchitsch, had been informed of the conspiracy."

Halder decided to strike on the night of Sept. 14. He sent a *Panzer* division to Berlin without arousing suspicion. Just when the coup seemed completely assured of success, London announced the umbrella-toting Prime Minister's impending visit to Hitler's mountain. Halder, shaken by this dramatic evidence of the Führer's political sagacity, called off the plot, thereafter toed the Hitler line. Later, Chamberlain's policy was defended as giving Britain time to prepare. Halder's statement indicated that it was Germany that got the time.

EFFICIENCY: Berlin was getting ready for the winter. Quickly, OCT. 1 before the earth froze over, shovel squads were digging extra graves—for some 100,000 Berliners expected to die of hunger and cold, or to commit suicide.

PATTON & THE DEVIL: General George S. Patton Jr. had kept mum for quite a while. It was unlike him. Last week in Bavaria, where he is U.S. military governor, he brandished his riding crop and informed the press: "Well, I'll tell you. This Nazi thing. It's just like a Democratic-Republican election fight." In his opinion, too much fuss was being made about denazification. Said Patton: "I'm not trying to be King of Bavaria."

He hated Nazis as much as anyone else, he said. But in trying to govern Germany "you'd be in a hell of a fix if you tried to remove all Party members." Patton's ideas on how to run Germany were: 1) restore normal conditions to prevent anarchy; 2) get German industry back into shape so that the U.S. taxpayer will not have to foot the bill; 3) show the Germans "what grand fellows we are."

Said Patton in his best grand-fellow manner: "To get things going, we've got to compromise with the devil a little bit."

OCT. 8 **"PATTON'S MOUTH":** Old Blood & Guts Patton was in Dutch again. He had made a fool of himself by pooh-poohing efforts to rid Germany of Nazis. He had also impugned the orders of his Supreme Commander, General of the Army Dwight D. Eisenhower, who ordered Patton to retract.

Patton called the press in for a retake, blamed the whole thing on his unfortunate "analogies" and the newspapers' "startling headlines." Then, chafing under his orders, he declared: 1) that what he had said should not "reflect on my commanding officer, General Eisenhower"; 2) that "so vile a thing as Naziism" could not be got rid of overnight. The net implication was that he was right the first time.

Lieut. General Walter Bedell Smith, Eisenhower's chief of staff, forthwith called a press conference of his own. Growling that General Eisenhower would tolerate no insubordination, General Smith then spoke as one professional soldier practically never speaks of another: "Patton's mouth does not always carry out the functions of his brain. George acts on the theory that it is better to be damned than say nothing —that some publicity is better than none."

DEC. 3 **"DEAR DIARY":** In one respect, at least, Adolf Hitler got exactly what he deserved: his devoted Eva Braun was as mean-spirited a doxy as his worst enemy could have wished. U.S. intelligence officers culled these bits from a 1935 diary:

"When he says he loves me he takes it about as seriously as his promises which he never keeps. I have just sent him a letter. If I don't get an answer by 10 o'clock I'll take my 25 pills and lie down peacefully.

"The weather is gorgeous and I, mistress of Germany's and the world's greatest man, have to sit at home and look at it through a window. If only I had a dog."

Russia

FEB. 5 **HISTORIC FORCE:** Barring the possible existence on earth of undetected saints and major prophets, about the most important person in the world last week was Joseph Vissarionovitch Djugashvili. He was better known to the world as

Joseph Stalin, Marshal and chairman of the Council of People's Commissars of the Union of Socialist Soviet Republics.

In Poland and the Reich, his gigantic armies were (in Winston Churchill's feral phrase) "tearing the guts out of the Germany Army." Yet, even as Britons and Americans followed the Red Army's advance on their war maps, they could not escape at least a visual uneasiness. The line of Russia's 800-mile military front practically bisected Europe. Behind Russia's drive and political aims was the stubborn fact that the Soviet Union had emerged as the greatest power in Europe, able (and probably willing) to fill the political void which would be left by the crushing of Germany, and which neither weakened Britain nor weakened France could hope to fill. Who was this man in whose hands lay so heavy a responsibility for the world's destiny?

He was a little man (5 ft. 5 in.), two inches taller than Napoleon. He speaks Russian with a thick Georgian accent; he has been thrice married; he travels in a bullet-proof automobile. There are also the stories of his bearish manners (if he is angry or suspicious), of his bearish humor (if he is pleased); of his ability to drink 22 vodka toasts with no audible thickening or loosening of the tongue.

And there are the stories of his adventures with the English language, which he does not speak. But he sometimes memorizes phrases by heart. General Pat Hurley (now U.S. Ambassador to China) taught Stalin the English phrase which he sprang on Churchill and Franklin Roosevelt at Teheran. Coming into a room, where the two had their heads together, Stalin loudly asked: "What the hell goes on here?"

SO SORRY, MR. SATO: At 3 p.m. on a cold and sleety day last APRIL 16 week, Japanese Ambassador Naotake Sato entered the Foreign Commissariat in Moscow. He had been summoned by Foreign Commissar Vyacheslav Molotov, who had some Jap-shaking news:

"The neutrality pact between the Soviet Union and Japan was signed April 13, 1941. Since that time the situation is entirely altered. Germany attacked the Soviet Union, and Japan, an ally of Germany, helped the latter in her war against the U.S.S.R. Besides, Japan is fighting against the

United States and Great Britain, who are allies of the Soviet Union.

"Under these circumstances the neutrality pact had lost its sense. The Soviet Government declares to the Japanese Government its wish to denounce the pact of April 13, 1941."

OCT. 1 **PILLOW & PISTOL:** Last week the U.S.S.R. was throwing its weight about as never before. It persisted in treating eastern Europe as a special Russian preserve and, though Moscow's *Pravda* insisted angrily that no issues between the great powers were insoluble, distrust and tension grew.

A bedroom story measured Soviet Foreign Commissar Molotov's own suspicions. When Molotov visited Clement Attlee at the Prime Minister's quiet summer home, Chequers, the Russian brought a Russian chambermaid. In stiff disapproval the regular Chequers maid looked on while the Russian woman made Molotov's bed. The eyes of the English maid nearly popped when the pillow was lifted. There lay a long, fat pistol.

NOV. 12 **UNHAPPY WARRIORS:** Millions of Russian soldiers were returning to Russia, and many brought back a problem for their leaders: how to keep them down on the collective farm, after they'd seen Paree. When Red Army men first streamed westward across Russia's frontiers, they entered a new world full of fascinations and dangers. Siberian trappers, Uzbek farmers, Cossacks from Kuban were so many children discovering toys they had never known in their Communist nursery.

In Poland, their discipline cracked. Some went wild, looting, raping, killing. The Red Army command took stern measures, but it could not change the basic fact which made for all the trouble: the discrepancy between the standard of living in Russia and in the rest of Europe.

Hard-working, hard-fighting Russian soldiers found what they considered luxury even in the poor countries of southeastern Europe. They discovered, in the shambles of war, the leftovers of great comfort. They saw in the U.S. and British zones of Germany the signs of wealth and ease.

Many, wanting all these things, deserted. In the Berlin region alone, thousands deserted each month. Some simply went to the U.S. zone and tried to stay there. Others roamed the countryside. The Red Army had to ask the U.S. and British Armies to help round them up.

Japan

APPLES & OCTOPUSES: The bomb-scorched Japanese took MARCH 26 what cheer they could from two advances in the science of aviation:

¶ Tokyo scientists have succeeded in increasing the alcoholic content of apple cider to a point where it is "usable as airplane fuel."

¶ "It has been discovered that octopus extract is an exceedingly efficacious remedy for relieving fatigue, as such will be indispensable to our flying men."

THE ENEMY SPEAKS: The unfathomable Japanese publicly APRIL 23 extended their sympathy to the U.S. people on the death of President Roosevelt.

In a broadcast from Japan, Premier Admiral Kantaro Suzuki [who had replaced Koiso] was quoted as saying, "I must admit that Roosevelt's leadership has been very effective and has been responsible for the Americans' advantageous position today. For that reason I can easily understand the great loss his passing means to the American people and my profound sympathy goes to them."

WAITING: Japan prepared feverishly for the U.S. invasion. JULY 9 Boasted Radio Tokyo: *Kamikaze* bases had been installed throughout the main islands, armed with secret weapons. A regional defense system had been readied; the invaders would have to reduce resistance district by district. The capital's flattened industrial areas were being converted into fishponds and rice paddies. Cried Radio Tokyo: "The sooner the enemy comes, the better for us, for our battle array is complete."

LAST DAYS: It was dawn on Friday, but dusk for Japan. Em- AUG. 20 peror Hirohito had approved a surrender proposal to the Allies. Five days before, the Japanese radio still talked of 100 years' resistance, and there seemed little question of Japan's ability to hold out for months. Then in shattering succession came atomic bombing and the Russian declaration of war. Japan's battered will to resist began to stiffen in rigor mortis.

No news of the surrender proposal was announced to the 70 million Japanese people. But the Tokyo newspaper *Yomiuri Hochi,* in a historic editorial, prepared the minds of the Japanese people for the news: "There is an ebb and a flow in the tides of the affairs of every nation. Individuals must have the courage of self-immolation, but it may be said that a nation does not have the right to commit suicide. Therefore there are times when statesmen must have the courage to save the nation at the cost of their own lives. What we should do at this critical moment is to wait for the great command from the throne."

AUG. 27 **TEARS:** Domei described the scene at which Emperor Hirohito decided to surrender to the Allies:

"On the personal initiative of His Majesty, an historical conference was held before the Throne at the Imperial Palace. After all stated their opinion, His Majesty was graciously pleased to make the final decision, stating that whatever the future may bring in regard to his personal safety, he should not like to see any more of his subjects killed and the country reduced to scorched earth."

Thereupon Hirohito broke down, sobbed, wiped his tears away with his white-gloved hand. His ministers and aides, "profoundly impressed by the gracious concern of His Majesty, silently bowed down and wept. Thus the final decision to accept the terms of surrender was taken."

Next day Hirohito broadcast an Imperial Rescript to his nation: "Despite the best that has been done by everyone the war situation has developed not necessarily to Japan's advantage. Moreover, the enemy has begun to employ a new and most cruel bomb. We have resolved to pave the way for a grand peace for all the generations to come by enduring the unendurable and suffering the insufferable."

HONORABLE SUICIDES: Died. General Korechika Anami, Army bureaucrat and War Minister in the Suzuki Cabinet; and Vice Admiral Takejiro Onishi, originator of *Kamikaze* ("divine wind") tactics; both by harakiri, induced by the Japanese surrender; in Tokyo.

General Anami was a military mystic. He once called on Japan's soldiers "to defend the Imperial land even after death with your souls." When he heard the news of his son's death in battle, his only visible emotion was to crush a flower bud in his hand. He had held out against surrender.

Vice Admiral Onishi left a note to the "spirits" of his *Kamikaze* corps: "With my death I desire to make atonement to the souls of you who fell gallantly as human bullets."

Emperor Hirohito visits General MacArthur. One day he is the Son of Heaven, the next simply a tired, bespectacled little man.

THE FROZEN HEART: The tired, bespectacled little man whom OCT. 8 the Japanese regard as the Son of Heaven emerged from his walled and moated palace for the first time since the conquerors had landed in his country. He wore a cutaway, striped trousers, a wing collar, a top hat. He climbed into an old, immaculate Daimler.

Convoyed by a small motorcade, Emperor Hirohito's car moved through the streets of Tokyo. At the gates of the U.S. Embassy, U.S. guards presented arms. Two U.S. officers escorted him to the huge living room where General Mac-Arthur was waiting. MacArthur, who wore a shirt open at the throat, shook hands and said, "Good morning."

Hirohito consented to pose with MacArthur for a picture.

Then he and the Supreme Commander talked alone (through an interpreter) for 38 minutes. When he came out, the Emperor saw a cluster of U.S. correspondents, doffed his high hat and just perceptibly bowed.

MacArthur had not invited the visit; the Emperor had asked to see MacArthur. As nothing else could, the imperial homage to MacArthur told the people that Japan was truly beaten. A railway ticket-seller, when he heard the news, dropped his rice bowl, laid his head on the counter and wept. He said: "My heart is frozen."

China

During the war against Japan, the stubborn conflict between the Chinese Communist and Nationalist forces had been played down. But by 1945 the Nationalist government of Chiang Kai-shek was seriously weakened by the war and by a raging inflation; in contrast the Communists, led by Mao Tse-tung, were growing in strength. As the war neared an end the stage was set for a resumption of the old struggle between Chiang and Mao for the leadership of China.

JAN. 1 **YAHOO!:** Big, jovial Major General Patrick Jay Hurley, who has been coal miner, cowboy, mule skinner, lawyer to the Choctaws, buck private and presidential envoy extraordinary, began his newest job: U.S. Ambassador to China. In the American Embassy Pat Hurley told reporters how he had taken part in parleys between Chiang Kai-shek's Government and the Chinese Communists.

Last October General Hurley sat in on go-between talks in Chungking. Then in November he flew north to Yenan, capital of Communist China. Pat Hurley sent ahead no advance notices. But a rush phone call summoned Communist Party Secretary Mao Tse-tung, Generals Chou En-lai and Chu Teh. They sped to the airport in Mao's car (a converted ambulance), ran across the field to greet their guest. Bugles blared. General Hurley snapped to attention, saluted. Then he gave China's Communists the Choctaw war whoop: "Yahoo!"

Having thus shattered the ice in a way more formalized diplomats would have disdained, General Hurley took an earnest part in the serious talks that followed. Later he brought Chou En-lai south for more parleys in Chungking. Chou returned to Yenan with a proposal from Chiang Kai-shek for a Chinese united front. But for all Pat Hurley's war whoops and readiness to act as an intermediary, the gulf between the Communists and the Central Government was still unbridged. Last week Mao Tse-tung angrily spurned the Generalissimo's offer.

FLIGHT THROUGH KWEICHOW: Before the Japs' latest drive JAN. 8 into east central China, half a million or more Chinese left their homes, fled deeper into the hinterland. Perhaps 70,000 of them perished. Last week TIME Correspondent Theodore H. White cabled this eyewitness report of their ordeal:

"There are certain clinical phenomena that characterize mass flight in China. First is exhaustion. Second is a beastlike silence broken only by children's chattering. You get technical after you have seen millions of people suffering for years. You examine the children's hair to see whether it is dry and brittle; when a child starts to go, his hair loses oil and it cracks easily. Most of all you listen to the quality of their silence. The longer the trek, the more intense the silence, the more deadly the apathy. The silence on this road was prodigious.

"Along the route of flight lay little towns, deserted by their inhabitants and now only stopping places for the refugees. Occasionally we saw what was left of a horse, donkey or cow. Always the carcass had been stripped to its skeleton, for the refugees fell on any dead thing and picked its bones clean. And there were the human dead as they had fallen, on roadsides, in ditches, and nearby paddies. They were shriveled and brown. One more thing we saw. Across our headlights' beam ran a wolf, a grey, lithe creature. He looked well-fed."

A HOUSE DIVIDED: Encouraged by U.S. Ambassador Hurley, FEB. 26 the Communists' ace negotiator, smart, suave General Chou En-lai, had flown down from Yenan for one more try after almost a year of bootless words over issues as broad as China itself. At the last moment, the Generalissimo personally took part in the talks. He could not, he pointed out, tolerate an armed state within the state. He was the steward of China's destiny. General Chou would not budge either. The crux of the matter was that Yenan's one-party dictatorship dared not, any more than Chungking, surrender control over the military forces on which its power is based and its survival depends.

JUNE 18 **BID FOR POWER:** As Generalissimo Chiang Kai-shek's resurgent army harried the retreating Japs, China's Communists were bursting out of their original area of power around Yenan. Their main objective: Shanghai and the China coast. The Communists' plan was to move in as the Japs moved out, to win U.S. military recognition and thereby take a long step in their bid for power in China. Should such a situation arise, the U.S. would face a momentous political decision.

JULY 9 **THE RAIN MAKERS:** In Szechwan Province (biggest city: Chungking), drought threatened the crops. Chungking patriots organized a "Praying-for-the-Rain Dragon Corps." They paraded in time-honored rain-making costume: short trousers, bare chests, bands of green grass around their heads. They shouted and beat gongs. A lama supplicated the heavenly waters by burning incense before an altar for three days.

Cried Chungking's press: ancient superstition. The idea of depending on heaven for food must be discarded. It would make a bad impression on China's allies. Rain making was useless nonsense.

Next day it rained.

AUG. 27 **CRISIS:** As the Japanese prepared to lay down their arms in China, Yenan still crackled with defiance. Communist Commander in Chief Chu Teh roughly rejected the nominal authority of Generalissimo Chiang Kai-shek. To Chungking he wired: your order not to take independent action in accepting Japanese surrender "does not conform to the national interest. You have issued the wrong order, and we reject it resolutely."

Cried Radio Yenan: "Chiang Kai-shek, the Fascist chieftain, whose policy has been to sit aside and watch others fight, really has no right to accept a Japnese surrender . . . Reactionary . . . stupid . . . sinister plot . . . to instigate civil war."

As Communist troops neared Peiping and Tientsin the good, grey New York *Times* summed up the situation in a stinging editorial: "The Chinese Communists are in open rebellion against President Chiang Kai-shek and his Government. They want domination. They are not a political party; they are a conspiracy to seize the Chinese Government."

A NEW ERA: At the very hour—about midnight—when the SEPT. 3 Japanese warlords were bowing to Hirohito's surrender decision, Joseph Stalin moved toward a new era in east Asian politics. Abruptly leaving a Moscow banquet for General Eisenhower, Stalin hurried to the final conference on a 30-year Sino-Russian pact.

When the terms were published this week, it was clear that China had achieved its greatest chance in modern times for peace, progress, and perhaps even prosperity. China agreed on her part to give up her "sovereignty" of Outer Mongolia where Chinese rule has been shaky for 50 years. Port Arthur will become a Russian naval base. And Russia gets the use of another port, Dairen, on equal terms with China. China and Russia will be co-owners of the two Manchurian railroads but Russian soldiers may not use the railroads except to fight Japan. Further, Russia would get Japan's half of Sakhalin Island and the Kuril Islands enclosing Russia's Okhotsk Sea. Russia's position in east Asia would return to about where it was in 1904 before the Russo-Japanese war. Stalin's imperialism had redressed the Tsars' imperial ineptitude.

In return, Russia promised China moral, material and military aid. More tangibly, Russia recognized the sovereignty of the Chinese National Government of Chiang Kai-shek over all of China, including Manchuria. That meant Russian aid to China would be sent only to Chiang's government. For the present, this kicked the props out from under the Chinese Communists.

HIS HUMBLE SELF: With the new Sino-Russian treaty in Chiang's pocket, last week the Generalissimo sent his second telegram of invitation to Mao Tse-tung: "To achieve national reconstruction and reap the fruits of the war will depend to a great extent upon your coming to Chungking to discuss and jointly formulate our national policies."

Mao replied that he would send the No. 2 Communist and veteran negotiator, General Chou En-lai.

The Generalissimo sent a third telegram (in Chinese tradition, to invite thrice is to prove sincerity): "I must talk to you in person. I have prepared a plane to bring you here. Please hasten."

At week's end Mao gave in, with Chinese punctilio: "Mr. Chiang Kai-shek. I appreciate your telegram. My humble self is most willing to come to Chungking. Chou En-lai is leaving as soon as your plane arrives. Your younger brother is preparing to come in the immediate future."

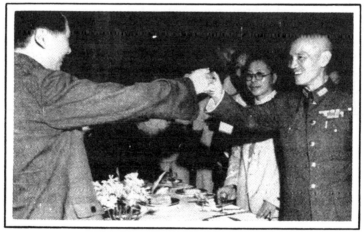

After years of quarreling, Nationalist Chiang Kai-shek (right) and Communist Mao Tse-tung drink a toast in yellow wine.

SEPT. 10 **REUNION IN CHUNGKING:** All Yenan flocked to the airfield to see nervous Mao Tse-tung take off for his unity conference with Chiang Kai-shek. U.S. Ambassador Hurley had flown up from Chungking the night before (with two cases of Scotch) to escort the Communist leader. Mao hugged his little daughter, kissed his young wife goodbye with the quiet desperation of a man going to be executed. Then he climbed aboard for the first plane ride of his 52 years, his first meeting with the Generalissimo in two decades of civil strife.

Chiang Kai-shek was not on hand when Mao deplaned at Chungking. Ambassador Hurley hustled Mao into his own black Cadillac. As they drove off, the high-spirited Oklahoma diplomat, whose Choctaw war whoops are the delight of Asia, yelled to the astonished crowd: "Olive oil! Olive oil!"

That night the Generalissimo and Mao toasted each other in yellow wine. The Communist leader quaffed his cup; the Generalissimo (a teetotaler) barely wet his lips. Said Chiang: "I hope we can have the cordial atmosphere of 1924."

The words brushed memories that went back to the beginnings of modern China, when the Communists were part of Sun Yat-sen's revolutionary people's party, the Kuomintang. Chiang, just back from military training in Moscow, had the job of organizing the nucleus of China's new nationalist army. Mao and Chou were his comrades and the army's political commissars. From Canton the three men marched together on the famed Northern Expedition (1926-27), which gave republican China its first taste of unity. They split in 1927 when Chiang broke with the Kuomintang's Communist wing. Now, with the signing of the Sino-Russian pact, a change had come over the Communist propaganda line. The Generalissimo was no longer a "fascist" defeatist but "President Chiang Kai-shek." The Generalissimo's regime was no longer the "reactionary Kuomintang clique" but the "National Government." Said a Communist spokesman: "We recognize Chiang as a national leader of the anti-Japanese war and we are prepared to recognize him as the leader of postwar rehabilitation."

ONE GOAL: OCT. 22

"One heart, one soul,
One mind, one goal."

Last week on China's lucky "Double Tenth"—the tenth day of the tenth month—came the 34th anniversary of the Republic. In Chungking, cheering crowds sang the unifying words of the new China's national anthem. For the first time in a decade they were not idle words. Peace had brought back a vision, a reunited China.

Then came the announcement of the results of Chiang's and Mao's long bargaining. On many of the secondary issues, the Generalissimo and Communist Mao were hearteningly close. But on the primary issues, the issues basic to China's national weal, they were still far apart.

Chiang and Mao put the maximum emphasis upon their area of agreement—in principle:

¶ Under Generalissimo Chiang's leadership both the Kuomintang and the Communists will do their utmost to avoid civil war and build a free, prosperous China.

¶ An all-party political consultative council will be formed to discuss the end of the one-party rule of the Kuomintang. The Government will recognize that all political parties are equal before the law.

¶ China will have freedom of person, speech, conscience, press and assembly. Postponed, as a concession to the Communists, so that its composition could be broadened, was the National Assembly originally called for Nov. 12 to draft a new constitution.

¶ Local self-government will be encouraged.

But no amount of well-meant gloss could conceal the remaining, fundamental area of disagreement:

Communists insisted on keeping control—through governors and mayors—of vital areas, mostly in North China. Chiang flatly rejected this concept of a dynamic, hostile state-within-a-state. Under Mao's minimum demands, Communist China would remain essentially intact north of the Yellow River and parallel to China's great Yangtze Valley. Such a settlement would effectively separate Nationalist China from Manchuria. Geographically as well as politically, China would be fatally partitioned.

NOV. 5 **MONTH OF TROUBLE:** The month of October, while much-publicized peace talks were going on in Chungking, saw plenty of fighting between the Nationalists and Communists. The Communists made bitter and partly successful efforts to seize North China and wreck the Nationalist chance of successful occupation. A fortnight ago in northwest Shansi, a Communist concentration ambushed 10,000 of Chiang's troops, killed several thousand of them before the rest could be extricated.

But the most serious trouble is not gunfire. For eight weeks now the Communists have worked tirelessly to chop up China's communications and paralyze Government progress into North China. The Chinese railway network north of the Yangtze River is cut in innumerable places. The Communists have also wrecked coal mines which supply the railways.

As the Nationalist-Communist conflict deepened, Ambassador Hurley resigned and the U.S. sent General George C. Marshall to China in the hope that he could negotiate a settlement of the Chinese differences.

ANOTHER TRY: The rugged, aging General of the Army, on DEC. 31 whose shoulders the hopes of East Asia rested, bore the burden confidently. As he stepped from the transport plane at Nanking, Special Envoy George Catlett Marshall was met by a solitary figure, beaming broadly and hand outstretched. Said Generalissimo Chiang Kai-shek: "I am very happy to meet you."

The next stop was Chungking. There, as the special envoy arrived, were gathered the delegates of China's new Political Consultative Council. Set up at last fall's talks between Generalissimo Chiang and Communist Chairman Mao Tse-tung, its members included eight Nationalist leaders, seven Communists and 23 minor-party men and independents. It was charged with the task of furthering a settlement of China's civil strife.

As they prepared to confer, the main contenders jockeyed to improve their standing, and to impress the American envoy with their conciliatory spirit.

Affable General Chou En-lai, No. 1 Communist delegate, announced that he would press first of all for an immediate truce in North China. Then General Chou quietly dropped the Reds' demand that reorganization of the National Government precede acceptance of the Government's authority by the Red armies.

By contrast, Liberal Shao Li-tse spoke for the Kuomintang. He reiterated the National Government's demand that the Communists withdraw from North China's badly snarled railways as a preliminary to a truce.

Said scholarly Dr. Lo Lung-chi, leader of the left-of-center Democratic League:

"For us General Marshall's coming is a case of what the Chinese call *hu ying,* or 'call and answer.' We have called and America has answered." [For more than a year General Marshall tried to mediate and prevent civil war. But his mission was a failure.]

Italy

When 1945 began, the German army still controlled northern Italy, but it was retreating fast. Dictator Benito Mussolini, who had been forced out of power in 1943, was in the north with the Germans. He had no authority, and was actually living under a kind of loose house arrest.

MAY 7 **DEATH IN MILAN:** Death came last week to Benito Mussolini, from the rifles of an Italian firing squad. As his body lay, reviled and spat upon, in a public square of Milan, TIME Correspondent Reg Ingraham sent this eyewitness report of one of history's raw spectacles:

"The first of the Fascist dictators was the first to meet death at the hands of the people he had so long oppressed. This Sunday morning in a sun-drenched square not far from Milan's center, where 22 years ago Benito Mussolini launched the Black Shirt March on Rome, his battered, bullet-riddled corpse sprawled in public display. His head rested on the breast of his mistress, comely Clara Petacci, who had died with him. Around him stretched the bodies of 16 of his Black Shirt henchmen.

"When other correspondents and I reached the scene, a howling mob was struggling for place beside the heap of cadavers. Partisan guards vainly fired rifle and pistol shots into the air to keep the crowd back. A civilian tramped across the bodies and dealt Mussolini's shaven head a terrific kick. Although Duce's upper teeth now protruded grotesquely, there was no mistaking his jaw.

"In death, Mussolini seemed a little man. He wore a Fascist Militia uniform—grey breeches with a narrow black stripe, a green-grey tunic and muddy black riding boots. A bullet had pierced his skull over the left eye and emerged at the back. Mistress Petacci, 25-year-old daughter of an ambitious Roman family, wore a white silk blouse. In her breast were two bullet holes ringed by dark circles of dried blood. One woman emptied a pistol into the Duce's body. 'Five shots!' she screamed. 'Five shots for my five murdered sons!' Others cried: 'He died too quickly! He should have suffered!' But the hate of many was wordless. They could only spit."

The bodies of Mussolini and his mistress hang in a Milan square. Once he had cried: "If I retreat, kill me!" Now it was: "Let me save my life!"

As nearly as can be pieced together, the last days of Benito Mussolini ran out in this fashion:

On Sunday, April 22, Milan's railwaymen went on strike. The city's German garrison correctly interpreted this as the prelude to a revolt, withdrew from the streets into their barracks. On Wednesday demonstrations against the Germans and Fascists swept through the city. That evening Mussolini met with Italian partisan representatives. Terms of surrender were discussed. Mussolini cried: "The Germans have betrayed me!" Bombastically he asked for one hour's time to inform the German High Command of his displeasure.

Before the hour expired, the Duce, who in his fustian prime had bellowed to his followers, "If I retreat, kill me!" was in headlong flight. At 9 p.m. he reached Como near the Swiss border. About 6 a.m. on Thursday Mussolini sneaked northward presumably in the hope of reaching Germany. According to one report he joined a German truck convoy, trying unsuccessfully to disguise himself in a German officer's overcoat. He was spotted near Dongo and held for arrest.

A partisan commander known by the *nom de guerre* "Eduardo" dispatched ten men and an officer to "settle the matter." They found the dictator and his mistress in a cottage on a hill outside the village. When he saw his countrymen approaching, Mussolini thought they had come to liberate him. When he learned that he was under arrest, his face turned yellow with fear and fury. He cried: "Let me save my life, and I'll give you an empire!"

The partisans bluntly informed him that he had been condemned to death. After a brief "trial," the 16 other Fascists in the Duce's party were also adjudged guilty. The Duce's last words as he faced the firing squad were: "No! No!"

The bodies of the 18 were loaded into a moving van and trucked south to Milan. There, at 3 a.m. Friday, they were dumped in the old Piazza Loreto. The bodies lay on the ground for many hours. Then, the partisans hanged Mussolini and Petacci by their feet from a scaffold.

Shortly before noon today the bodies were removed to a mortuary. Mussolini and Petacci were dragged like sacks of grain into a high-walled courtyard. Men, women & children followed, climbing the brick wall and peering over at the shapeless pulp that was the Duce's face. "At last, it is finished," said one quietly.

JULY 23 **WAR:** With the approval of the Allies, their co-belligerent, Italy, this week declared war against her ex-Axis ally, Japan. Said Alberto Tarchiani, Italian ambassador to Washington: "We hope soon to become Allies ourselves."

NOV. 26 **RETURN OF THE NATIVES:** The prisoners of war returning from Russia were thin, unkempt, hungry, tired. Relief workers greeted them with what poor Italy could afford: a cup of minestrone, two small loaves of bread, an apple. At Folano the local Communist party turned out with red flags to welcome the travelers from the Soviet fatherland. The POWs remembered scanty rations, hard marches through the snow and Russian favors to Italians who embraced Communism. They fell upon the welcomers, killed three, injured 50.

FALL: Italy's coalition government fell apart. Deserted by the DEC. 3
right wing of his Cabinet, Premier Ferruccio Parri resigned.
To Italy's fractious factions he addressed a warning:

"Beware of civil war, of reopening the door to fascism.
There are rumors that Washington and London had no trust
in me. The real reason for this lack of trust is that Italy has
only a fragile front of anti-fascism. I hope my successors will
follow the only worthy policy for Italy: left of center."

CURE: Scholarly Alcide de Gasperi has one hobby: mountain DEC. 17
climbing. But no rock wall he ever encountered gave him the
trouble he experienced last week in forming a new government for Italy.

When Crown Prince Umberto, Lieutenant General of the
Realm, named him Premier to succeed Ferruccio Parri, De
Gasperi was ill with influenza. At first, propped up in bed,
sneezing and rheumy-eyed, he haggled with fellow politicians.
Then, pale and weak, he left his bedchamber for day & night
sessions in the Chigi Palace. Punctually at 7 each morning a
neighbor's phonograph woke him up.

Sleepless De Gasperi wanted to continue coalition government. Communists, Socialists, Christian Democrats, Action-
ists, Labor Democrats agreed, but the Liberals insisted that
De Gasperi promise to call off the purge of Fascists. His wife
Francesca had never seen De Gasperi in a more abominable
temper. He threatened to exclude the Liberals and form a five-
party government. While the neighbor's phonograph played,
he drafted a tentative list of ministers. Then much-enduring
Alcide de Gasperi fainted.

This week the Liberals capitulated. The purge of Fascists
would continue. As he and his ministers took their oaths,
Alcide de Gasperi cried out in relief: "You wouldn't believe
it, but now my cold is cured!"

International

THE YALTA DOCTRINE: No doubt about it—the Russians were FEB. 26
changing. At Yalta, as at earlier conferences, Stalin and other
Soviet bigwigs shed a little more of their personal isolation.

Stalin mugged for the cameras, patently loved to show off his fine grey uniforms. His stock of English phrases had grown: "So what?" and "You said it," had been added to "The toilet is over there!" and "What the hell goes on here?"

Stalin, Roosevelt and Churchill bluntly said that the three powers who had "made victory possible and certain" proposed to administer the victory. Big Three unity for this purpose was "a sacred obligation which our Governments owe to our peoples—and to all the peoples of the world."

This assertion of high purpose was a logical expression of Stalin's cold certainty that only power counts. (Said he once of the Pope, "How many divisions has he got?") It was an equally natural extension of President Roosevelt's recent assertion that the U.S. intends not only to take a responsible part in world affairs but to shape the decisions for which it shares responsibility.

JULY 23   **IN THE WOODS:** People who had nothing better to worry about last week noted a strong dendrophile tendency in the Big Three. They could not stay away from trees. There had been the economic conference at Bretton Woods and the conference setting up the United Nations at Dumbarton Oaks. Now they were at Potsdam, a German version of the old Slavonic name, Poztupimi, which means "under the oaks."

JULY 30   **MINUET IN POTSDAM:** In Potsdam's rococo rooms the great Emperor Frederick had played his flute (not badly); in its disciplined gardens he had schemed to confuse and divide his enemies. Now a humbly born President of the U.S., a midwestern Missourian, was top man at Potsdam. Winston Churchill, the descendant of Marlborough, and Joseph Stalin, the Bolshevik dictator, made Harry Truman the chairman of their formal meetings. One evening he gave a state dinner for the other two, and afterwards he sat at a piano and played a minuet in G for them. Joseph Stalin turned up at Truman's dinner in a fawn-colored uniform with scarlet epaulets and the big Gold Star of a Hero of the Soviet Union. Churchill, who had seen and envied Stalin's fawn outfit at Yalta, remembered that as Lord Warden of the Cinque Ports he also was entitled to wear a fawn-colored uniform. So he did. Truman wore a brown business suit.

Churchill, Truman and Stalin meet at Potsdam. After dinner and "The Missouri Waltz," the President entertains with a minuet in G.

After dinner Sergeant Eugene List of the U.S. Army preceded Truman at the piano. Pianist List angled most of his program for Stalin: some Tchaikovsky, three Shostakovich preludes, folk songs of the Volga, the Caucasus and the steppes. Stalin sprang up, shook List's hand, drank a toast to him and asked for more. Churchill, well briefed on Truman and his ways, broke up the twosome by asking List to play *The Missouri Waltz*. Truman listened happily. Then, aglow with camaraderie and his own bourbon, he went to the piano and played the minuet. Churchill and Stalin were enthusiastic.

PLAN FOR A CONTINENT: How to keep Germany from making war again was the central question of Potsdam. To destroy Germany utterly and forever might put Europe back a century economically and leave a political vacuum into which Big Three rivalries would rush. To preserve the old Germany was to run an all-too-familiar risk. The Potsdam conference had to thread a way between.   AUG. 13

Politically, the Potsdam planners put their trust in 1) that vague and aleatory something called "re-education," 2) a determination to permit no central German government to function for a long, long time.

Economically, said the communiqué, "primary emphasis shall be given to the development of agriculture and peaceful domestic industries." Perhaps the most significant point in the Potsdam communiqué was its provision for a Germany that was completely demilitarized and forever forbidden to put its energy into armaments and thus fundamentally changed.

AUG. 27 **POTSDAM POSTSCRIPT:** From a credible source came a belated report on personal relations among the top men at Potsdam:

Harry Truman and Joseph Stalin got along strikingly well. Stalin's dislike of Winston Churchill and his long-winded speeches was never more apparent. Once, when Churchill voiced a detailed bill of complaint against Russian plundering in southeastern Europe, Stalin merely grunted; his interpreter said that he had no comment. Truman sprang up, said that he had investigated the British charges and was prepared to substantiate them. Stalin twinkled, pointedly replied: "I will believe the Americans."

War Crimes

Long before the fighting ended, teams of investigators had begun compiling evidence to prove that enemy leaders had consistently and purposefully committed crimes against humanity for which they could be brought to trial under international law. Some of the trials that resulted were held by the nations in which the alleged crimes were committed. But the top Nazis were rounded up and taken to Nürnberg, Germany, there to stand trial as a group before a tribunal presided over by U.S., British and Russian legal experts.

HERR KRUPP: The great Krupp works at Essen, arsenal of Kaiser and Führer, lay dead. For five years this steel heart of the German war machine had been a prime target of Allied bombers. Last week U.S. Ninth Armymen rolled past the debris, a few miles farther south overran the high-walled Villa Hügel, secluded estate of Alfred Krupp von Bohlen und Halbach, Herr President of Krupp, silent partner of Naziism, now wanted by the Allies as a war criminal.

A brace of Villa Hügel retainers blocked the door. Strapping (6 ft. 5) Lieut. Colonel Clarence Sagmoen merely drew his Colt 45, and a passage opened. Colonel Sagmoen soon had his captive in tow—a thin, nervous man, balding at 37 and trimly dressed in a pin-striped business suit. The American growled: "You bastards started this war and we'll show you who's finishing it!" He ordered the prisoner into the back of his Jeep.

Later Krupp was interviewed by U.S. officers who asked: "What are your plans after the war?"

Herr Krupp pondered. For five generations his family had forged arms—for Napoleon, for the Habsburgs, for the Hohenzollerns, for the Nazis, for any customers with cash. Herr Krupp, merchant of death, answered: "I hope to rebuild the factories and produce again." [Krupp was found guilty of war crimes and spent six years in prison, after which he was allowed to rebuild his family's firm as an essential element in the economic recovery of West Germany. However, in 1967 he ran into credit difficulties, and after 156 years of uninterrupted family control, Krupp was forced to convert his steel empire into a publicly owned company.]

HORROR: As the U.S. armies penetrated the dark heart of Germany last week, they discovered and revealed to the world some examples of the most highly organized horror of all time—a series of concentration camps for political prisoners, from most of the nations the Nazis had conquered, including the German nation.   APRIL 30

The evidence of the camps at Buchenwald, Belsen and Nordhausen was as irrefutable as death, as monstrous as human degradation. From the camps, TIME & LIFE correspondents described these horrors.

¶ *Belsen*—From the Belsen camp LIFE Correspondent George Rodger reported: "The six-square-mile, barbed-wire enclosure in the heart of a rich agricultural center has been a hell on earth for 60,000 men, women & children of a dozen different nationalities who were being gradually starved to death by *SS* guards under a brutish, pig-eyed leader, Captain Krämer. During the month of March, 17,000 people died of starvation. Under the pine trees the scattered dead were lying, not in twos or threes or dozens, but in thousands. Little children rested their heads against the stinking corpses of their mothers, too nearly dead themselves to cry. A man hobbled up to me and spoke to me in German. I couldn't understand what he said and I shall never know, for he fell dead at my feet in the middle of his sentence.

"Women tore away their clothing and scratched the hordes of lice which fed on their emaciated bodies; rotten with dysentery, they relieved themselves where they lay and the stench was appalling. Naked bodies with gaping wounds in their backs and chests showed where those who still had the strength to use a knife had cut out the kidneys, livers and hearts of their fellow men and eaten them that they themselves might live. Perhaps it can all be summed up in the few croaking words that came from a pitiful pile of rags and bones that lay at my feet: 'Look, Englishman, this is German culture.' "

¶ *Buchenwald*—From the camp at Buchenwald Correspondent Percy Knauth reported: "Buchenwald is acres of bare ground on a hillside in Thuringia where woods and fields are green under warm spring sun. It is miles and miles of barbed wire once charged with electricity and guarded by machine-gun towers built of creosoted pine logs. It is barracks after barracks crowded with 21,000 living, breathing human beings who stink like nothing else on earth and many of whom have lost the power of coherent speech. It is gallows standing in desolate courtyards, ropes still swinging from the hooks, pillories standing in the great parade ground just beneath the main gate, where men were tied down and beaten until they blubbered.

Buchenwald is a fact which has existed for eleven years, and it is a fact which will stink through the years of history as long as generations of mankind have memories.

"There were two ovens here, each with six openings. The ovens are cold now but before the Americans came their clean bright flame consumed between 150 and 200 people daily. And there are down in a cellar on a clean, whitewashed wall many hooks jutting out near the low ceiling. Before we came men were strung up on the hooks, pulled up till they choked. It took them a long time before they gave up the instinctive fight for breath, and there are scratches on the walls where they clawed vainly for support.

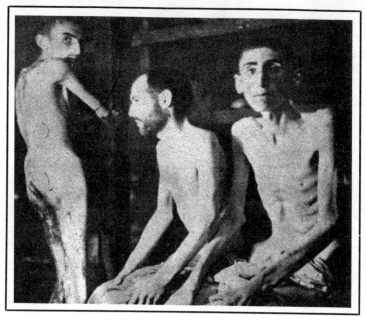

Survivors of Buchenwald. "There were two ovens, each with six openings. There were bodies stacked like firewood. There were men and some were naked."

"We came up from the cellar and passed into another yard fenced in by a high wooden wall. There was a pile of bodies there, stacked more or less the way I stack my firewood back home, not too carefully. There were men and some of them were naked. They looked strange. Their mouths were open as though in pain and little streaks of blood flowed from their noses. A G.I. stared and stared and couldn't get one thought out of his mind, repeating it over and over: 'Those guys just starved to death. They just starved.'"

DACHAU: When all other German prison camps are forgotten the name of Dachau will still be infamous. It was the first concentration camp set up for Hitler, and its mere name was a whispered word of terror through all Germany from the earliest days of Nazi control. Last week the U.S. Seventh Army entered Dachau and liberated 32,000 of its still living inmates. With them went TIME Correspondent Sidney Olson. His report:

"Beside the highway into Dachau there runs a spur line off

MAY 7

the Munich railroad. Here a soldier said: 'I think you better take a look at these boxcars.' The cars were filled with dead men. Most of them were naked. On their bony, emaciated backs and rumps were whip marks. Most of the cars were open-top cars like American coal cars. I counted 39 of them which were filled with these dead. The smell was very heavy.

"The main entry road runs past several largish buildings and now we began to meet the liberated. Several hundred Russians, French, Yugoslavs, Italians and Poles were here, frantically, hysterically happy. They began to kiss us, and there is nothing you can do when a lot of hysterical, unshaven, lice-bitten, half-drunk, typhus-infected men want to kiss you. Nothing at all."

OUT OF THE PIT: The first shock of horror had been absorbed, but this week came news of a monstrosity that appeared to top all previous tales of Nazi inhumanity.

To U.S. Army questioners a captured German doctor, Gustav Wilhelm Schuebbe, casually admitted that the Nazi Annihilation Institute at Kiev had killed from 110,000 to 140,000 persons "unworthy to live" during the nine months he had worked there. Dr. Schuebbe, a crippled drug addict who was head of the Institute, added coolly that he himself had killed 21,000 people.

The human material included epileptics, schizophrenics, Jews, foreigners, gypsies. Each doctor on the staff "processed" about 100 persons per working day with injections of morphine tartrate. Explained Dr. Schuebbe: the subject showed "breathing difficulties and a shrinking of the eye pupils; the face assumed a blue color; there was sporadic breathing; then a breathing stoppage and a heart stoppage. *Exitus lethalis.*"

Dr. Schuebbe was scientifically detached in his motives. Said he:

"I still maintain that, just as one prunes a tree—by removing old, undesirable branches in the spring- so for its own interest a certain hygienical supervision of the body of a people is necessary from time to time."

MAY 21 **THE FAT'S IN THE FIRE:** Reichsmarshal Hermann Göring surrendered in state. The 36th Infantry Division's assistant commander, Brigadier General Robert Stack, met him by appointment on a country road in Bavaria, saluted smartly, and escorted him to division headquarters. Afterward the biggest Nazi scoundrel so far bagged by the Allies lunched on chicken, changed into a fresh uniform with twelve medals, and put up for the night at a nearby castle with Frau Göring.

A few days later Göring met the Allied press. According to Göring, only Göring made any sense in the Nazi hierarchy, and only he understood the Allies. Hitler was "narrow and ignorant." Joachim von Ribbentrop, the Reich's deposed Foreign Minister, was "a scoundrel." After the attempt to kill Hitler last July, even Heinrich Himmler fell from grace. At the last, the man closest to the Führer was Martin Bormann.

On April 24, said Göring, he asked Hitler to let him take over the collapsing Reich and negotiate a surrender to the Allies. According to one of Hitler's stenographers, the Führer had already nominated Göring for his job. Göring's own account differed: he said that Hitler raged, condemned him to death, reprieved him when Göring promised to give up all his honors and titles. At Berchtesgaden, Göring added, the *SS* seized him and would have killed him if loyal *Luftwaffe* men had not rescued him. Just when he found time to arrange the loading of a 20-car armored train with looted art and treasure, Göring did not say.

NAMES FROM HELL: The final convulsions of Nazi Europe continued to cast up a collection of murderers and innocents, thieves and victims, such as the world has seldom seen:

¶ General Heinz Guderian, tank expert, belittled U.S. tanks and Lieut. Gen. George S. Patton ("he followed the same principle that I used in Poland, France and Russia"), declared U.S. and German soldiers should shake hands and make up ("just like after a football match").

¶ Edward Waiter, head of the Dachau death camp, shot himself through the heart, still lived, shot himself again through the head and died. Priests refused to touch his body.

¶ Hans Frank, who as Nazi governor of Poland had been responsible for the death of millions, had to be forcibly restrained by his American captors from slashing his wrists.

¶ Hitler's maidservant, Gertrude, found at Berchtesgaden, declared of her ex-boss: "He was a nice man, really. Of course he was mad."

MAY 28 **COLLECTORS' ITEMS:** A few of the German Nazis caught last week distinguished themselves by admitting that they were Nazis:

¶ Dr. Robert Ley, leader of Hitler's Labor Front and "Strength Through Joy" movement, turned up in a four-day beard, blue pajamas, a green hat, relinquished a vial of poison and told his U.S. captors: "I will always believe that Adolf Hitler was Germany's greatest man. You can beat me; you can torture me, but I'll never doubt Hitler's acts."

¶ Protested Adolf Hitler's onetime protegée, Nazi cinemactress Leni Riefenstahl, when U.S. troops ejected her from Foreign Minister Joachim von Ribbentrop's hill villa at Kitzbühel, Austria: "Some of my best friends were Jews."

JUNE 4 **A GRAVE ON THE HEATH.** On his last trip, from Berlin to the north German moors, Heinrich Himmler had shaved his Hitlerian mustache, replaced his scholarly pince-nez with a black eye patch. He had become Herr Hitzinger. His papers were in perfect order.

But perfect order was a noticeable incongruity in conquered Germany. British guards, noting and suspecting the perfection of Herr Hitzinger's papers, dumped him in a prison camp. After three days he declared to the camp commandant: "I am Heinrich Himmler."

Security officers stripped him, found a tiny blue glass vial of poison in his clothes. Then a British sergeant major and a doctor searched him—under his arms, in his ears, his hair. Finally the doctor decided to look into Himmler's mouth. The prisoner quickly ground his jaws, and fell to the floor. He had concealed a second poison vial in his mouth, and had broken it with his teeth. The potassium cyanide worked quickly: in 15 minutes he was dead.

Cheated of a formal inquisition and execution, Himmler's captors let his body lie for two days on the floor where he had fallen. Medical authorities removed the brain, took plaster casts of the skull. Finally, a British Army detail, sworn to secrecy, buried the unembalmed body in a grave on the heath near Lüneburg. There was no coffin, no marking on the grave, for a martyr's monument.

The only words spoken at the graveside came from a British Tommy: "Let the worm go to the worms."

POOR GÖRING: Prisoner Hermann Göring was a mountain- AUG. 6
ous wreck. His drug dosage had been cut from 40 tablets of
paracodeine to 26 tablets daily. Mostly he kept to his cot or
his chair (he had to have an outsize one; a small one had
crumpled under his 270 lbs.). He alternately bragged and
wept. Last week he went completely to pieces during a thun-
derstorm—which scared the daylights out of him—and suffered a heart attack.

DEFINITION: The Big Three, with the addition of France, final- AUG. 20
ly decided what constituted a war crime. Three categories were
established, all punishable by death:
¶ Crimes against peace: *i.e.,* planning, preparing, initiating
and waging wars of aggression or wars in violation of international treaties or agreements.
¶ Violation of the laws and customs of war: *i.e.,* maltreat-
ment of prisoners and of civilians in occupied countries, murder of hostages, plundering, wanton destruction of cities or
devastation not justified by military needs.
¶ Crimes against humanity: *i.e.,* murder, extermination, en-
slavement, deportation, or persecution on political, racial or
religious grounds in the execution of or in connection with
any crime within the jurisdiction of the tribunal.

For Supreme Court Justice Robert Houghwout Jackson,
chief U.S. prosecutor of war crimes, last week's declaration
was a personal victory. He had argued long & loud that a war
of aggression must, per se, be considered a crime.

The agreement made other milestones in international law.
One was that entire organizations, such as the *SS,* could be
adjudged guilty collectively. Another was that obedience to
orders from above was no excuse. Loopholes such as this had
nullified most war-crime trials after World War I (of 896
Germans accused, only six were convicted).

THE 24: As the Allies prepared to try the top Nazis as a group SEPT. 10
at Nürnberg, all but one of the 24 were in custody. The exception was Martin Bormann, Hitler's deputy and closest
adviser in the final days.

In Nürnberg jail, where most of the accused were held,
there was a decided religious trend. More & more of the Nazis
asked for Bibles and the services of the U.S. Army chaplains.

NOV. 5 **THE BLACK DAYS:** Among the opportunists, perverts, gangsters and men of distorted genius who rose to power in Hitler's Germany, Dr. Robert Ley was an exception. The boss of Germany's Labor Front was a rather ordinary little man, fond of his bottle and frantically fervent in his adulation of Hitler and Naziism. "National Socialism has made an end to the bone-softening doctrine of life negation," he once said. "Germans are fanatics of life." When he was arrested last May, he moaned: "Life [without Hitler] does not mean a damn thing to me."

He meant what he said. One evening last week, in his war criminal's cell at Nürnberg, Robert Ley hanged himself.

He left a testament to "My German People." It told them that their worst mistake had been anti-Semitism, counseled them to make amends: "The Jew should make a friend out of Germany and Germany a friend out of the Jew." He also gave his reason for suicide. "I was with Hitler in the good days and I want to be with him now in the black days."

DEC. 10 **DEFENSE MOMENTS:** The war crimes trial at Nürnberg was not all the prosecution's show. The defendants had their moments. There was a half hour of bickering between defense and prosecution over whether Rudolf Hess, supposedly an amnesia victim, should be tried. Hess rose, informed the court that he had faked his amnesia for tactical reasons, that he now wanted to be tried with his comrades. Said he: "Mr. President, as of now, my memory is again in order."

Göring laughed, bowed, took notes, eyed pretty girl reporters in the gallery. He gave an interview to the Associated Press in which he defiantly proclaimed himself a "true paladin of my Führer" and declared that, if he had the choice, he would do the whole thing over again.

The most impressive piece of prosecution evidence was an hour-long film record of German concentration camps. The courtroom lights were dimmed for the first time since the trial started, and the defendants sat in semi-darkness. Across a motion picture screen moved what veteran correspondents called the most terrible pictures of mass slaughter and torture they had ever seen.

The accused in the dock were gripped by the horror they had created. Hess watched in tense fascination. Göring reddened when the film was three-quarters through, gazed fixedly at his lap until the film was over. Keitel mopped his brow and covered his eyes. Ribbentrop remained calm, shook his head in disbelief. Hans Frank, ex-Governor General of Poland, wept.

When the lights went up, the courtroom was silent. Then, in the gallery, someone muttered: "Oh, God, why can't we shoot the swine now?" [When the trial ended in 1946, ten of the Nazi defendants were sentenced to prison terms ranging from ten years to life; three were acquitted. The remaining twelve—including Göring, Von Ribbentrop and General Jodl —were sentenced to hang. Göring committed suicide a few hours before his scheduled execution.]

United Nations

In 1943, in the midst of the fighting, the U.S., Great Britain, Russia and China had agreed on the need for an international organization after the war to maintain peace and security. Representatives of the four nations met at Dumbarton Oaks in late 1944 to draw up plans for such an organization, and it was agreed at Yalta, in February 1945, that an international conference would be called at San Francisco in April to sign a formal charter. In the meantime, an international organization known as UNRRA (United Nations Relief and Rehabilitation Administration) was set up in 1943 to provide immediate relief and food to the liberated areas.

CHIEF CLERK: The Secretary-General for the San Francisco APRIL 16 conference was announced last week—lanky, Harvard-trained Alger Hiss, one of the State Department's brighter young men. Alger Hiss was one of the Harvard Law School students whose records earned them the favor of Professor (now Justice) Felix Frankfurter and a year as secretary to the late Justice Oliver Wendell Holmes. He joined the State Department in 1936, accompanied President Roosevelt to Yalta.

At San Francisco he and his secretariat of 300 (mostly Americans) will have the drudging, thankless clerk's job of copying, translating and publishing, running the thousands of paperclip and pencil chores of an international meeting. But Alger Hiss will be an important figure there. As Secretary-General, managing the agenda, he will have a lot to say behind the scenes about who gets the breaks. [Hiss would be convicted of perjury in 1950 after denying that he had passed government secrets to a Soviet spy ring. He served nearly four years in prison.]

MAY 7 **THE SECOND BEGINNING:** It had been warm and bright in the morning. By mid-afternoon clouds hung in the blue sky, and their shadows lay on San Francisco. Outside the Opera House, where the modern world was about to begin its second quest of planned peace, police horses soon glistened in the rain. The flags, half-staffed for Franklin Roosevelt [whose death had occurred two weeks previously], nodded damply downward.

A band had been stationed backstage to entertain the galleries while the delegates were arriving. Conditioned to *The Star-Spangled Banner* [which had preceded virtually every meeting and performance during the war], hundreds rose when the first bars sounded. It was a false alarm. For reasons unknown, the band successively played *Lover, Come Back to Me; Stout-Hearted Men; Wanting You*. When the band got to *The World Is Waiting for the Sunrise* the galleries were giggling.

THE SPEECHES: The voice that all had hoped to hear was stilled. No speaker stirred the conference as Franklin Roosevelt would have stirred it. But that was no great reflection on those who did speak. Like the war which had brought it forth, this was a conference without banners.

President Truman, speaking from Washington in a dry, hurried voice, used the words "just" and "justice" seven times ("Justice remains the greatest power on earth. To that power alone will we submit").

Viacheslav Molotov, in blunt Soviet fashion, asserted the Big Three's prime responsibility, and added: "The point at issue is whether other peace-loving nations are willing to rally around these leading powers to create an effective international security organization."

Anthony Eden, usually no great orator, outdid himself and brought his audience up cheering. His best (and final) lines: "In the last six terrible years, unnumbered men have died to give humanity another chance.

"We too have a job of work to do if we are not to fail those men.

"Let us do it with courage, modesty and dispatch.

"Let us do it now."

WHY IT IS SO TOUGH: People were getting bored and a little JUNE 4 impatient with the San Francisco conference. The goal—security—was so plain and good that the difficulties in drafting a charter seemed remote, artificial, vexingly technical and hard to understand.

Yet every week at San Francisco made it clearer that beneath the rivalries, the petty legalisms and the quibbling in committee rooms lay real problems related to the real world outside. Chief among these was the sovereign state. Every delegate represented one, and, as a public official, was sworn to uphold its sovereignty. Many of the states represented at San Francisco had just been through a war in which they obtained a victory which each thought of as a national achievement. Sovereignty had reached a new high on V-E day.

In some important respects, most of the small states were willing to delegate to the central organization more sovereign power than the large nations would give up. As agreed at Yalta, the Security Council could not act if one of the Big Powers said no. Russia insisted on retaining this veto because it feared that the majority of nations on the Council would be basically unfriendly. The U.S. also wanted the veto; few politicians believed that the charter could pass the Senate without it.

"GOOD AND DUE FORM": JULY 9

We, the peoples of the United Nations, determined

To save succeeding generations from the scourge of war, which twice in our lifetime has brought untold sorrow to mankind . . .

Do hereby establish an international organization to be known as the United Nations.

It would never be set to music. Nevertheless, the final draft of the Preamble to the United Nations charter went a long way toward that universal appeal of language which many of the delegates thought essential.

Some of the earlier versions read like real-estate deeds. At one point Poet Archibald MacLeish, U.S. Assistant Secretary of State, returned to San Francisco and was assigned the re-drafting job. He tried to boil the whole thing down to 100 words, but the coordinating committee threw his version out. It was too literary.

A committee composed mostly of lawyers wrote the final draft. Phrases and concepts were borrowed from all over. There were Lincoln's "scourge of war" and Pope Leo XIII's "dignity of man." The committee achieved one fine clause: "to practice tolerance and live together in peace with one another as good neighbors."

DEC. 10 **IN THE U.S. TRADITION:** Which town will get the county seat? Rich and raucous is the American tradition of debate on such matters. It sounded a little odd last week in the oak-paneled, semi-ecclesiastical room of London's Church House, where world statesmen were considering where the world's capital—the permanent seat of UNO—should be.

American boosters, as stiffly confident as high school valedictorians, trooped one by one to the lectern to air their local prides. First came Atlantic City's A. W. Phillips, in a neat blue suit and rimless glasses. He spoke for only three and a half minutes, since the committee was already well briefed by an elaborate brochure which included a spread of the Atlantic City beauty pageant.

Chicago's Barnet Hodes claimed that Chicago's libraries had 125,000 more books than Boston's had. Chicago, like the other delegations, had a newsreel to show its beauties. As the commentator said "This is the sort of thing worthy of study in Chicago," the reel stuck, and a bevy of fan dancers on ice skates froze on the screen, grinning toothily at the statesmen.

The star performer was Paul Bellamy, a bull-necked businessman who represented no city, but the bleak Black Hills of South Dakota, where men are men and steaks are three inches thick. Bellamy's best argument had a pessimistic undertone:

Boston, Philadelphia and the other coastal cities were within easy reach of atomic bombings. "In the Black Hills there are no military objectives, and the gentlemen who are striving for the peace of the world can live at peace while the atomic bombs are falling."

"A LITTLE QUICKLY": Men could look hard at UNRRA. They could suspect—and in some cases rightly—that there was waste; that sometimes supplies filtered into the black markets; that other mistakes were made. DEC. 31

But in the nine war-ravaged countries of Eastern Europe and the Far East, where UNRRA's rows of ciphers turned into living people, the view was different. Stalled until V-J day by lack of men, ships and supplies, UNRRA was working at last. Grain that may save 400,000 lives was now moving along the Dalmatian coast. Hungry men worked slowly and happily, unloading UNRRA ships in Greek and Italian ports. Missouri mules made themselves at home on Yugoslavia's tiny farms. Pure-bred bulls had been sent to rebuild herds slaughtered during the war. Tractors and plows were on hand to turn the earth of hundreds of farms. Pumps and pipes from the U.S. and Britain have restored Athens' water supply.

At last UNRRA was beginning to respond to the plea of a Partisan widow who told an UNRRA worker in the ruined Czechoslovak village of Zlata Bana: "We don't need much, but we need a little quickly."

"WHERE THERE IS WINE": After London's meeting of the UNO Preparatory Commission decided to place UNO's capital in the U.S., the fight narrowed down to San Francisco v. the East. Said Antonio Parra Velasco of Ecuador: "San Francisco is a city of wine, and where there is wine there is civilization, culture and the spirit of enthusiasm which we need." Professor C. K. Webster, the United Kingdom's alternate delegate, said he had found the wines of the Hudson Valley equal to those of California.

On a vote, the admirers of California wine lost, 25 to 5. The new international center would be in the U.S., somewhere east of the Mississippi. [In 1946, the Commission decided that the headquarters would be located in New York City.]

Argentina

A bloodless revolution in 1943 had put into power a group of army officers who ruled the country with an iron hand and maintained a pro-Axis policy throughout the war. The most prominent among them was Colonel Juan Domingo Perón, who ran the government from behind the scenes as War Minister and Vice President.

SEPT. 3 **THE RETURNS:** Strong Man Juan Domingo Perón, the soldier-opportunist who yearned to be President-Dictator, had tried everything: the trappings and struttings of Fascism, anti-U.S. nationalism, an anti-Communist witch hunt. He had promised the moon to the Argentine working man, the same moon to Argentine industrialists. He had made gestures toward U.S. democracy, and had hinted at lining up (if worst came to worst) with the U.S.S.R. By last week's end, the returns were pouring in and they were not pleasant reading for Colonel Perón.

His country was in an uproar. Only the soldiers and cops seemed to be still loyal to the strong man. To Buenos Aires from Montevideo flocked some of Argentina's most important political exiles. Cheering crowds met them at the dock; so did police armed with sabers. In the capital, students went out on strike—while their sympathetic teachers resigned or were fired in droves.

Then from faraway Boston came a body blow. Nelson Rockefeller, the conciliatory U.S. Assistant Secretary of State in charge of Latin American affairs, stood up at a Pan-American dinner and denounced Argentina as "the black sheep" of the hemisphere family. Argentina's Government, said Rockefeller, had not kept the promises it made before admission to the San Francisco Conference. Fugitive Axis nationals and funds had not been hunted down. The Government ruled by naked force, with no elections in sight. Rockefeller's prescription for the Argentine people: kick out the militarists.

SEPT. 17 **NEAR MISS:** Heading northwest across the pampas toward Córdoba one day last week, Argentina's Vice President and Strong Man Juan Domingo Perón looked out from his airplane seat at fleecy clouds and the three-plane fighter escort close at hand. Suddenly one of the fighters veered away from a fog bank, shot toward Perón's DC-2. The fighter whipped overhead, barely missed crashing squarely into the transport's fuselage. There was a sharp bump and it thundered into a spin. One of the transport's propellers had cut off its tail assembly.

Three miles beyond, the DC-2 landed. There Perón learned that the fighter pilot had been killed. Said the Strong Man, chalk-white and shaken: "We have been born a second time." Later he took a train back to Buenos Aires, where imaginative Argentines were already calling the fallen pursuit pilot a home-grown version of Japan's *Kamikaze* pilots. One proposal: a monument to the man who had scored a near miss.

ELECT OF GOD: Through the Venetian blinds of his fifth-floor office in the Ministry of War, Juan Domingo Perón last week looked down upon half-a-million of his countrymen. They shouted "Down with Perón!" "Death to dictatorship!" For three hours, they marched through Buenos Aires' Calle Callos. They whistled, hooted and cat-called. It was Perón's longest raspberry. Young students and elderly aristocrats, Army and Navy officers in mufti, even women had broken through barriers to demonstrate their common disgust with Colonel Perón and his heavy-handed military dictatorship. OCT. 1

BACK TO NORMALCY: Argentina was back to normal. Anybody who was anybody was in jail. After 52 days of abnormal freedom, Vice President Juan Domingo Perón had again imposed the repressive "state of siege" under which Argentines had suffered for almost four years. The resounding demonstration staged in the streets of Buenos Aires last fortnight by 500,000 irate Argentines was the tip-off to Perón that he had better get tough or get out. OCT. 8

THE CRACK-UP: Argentines rid themselves of their military dictator last week. But they were not rid of the military. Out of the turbulence of armed revolt and panic which rocked the Argentine nation, three facts emerged: 1) Colonel Juan Domingo Perón was out cold; 2) General Eduardo Avalos, new Minister of War, held the sword-hand; 3) democratic Argen- OCT. 22

tines, united in a common front, were in no mood to accept anything less than the full restoration of constitutional government.

A clique of colonels had sprung Perón into power in 1943. Last week it was Argentina's younger officers, the lieutenants, captains and majors, who had told potent General Avalos that the country was threatened with civil war as long as Perón dominated the Government. They demanded a showdown. Avalos agreed. Perón had no choice but to resign as Vice President, Minister of War and Secretary of Labor.

But the cheers were short-lived. The press was still gagged and citizen Perón took to the air, intimated that he might run for the Presidency in the April 7 elections. Again the young officers forced action on General Avalos. Perón's arrest was ordered. In a second-rate hotel near the Plata estuary, where he was hiding with his mistress, ex-actress Eva Duarte and $50,000 in cash, the late master of 14,000,000 Argentines meekly surrendered. Twenty-four hours later, Perón was duly packed aboard a small naval vessel, shipped off to a concentration camp where he joined the company of political prisoners whom he had locked up.

OCT. 29 **PRODIGAL'S RETURN:** The Hemisphere's No. 1 authoritarian was back in power. After one brief day in his Argentine Elba, the federal prison on Martín García Island, Juan Domingo Perón overturned the moderates who had forced his resignation and vaulted back to the balcony of Government House. Thousands of Perón-struck workers cheered: *"Viva Perón! Viva labor! Viva Argentina!"*

The abrupt collapse of Argentina's week-old fumbling interim government came as a surprise. What manner of country was this, where a ruling clique and a single city, Buenos Aires, seemed to decide a great nation's political destinies?

Argentina lived last week, as it had for the past century, in two worlds. One world was the cosmopolitan, factory-packed port of Buenos Aires. The other was the land of rich green pasturage which stretched west to the Andes, south to Patagonia. Those who peopled the two worlds—the *porteños* of the port and the *peónes* of the countryside—had little in common. But both worlds had long been ripe for change. In few other lands in the Americas had the feudalism of a landholding aristocracy persisted so long. And, as Secretary of Labor and Social Welfare, Perón had won the backing of both *peón* and *porteño.*

He upped *peónes'* wages to as much as $30 a month, guaranteed them a two-hour rest after lunch (called the "Siesta of Perón"). Perón upped the *porteño's* wages an average 10%-20%, rolled back rents and clothing costs. Few of Buenos Aires' old-line, socialist-controlled workers went into the Perón camp. But on the poorest fringe, Perón found a following. It was this element that Perón's Labor Secretariat last week turned loose on Buenos Aires.

SEÑORA?: Argentines heard last week that their 50-year-old NOV. 19 Strong Man, Juan Domingo Perón, had legalized a two-year companionship: he had married his 26-year-old mistress, Actress Eva Duarte. If the story was true, Strong Man Perón was a stronger prospect for the presidency. [With the help of Eva Perón, who won great popularity with the masses by promising them extensive social reforms, Perón was elected president in 1946 and remained in power until 1955.]

The Bahamas

ABDICATION FROM ELBA: London's Colonial Office stiffly an- MARCH 26 nounced: His Royal Highness the Duke of Windsor has resigned as Governor and Commander in Chief of the Bahamas. The resignation, said the Government, need occasion no surprise: the Governor's "normal tenure" of five years is almost up. For half a day the Duke of Windsor was not at home to any queries. Then he donned a dapper, grey check suit, pinned a red carnation in his lapel, and with his well-dressed Duchess at his side, gallantly went forth to meet the press and explain his second abdication.

There was not much to explain, really. Even with the woman he loved, the onetime King-Emperor who had ruled over a domain on which the sun never sets could not be very happy ruling 29 islets, 661 cays and 2,387 sandspits. In public, however, he was always correct. Only in private did he say "This Elba!" and she echo "This St. Helena!"

Brazil

APRIL 16 **COMMUTERS' REVOLT:** Millions of wartime commuters have longed to do it; last week a few hundred Brazilians did it.

Clanking and wheezing, a spavined suburban train crept out of Rio de Janeiro. Late as usual, packed to the gills with the sweating homeward-bound, it broke down outside the city. For a while the passengers endured with true commuter calm. Then, like an oilfield fire, wild revolt swept through the train. The long-suffering customers tore out the seats, dragged down baggage racks, turned the train into a shambles.

The worm-turning spirit spread to a crowd at a nearby station, who joined in the fun of tossing rocks to destroy signboards. When the train began to move again, the rebellious commuters clambered aboard—but at every stopping place they spread the revolution and left behind a trail of mob-torn stations.

One worm-turned-dragon finally went too far: he set the train on fire. As the flames crept forward, the driver unhitched the engine, sped up the line for police.

MAY 28 **SMALL CHANGE:** "Your change, senhor," said the waiter, tossing onto the marble-topped coffee table: some aspirin tablets, a string of trolley-car tickets and a postage stamp. For months, metal change has disappeared from Brazil's inflation-ridden economy.

It became scarce when hoarders buried and manufacturers melted down copper and nickel coins. Paper *cruzeiros* were ordered printed in the U.S., but German submarines sank the entire shipment. Last week frantic officials had rushed a ton of new one and two *cruzeiro* notes (value: 5¢ and 10¢) from the U.S. to Rio, hoped presently to retire the aspirin tablets.

JULY 9 **UNANIMOUS:** Twenty rugged Brazilian flyers, veterans of the Allied campaign in Italy, sat in a conference room in Washington's Pentagon Building. Asked a reporter: "Are you going to fight Japan now?"

"Well," answered Lieut. Alberto Martins Torres, "90% of us would love to go."

"What about the other 10%?"

"They were killed in Italy."

Canada

A.W.O.L.: It was a national humiliation—thousands of Cana-   JAN. 29
dian soldiers were deserting to avoid combat. Defense Minister Andrew G. L. McNaughton confessed:

"A high percentage of absenteeism was reported during the
movement of the various units in Canada over the Christmas
and New Year holidays. Of 15,600 draftees warned for overseas service, 7,800 were at one time overdue or absent without leave. Approximately 6,300 are still unreported."

All over Canada, police were so busy rounding up deserters
that a provincial police official remarked: "The nearest approach man's ingenuity has made to perpetual motion is the
process of draftees going A.W.O.L., being picked up by police and put back in barracks, to go A.W.O.L. again."

RUSH TO BUY: As U.S. shortages have mounted, more &   FEB. 12
more Detroit shoppers have been crossing over to Windsor to
buy goods that are plentiful and unrationed in Canada. Last
week they threatened to sweep the shops bare. They bought
dress goods, rubbers and overshoes, canned goods, cosmetics.
They bought Canadian cigarets at 35¢ a pack. But most of
all they wanted meat. With arms laden with bacon, beef, ham,
canned meats, chicken, and even rabbit, they headed back to
the U.S. On the U.S. side, shoppers had to stand in line while
customs men opened all packages, weighed the meat, collected ration points and duty.

Windsor housewives wailed that Americans were not only
greedy but "pushy." But customs men claimed that more &
more Canadian women go into the U.S. for such goods as
infants' wear, towels, women's underwear (all scarce in Canada), and that they frequently evade Canadian customs rules
by wearing their purchases home.

AN INDUSTRIAL NATION: In sharp outline Canadians saw this   DEC. 3
week how two World Wars had buttressed the Dominion's
agricultural economy with a fine manufacturing industry. The
lesson was recited by Reconstruction Minister Clarence Howe,
who gave a final report on Canada's World War II output.

The war record was impressive. As an arsenal of the Empire
Canada had produced 16,200 aircraft, 28,000 heavy field and

naval guns, 1,500,000 machine guns and rifles, 8,000 ships, 800,000 vehicles, ammunition in the millions of rounds. Said Howe with pride: "This has resulted in manufacturing becoming the leading industry of the country."

Greece

During the Axis occupation, a Communist group called EMA had eliminated its political rivals and set up a provisional government in the mountains under the protection of a Communist guerrilla army known as ELAS. When the Greek government-in-exile returned in October 1944, it ordered the Communists to disband. The Communists refused and civil war broke out two months later.

JAN. 1 **"WITH ALL ARMS"**: Still there was no pause in the Greek civil war. The truce talks continued. So did the shooting. Now Athenians in their cellars caught another sound in the cacophony of conflict: the whoosh of rockets from British strafing planes. In the barricaded streets and around the ruins on the storied hills the tide of fighting ebbed & flowed. British Lieut. General Ronald M. Scobie warned ELAS that he would attack "with all the arms at my disposal," did so next day. Sherman tanks, spitting shells, dispersed ELAS troops in Mount Lycabettus. But ELAS had their successes too. In the fashionable Kifissia suburb they dynamited their way into R.A.F. headquarters. In central Athens they stormed into forbidding Averoff prison where scores of political prisoners passed from British to ELAS custody. But by week's end the British had cleared about a third of Athens.

UNRRA OUT: A prime casualty of the civil war was UNRRA. Last week, before it had begun its mission, it was ordered back to Cairo till the shooting ended. The little men & women of Athens, round whose homes the battle swirled, went mostly hungry. Inside their area the British were feeding tinned meat every day to one in 25 of the city's population. Less fortunate Athenians subsisted on herbs and grasses.

MISSION TO ATHENS: Prime Minister Winston Churchill and JAN. 8
Foreign Secretary Anthony Eden had planned to spend
Christmas at home with their families. Instead, they spent it
in Greece trying to end a civil war. The long winter flight from
London to Athens held hazards to life & limb. But it was the
greater hazard to Britain's power & prestige that spurred
Churchill to fly impetuously to Greece.

The situation there had grown almost out of control. Four
weeks of vicious battles between two sides, both of which
claimed to serve democracy, had established that: 1) the British might clear Athens but ELAS firmly held the rest of
Greece; 2) clearing the rest of Greece would require a major
operation for which Britain was neither militarily nor politically prepared.

The big plane landed in Athens on a chilly Christmas Day.
In their homes, Athenians were burning furniture to keep
warm. A few Greek civilians recognized and cheered the
portly figure in the R.A.F. commodore's uniform as he
stepped out of an armored car. Before a pink stucco building
Churchill paused, waved and smiled.

British security officers tore their hair. Their charge—the
Empire's No. 1 man—was blithely disdainful of personal precautions. Even as Churchill arrived at the conference a distant
sniper pinged in his direction. Doorways bristled with guards,
tanks watched every intersection. Overhead Spitfires pa-
trolled.

In a large, unheated room lit only by flickering oil lanterns,
the delegates faced one another across a table. At the head,
in his flowing black robes of office, sat the chairman, tower-
ing, bearded Archbishop Damaskinos, primate of the Greek
Orthodox Church. Down one side sat lanky, leonine Premier
George Papandreou with members of his Government. The
ELAS seats were vacant.

The conference began. Churchill was speaking when the
ELAS men finally turned up. All were relieved of their pistols.
Then the door was locked.

Churchill started over again. Each sentence was painstakingly translated. The Prime Minister was grim, his jaw set. He
thumped the table. The burden of what he had to say was:
"Settle it among yourselves, or we shall settle it for you."

Next day he stepped out to watch the war. A burst of

machine-gun fire hit a wall 30 yards away. Said Churchill, with disdain: "What cheek!" He went on watching.

In the conference room the second session grew so stormy that the Archbishop adjourned the meeting before blows were struck. From the spate of tempestuous talk emerged only one point of unanimity: Archbishop Damaskinos was acceptable to all parties as Regent for George II of Greece, waiting in London's swank Claridge's. The Prime Minister was confident he could persuade the King and was whisked off again to England.

In London Churchill wasted no time. He sent for King George. The 54-year-old Greek monarch was apprehensive that a temporary relinquishment of his throne might become permanent—that he might be signing his abdication. But after Churchill had talked with him he consented to the Regency. A royal proclamation announced that the King would not return to Greece "unless summoned by a free and fair expression of national will."

JAN. 15 **FLOWERS AGAIN:** The silence was startling. For the first time in five nightmare weeks there was no fighting in Athens. Tommies in tanks had recaptured the ruins of the Averoff prison which ELAS had used as a fort. After it fell, resistance collapsed. In driblets ELAS riflemen melted away into the countryside. Into the streets, behind them, marched British troops and Greek Government Militia, pelted by flowers from shattered windows. Said a perplexed Tommy: "Blimey, I'll never get the hang of these people. First flowers, then bombs, then flowers again."

JAN. 22 **TRUCE:** It was late at night. In the austere conference room of the British military headquarters in Athens stood four dejected Greeks. Three were dressed in ragged civilian clothes. The fourth wore the dirt-stained uniform of the guerrilla forces. All were haggard and unshaven. They were the delegates of the ELAS Central Committee.

Suddenly the door opened and Lieut. General Ronald MacKenzie Scobie, tall and trimly military, entered briskly and sat down at the head of a long, polished table. Without a word or glance at the Greeks, the British Military Commander began rapidly affixing his signature to documents his chief of staff handed him. When he had finished, he rose abruptly and left the room.

Still silent, the four Greeks sat down at the table and one by one added their signatures. Thus was signed the truce which formally ended Greece's 42-day civil war. By its terms, ELAS would withdraw from a wide area around Athens and fighting would end within three days.

Signatures on the documents were scarcely dry before a new difference arose. ELAS was holding thousands of Greek civilians as hostages. They would be held, said ELAS leaders, against the release of sympathizers of their movement. By week's end that bitter question was still undecided. [In 1946, the Communists stepped up their guerrilla operations. The British, exhausted by six years of war, were forced to discontinue their aid; the U.S., under the Truman Doctrine, took up the task of helping Greece defeat the Communists.]

Hong Kong

PEACE IS HELL: When the conquerors took over the swank NOV. 19 Hong Kong Club in 1941, they sawed six inches off the legs of the Club's billiard tables, so that stubby Jap officers could play. Last week, long-legged Britons were back at their billiards, kneeling and stooping to cue.

India

URSULA AND THE NAKED NAGAS: *"Aré wa ittai nan dai?"* JAN. 1 (What on earth is that?) cried a startled Japanese officer as a burst of elephant-gun fire whistled past his ears and a troop of half-naked Naga tribesmen leaped out of the bushes. He found out, but too late. He and his jungle patrol were wiped out. But last week other Japs who had survived the fight in northern Burma knew more about the Naga raiders and their leader. The half-naked tribesmen from northeastern India were directed by a white woman: pert, pretty Ursula Graham-Bower, 30.

In 1939 Miss Graham-Bower went out from England to India as an archaeology student. She disappeared into the hills to study the Nagas. These lithe-limbed warriors live in fortified hilltop villages, lead a somewhat humdrum existence punctuated by occasional raids to cut off their neighbors' heads, which they carry about in wicker baskets.

Miss Graham-Bower managed to keep her own head on, and presently won the friendship of the chieftains. Some of the more pretentious Nagas wore a little apron in front, but most just wore bracelets. They begged Miss Graham-Bower to name their babies. She named most of them Victoria Elizabeth.

When the Japanese armies surged across the Burma border and threatened to spill into India, Miss Graham-Bower declared personal war on Japan, and placed herself at the head of the mobilized Nagas. By her orders guards were posted on main and secondary trails, a watch-and-warn system was established. Over these trails escaped prisoners and bailed-out airmen fled from Burma to India. Miss Graham-Bower also directed Naga ambushes of Japanese search parties.

Back in England, Miss Graham-Bower's mother commented proudly: "An extraordinary girl; she never would sit still."

JUNE 25 **PLAN:** For three years India had been in a state of suspended political animation. Some 3,000 nationalists were in jail, their pleas for Indian independence silenced by the insistence of the British Raj that constitutional reform must wait till the war is won.

Last week, from his palace in New Delhi, Field Marshal Viscount Wavell, Viceroy of India, broadcast a new proposal to break the country's political deadlock and put her "on the road to self-government." High points:

¶ All posts in India's Executive Council—the equivalent of a national cabinet—will henceforth be filled by Indians, except those of Viceroy and the Commander in Chief (who sits as defense minister). This means that the three key portfolios of Finance, Home Affairs and External Affairs will be Indian-administered. India's diplomatic service abroad will be staffed by Indians.

¶ Indian members of the new Executive Council must cooperate in "carrying through the war against Japan."

¶   A British High Commissioner will be appointed from London to represent British commercial interests in India.

The British Government considered its new plan as a "step forward during the interim period" before the granting of Dominion status. To show that the British Government meant what it said, Lord Wavell ordered the release of eight Congress party leaders interned since 1942. Heading the list was Pandit Jawaharlal Nehru, leftist disciple of Mohandas K. Gandhi.

INAUSPICIOUS WEATHER: At India's summer capital, states- JULY 9 manship and wisdom were on trial. For in Simla's viceregal lodge the momentous conference of Viceroy Lord Wavell and India's nationalist leaders was about to begin. At stake was the future of India and the Wavell Plan, leading to eventual Indian self-government.

First, on a lawn overlooking the valley, there was the viceregal reception. The Viceroy and Lady Wavell shook hands with the delegates, chatted about the delightful weather. This was not just chitchat. Astrologers had claimed that the conference's opening day (June 25) was inauspicious, since there would be a partial eclipse of the moon. Hindus believe that anything begun on the day of an eclipse is doomed to failure.

For two days, Simla seethed with secrecy, bubbled with optimism. Then the conference suddenly stalled. Mohamed Ali Jinnah, president of the powerful Moslem League, disapproved the Wavell Plan's proposal for parity between caste Hindus and Moslems in the new government. He charged that the Untouchables and Sikhs would always vote with the Hindus, thus putting the Moslems in a permanent minority.

Almost as cantankerous was Mohandas K. Gandhi. When he reached Simla, Gandhi was exhausted. Huge crowds had surrounded his third-class railway coach at almost every stop from Bombay. Then he was closeted for nearly two hours with Lord Wavell.

On his way out of the viceregal lodge, Gandhi was mobbed by uncontrollable crowds. A bearded Sikh photographer pointed a camera at him. The non-violent Gandhi grabbed the camera, tried to smash it, failed. The astonished Sikh resorted to passive resistance, made no effort to recover his camera.

Later Gandhi, who for years has been playing political puss in the corner, startled newsmen by announcing that he would not attend the conference. He explained that he would act as adviser but would not be a delegate.

JULY 23 **FALSE DAWN:** Last week the 21 Indian delegates, gathered around the long teak table in the Simla conference room, learned that the hope of self-government for India had been a false dawn.

Lord Wavell, his face showing the strain of a fortnight's recurring crises, announced that his present effort to give India self-government had failed. Then the Viceroy made a remarkable statement:

"I wish to make it clear that the responsibility for the failure is mine. The main idea underlying the conference was mine. If it had succeeded, its success would have been attributed to me, and I cannot place the blame for its failure upon any of the parties."

NOV. 26 **PREDICTION:** Two members of TIME's London Bureau joined last week in sending their editors the following prediction:

"We hesitate to predict a revolution or revolt so far in advance, but all evidence points to the alarming conclusion that there will be a historic blowup in India after the elections end. We are firmly convinced that great trouble is in the making and further feel it highly significant that the British are keeping such large numbers of troops there instead of demobilizing them." [In 1947 India was divided into two independent nations—the Dominion of India, which was predominantly Hindu, and the Moslem state of Pakistan. The partition was the signal for mass migration from one state to the other and for bloody religious riots that resulted in the massacre of some 200,000 people in three weeks.]

Indonesia

OCT. 15 **PARTNERSHIP, NO:** Southeast Asia's contagion of nationalism plagued the Dutch last week. The rich tin mines and oil pools of The Netherlands East Indies had been prize loot for the Japanese. Dropping all such stolen property last month, the Japs took time to throw a sharp tack in the path of the former owners. On Java they granted independence to a "Republic of Indonesia." Its head: Dutch-educated Soekarno, 40, a longtime, long-winded nationalist orator.

When Britain sent troops to help out the Dutch, rioting broke out. The islands had Queen Wilhelmina's promise of eventual, postwar "partnership" in a Netherlands Commonwealth. But nationalists cried that the time was ripe for something more. They served notice that if British and Indian occupation forces brought along any Dutch troops, the Dutch would be shot.

Dutch tempers flared. Soekarno, the Netherlanders roared, was a puppet and an opportunist. The Dutch Government would talk nothing over with him; more likely it would try him as a war criminal.

ARSON & SNAKES: On Java, richest and most densely populated of the East Indies, the native faction which calls itself the Indonesian Republic declared war on the Dutch. Weapons (according to Indonesian People's Army headquarters): "All kinds of firearms, also poison, poisoned darts and arrows, all methods of arson and wild animals, as for instance snakes." OCT. 22

THE COURSE OF EMPIRE: Fighting flared anew in The Netherlands East Indies last week. The nationalist movement seemed to be getting out of its leaders' control. President Soekarno of the "Indonesian Republic" flew from Batavia to give a ceasefire order. But British reconnaissance showed that up to 100,-000 Indonesian troops, using Jap tanks and planes, were massing in central Java. The British rushed up more warships and planes. NOV. 12

Trim, smooth-talking Soekarno, meanwhile, was settled in a luxurious house in Batavia's European section. There he gladly poses for homey pictures with his beautiful Javanese second wife and ten-month-old son. He brushes aside queries about his anti-Allied broadcasts during the war by claiming that he merely cooperated with the Japs to get concessions for his people.

DEC. 3 **"THE GLOVES ARE OFF":** The fighting grew fiercer in Java last week. The Indonesians charged the Dutch with "burning our villages and murdering our people." The Dutch accused the British of refusing to let them land their own troops. The British listed 56 killed in three "atrocities," and said grimly: "The gloves are off now." [The Dutch would grant complete independence to Indonesia in 1949.]

Norway

SEPT. 3 **TRAITOR'S DAY:** Vidkun Abraham Quisling had provided the name for so many other base men that somehow he seemed almost to have lost personality. At the end of the first day of his trial last week in Oslo, only 21 hard-eyed Norwegians turned out to watch him as he was led back to his fortress-prison.

By day, the man whose name had become a word for venal treachery sat lumpily in the prisoner's box, his reddish, thinning hair unkempt, his neck shrunken in an oversize collar, his blue eyes beady in a suet face. In sullen silence he listened while the prosecutor read the charge—a catalog of shame reaching to high treason and murder.

"What have you to say for yourself, Herr Quisling?" asked the Presiding Judge when cross-examination began.

"I am Norway's martyr," he thundered. The court smiled.

What about his letter to Adolf Hitler urging "a great Germanic community, with Norway's voluntary affiliation to the Greater German Reich"? A forgery, muttered Quisling.

What about Major Quisling's refusal to serve in the Norwegian Army at the time of invasion? His answer: he could not serve a government he disapproved.

SEPT. 17 **A TRAITOR IS CONDEMNED:** Vidkun Quisling sobbed last week as his defense attorney pleaded his hopeless case, tried hard to list his virtues. Then, pale as death, Quisling himself launched into a two-day plea for his life. He claimed to have saved Norway from becoming a battlefield. He even boasted of his sentimental friendship with Hitler. With evangelical fervor he called himself a prophet and a patriot. His last feeble shout: "If my activity has been treason, then in God's name I hope that for the sake of Norway many of her sons will become the same kind of traitor."

Then the trial was over. Seven judges and jurors (among them a plumber, a factory worker, a bookkeeper, a barber) retired for three days and three nights to judge a man long ago judged by the world.

Then, frowning and blushing slightly, he heard the unanimous verdict: guilty. The life he claimed to have sacrificed for Norway would be ended by a firing squad.

JUSTICE: Vidkun Abraham Lauritz Quisling was awakened at NOV. 5 2 a.m. and hurried from his cell to a square in Oslo's somber Akershus Fortress. Awaiting him were a clergyman, a state prosecutor and a firing squad.

At 2:40, the officer commanded: *"Fyr!"* The soldiers obeyed.

Thus died the man whose name had become a worldwide synonym for traitor. The police had to keep the ashes of his cremated body; his native village refused to accept them for burial.

THE LITTLE CHILDREN: Alone among the occupied countries DEC. 24 of Europe—the rest of which have turned their backs on the problem—Norway has dared to look frankly into the eyes of its "war babies." Nine thousand offspring of Norwegian mothers and German fathers born during the German occupation will bear no stigma when they grow up. The children's origin will be purposely obscured in order to protect them against Norwegian resentment toward their parents.

The Government had proposed a special "war-baby law" changing the babies' names and providing for their adoption by Norwegian families; where necessary, costs will be paid by the state and added to reparations claims against Germany.

Saudi Arabia

DESERT WIND: The U.S. destroyer, her taut beauty leashed in MARCH 5 Jidda Bay, had dressed for the King of Saudi Arabia. The

King's rugs covered the steel deck. The King's gilded chairs gleamed against the grey turrets. On the forecastle deck, the King's tent stood in the somnolent heat. On the fantail, the King's sheep bleated in an improvised pen, making royal problems for the swabbers.

When all was prepared, King Abdul Aziz Ibn Saud embarked with his courtiers, guards, cooks and other retainers to the number of 48. On this, his first journey outside his own country, the exigencies of space on a destroyer cramped the King's style. Traveling in his own deserts, he would be more likely to have 2,000 retainers.

The U.S. officers and sailors saluting their guest at the rail saw one of the few living rulers who look the part. Looming over them was a robed, resplendent Arab, 6 ft. 4 in. tall—the absolute monarch of some 3,000,000 subjects, the overlord of 3,500,000 more, the master of a few oases and of many deserts and mountains whose combined area is about one-fourth that of the U.S., the dominant Arab of the Middle East's Arab heartland.

Ibn Saud was a kingly guest. As the destroyer coursed northward through the livid heat of the Red Sea, he sat in his tent, scorning a cabin. Mustachioed desert warriors, armed with daggers and clad in brilliant *abbayat,* roamed the deck. Arab servants squatted in every corner, butchered sheep and cooked them on glowing charcoal braziers.

Journey's end was Great Bitter Lake in the Suez Canal. There, aboard a U.S. cruiser, the President of the U.S. awaited.

What said the Squire of Hyde Park, schooled at Groton and Harvard, to the Lord of Arabia, schooled in the Koran, the desert, the raid, the running horse, the harem? The only direct news was official, and it was sparse:

"The discussions were in line with the President's desire that heads of Governments should get together whenever possible to talk as friends."

Ibn Saud is a strict adherent of the fanatically strict *Wahabi* sect of Islam. He neither practices nor permits smoking, drinking, or dancing. His justice is swift and sure: thieves have their hands chopped off; murderers, their heads. But he has his pleasures, the chief of which he considers a national duty. He once said: "In my youth and manhood, I made a nation. Now in my declining years, I make men for its population."

Nobody knows just how many sons he has sired; the usual estimate is 40.

He stays strictly within the Moslem maximum of four wives at a time, divorces frequently and usually keeps one place in his harem open for any comely virgin who may catch his sickly brown eyes. A favorite campfire story is about the time when he was wounded in the groin during a desert raid. To spike any calumnies against his manhood, he selected a maiden, married her on the spot, consummated the marriage that night.

Ibn Saud's Arab world is more important because of where it is than because of what it has. Within it lie the eastern Mediterranean and the Red Sea, parts of Britain's essential passages to the old treasure house of India and to the new, possibly greater treasure house of Africa. The Arabian Sea (northern part of the Indian Ocean) and the Persian Gulf flank India, reach into some of the world's richest oil areas. In this explosive area last week a new force was rising—the force of Pan-Arabianism—and Ibn Saud was at its crest.

MILESTONES

MARRIED: Technical Sergeant Charles E. ("Commando") Kelly, 24, rugged, rusty-haired "one man army," Congressional Medal of Honor winner (for killing 40 Nazis with assorted weapons in a single engagement); and plump brunette May Frances Boish, 19, whom he met last year when their home town Pittsburgh celebrated his homecoming.

DIED: David Lloyd George, Earl of Dwyfor, 82, Britain's Prime Minister during World War I, last surviving member of the first Big Three (the others: Woodrow Wilson and France's Clemenceau); of complications following influenza; in Llanystumdwy, Wales. Through five reigns and three wars, the fiery, witty, flamboyant Welshman enlivened the House of Commons. Even in his old age, friends & foes claimed that Lloyd George could still "talk a bird out of a tree." Of him Winston Churchill said: "There is no history like his in living memory."

MISCELLANY

OUT COLD: In Regina, Sask., Ethel Sheffield swerved around a slippery curve, crashed into a lamppost, slumped unconscious in the seat, would have frozen to death in the 16-below-zero cold if the lamppost had not upheld a fire alarm, which went off, bringing rescuing firemen.

LONG DIVISION: In Manhattan, Jean A. Brunner asked his niece what she did in her Washington war job, was told: "I work in the data-analysis group of the aptitude-test sub-unit of the worker-analysis section of the division of occupational analysis and manning tables of the bureau of labor utilization of the War Manpower Commission."

PEOPLE

"Names make news." In 1945 the following names made the following news:

WINSTON CHURCHILL, one of the world's most talked-about men, had another anecdote told about him. Sipping a glass of brandy one day aboard his private railroad car, he observed that he had drunk a "really formidable amount of brandy in my life, enough to fill a car as big as this—probably two or three this size." When this claim was challenged, he put one of his economists to work on the problem, learned that he had consumed only about a fourth of a carful. Said the Prime Minister: "For a man of my years, it *is* a bit disappointing."

KATHLEEN WINSOR, ornamental author of the sexy bestseller, *Forever Amber,* denied that her book was in any sense autobiographical: "If it were, would I have time to write a book?"

CHARLES A. LINDBERGH, abroad on a technical mission, made his sixth visit to Paris since the liberation, found it unlike the old days (1927). He reported: "I've been stopped on the street only once."

PRINCESS ELIZABETH, Britain's 19-year-old heiress presumptive, recently gave an inkling of what goes on in her pretty young head by choosing BING CROSBY as her favorite crooner.

NELSON ROCKEFELLER, whose father always told him to watch his dollars & cents, got a carefree feeling during the Mexico City Conference. Handed a 7,000 peso ($1,449) check for a diplomatic party, the Assistant Secretary of State cracked: "Who do you think I am, Rockefeller?"

SPORT

HOPES IN THE WIND: Chill wartime winds from Washington JAN. 22
had numbed the sports outlook for 1945, but there were luke-
warm currents in the air:

¶ The War Production Board said that its forthcoming order
curtailing nonessential use of electricity would not be applied
to night baseball. The hopeful saw it as an indication that the
Government would not extend its horse-racing ban [institut-
ed on January 3 to other sports].

¶ The Eastern Lawn Tennis Association decided to continue
its 1944 policy of playing all possible tournaments this year.

The lone cold breeze of the week blew out of the annual
meeting of the U.S. Golf Association, which found the idea
of reviving the U.S. Open distinctly premature. Too many
would-be competitors were still in uniform.

BIG DEAL: Ever since the death of Owner Jacob Ruppert six FEB. 5
years ago, the New York Yankees had been on the auction
block. Last week it finally happened: the Yankees changed
hands—and personality.

The new Yankee bosses brimmed with dollars and ideas.
Supplying a heavy piece of change was slender, soft-spoken
Del Webb, ex-minor-league pitcher who 16 years ago moved
to Phoenix, Ariz., parlayed a saw and hammer into a million-
dollar construction business. The other big moneyman was
Marine Corps Captain Dan Topping, heir to a tin-plate fortune. The man with the ideas was baseball's brilliant screw-
ball, redheaded Colonel Leland Stanford ("Larry") Mac-
Phail, who got a juicy ten-year contract as president and general manager. The once-conservative Yankees will never be
the same with him around.

As boss of the Cincinnati Reds a decade ago, Larry the Red
painted the park orange, introduced usherettes and night
baseball. Attendance figures doubled. When MacPhail took
over the seventh-place Brooklyn Dodgers, who were in hock

to bankers for a half-million dollars, he talked the banking gentlemen out of another $300,000, peeled off dizzy amounts for new players, promoted crowd-drawing grudge fights with every club in the National League. When he quit Flatbush for the Army three years ago, he had won a pennant and paid off a million dollars in debts. Now for the first time Larry MacPhail takes over a baseball business that is making money.

FEB. 26 **BIG SPLASH:** The world's greatest swim sprinter is knock-kneed, rusty-haired Alan Robert Ford. During the past month, his last at Yale, he has taken a final fling at rewriting the record books. Result: eleven new American free-style and backstroke marks. Last week he made the biggest splash of all. Keeping his stroke long and easy, Ford traveled 100 yards in 49.4 seconds, faster than any human ever swam before. It shattered Johnny Weissmuller's 17-year-old record by four-tenths of a second.

After 16 years of painstaking practice, Ford is pretty well fed up with swimming. Said he before his final record-breaking dash: "I got engaged last week. I want to get my Navy commission. I would like to find a nice quiet spot and drink lots of beer."

APRIL 2 **TALL BOY:** He was bounced from his high school team because "his feet didn't match." Now he is the glamor boy of college basketball. George ("Scaffold") Mikan stands 6 ft. 9 in his socks, weighs 227 lbs., sleeps in an 8-by-6 bed and looks like a gangling Harold Lloyd, even to the horn-rimmed spectacles. To keep his elongated bones together, De Paul University's mild-mannered Mikan makes away with a daily breakfast of oatmeal, a half-dozen eggs, ham, angel cake, three cups of coffee, a cod-liver pill.

His lumbering height and nearsighted eyes almost ruined George's basketball career before it began. But Coach Ray Meyer, hard pressed for a center, drove his clumsy recruit through dozens of daily dozens until Mikan cried: "What do you want, Coach, my blood?" Slowly Mikan's muscles learned to obey and the one-time marble-shooting champion of Will County, Ill. eventually got the hang of shooting baskets with a marble champion's sharp accuracy.

Outfielder Pete Gray of the Browns is a one-armed wonder.

Jackie Robinson, football flash, makes baseball history. Page 201.

Last week, De Paul's tall boy gave a basket-making exhibition in Manhattan's Madison Square Garden. With 18,253 admiring fans looking on, he piled up 21 field goals with his lazy lay-up shot, added eleven free throws for a total of 53— exactly as many as the whole opposing Rhode Island State team made. [Mikan, who later turned pro, was appointed Commissioner of the American Basketball Association in 1967.]

ONE-ARMED ROOKIE: With most baseball rosters as full of APRIL 9 unknown names as Y.M.C.A. hotel registers, everybody agreed that the caliber of big-league 1945 baseball would be somewhere between AA and A—but it would still be baseball.

In the American League, the St. Louis Browns had to be figured as favorites again—at 8-to-5 with the bookmakers. Their one weak spot, Manager Luke Sewell hoped, would be plugged by Pete Gray (up from Memphis), the most talked-about rookie of the year. Pete is a one-armed outfielding wonder who can hit some and drag bunt to perfection.

MAY 14 **GOLF AT ANY PRICE:** The supply of reprocessed golf balls (some going through the mill for a second and third time) was 25% below last year's bottom. On the black market, pre-war golf balls that once sold for $10 a dozen were bringing $40, $50, $60 a dozen, and were hard to get at any price.

Partial relief for the war-shortage headache was prescribed in Washington last week: WPB approved the manufacture of some 500,000 dozen new golf balls with synthetic (neoprene) rubber centers. Tests showed that the new balls were 15 yards short of the real thing on a 225-yd. drive. And production was a drop in the bucket compared to the yearly peacetime output of 3,000,000 dozen.

JULY 2 **EVERYBODY'S BALLPLAYER:** In 1941 the New York Giants got a new manager: Melvin Thomas Ott, the club's slugging right fielder with a peculiar but potent cocked-leg stand. A soft-spoken, brown-eyed little (5 ft. 9 in.) guy with a Southern accent, Playing Manager Mel has long been a favorite of fans everywhere. He even got along with umpires—until arguing with umpires became part of his managerial business. Umpire Bill Klem once called a doubtful third strike on him, and added: "You can't hit 'em without swinging at 'em, you Mississippi runt." Ott replied: "That kind of hurts me. Everyone ought to know I come from Louisiana."

By last week, the smile that helped make Ott everybody's ballplayer was being strained to the limit. After racing to the longest lead of any big league team in a quarter century (25 wins against seven defeats), his Giants fell flat on their faces. They lost 21 out of 29 games. Ott cajoled, threatened, finally fined players. The only thing still left untried: hiring a hackman to drive a wagonload of barrels (a traditional omen of good luck) around the Polo Grounds. But there was a shortage of barrels.

Despite the wear & tear of managing, Ott's own batting average is a hefty .341. With his game legs soaked in olive oil, he is clearly the best of the few remaining big leaguers. Some record-breaking reasons:

¶ He long since topped Rogers Hornsby's runs batted in mark. His 39 this year have boosted his grand total to 1,816.

¶ Early this year, he broke Honus Wagner's mark of 4,888 total bases, now has 4,923 to his credit.

Mel Ott of the Giants crowds the plate with feet apart, then rears up his front leg not unlike a dog leaning into a hydrant.

¶ He has had more walks (1,672), scored more runs (1,825), made more hits (2,809), and more extra base hits (1,048) than any player who ever wore a National League uniform.

Ott squares away to a pitch as though he were going to beat a rug. Crowding the plate with feet apart, he rears up his front leg (not unlike a dog leaning into a hydrant), pulls back his bat, then steps forward and swings. Whenever he faces a high-kicking pitcher, the game looks as leggy as ballet.

SAME OLD FELLER: Back with Cleveland's Indians last week SEPT. 3 after 44 months in the Navy, Bob Feller brought out Cleveland's biggest baseball crowd in three years (46,477). Poky as ever, Feller ambled out to the pitching mound, tugged up his pants in the old way, fired a fast-ball which was perhaps better than it used to be. After three pitches, his shirttail came out, just like old times.

Feller struck out twelve of the league-leading Detroit Tigers (including Hank Greenberg and Rudy York twice apiece), gave only four hits, walked five, won in a 4-2 breeze.

GRAND SLAM: Big Hank Greenberg rubbed a lucky piece of OCT. 8 bone on his bat, strode thoughtfully to the plate, and slammed a grand-slam homer into the left field bleachers. That did it: Hank's 13th home run (in 78 games since his

Army discharge) clinched the American League pennant for the Detroit Tigers, on the last day of the season. [In the World Series that followed, Detroit beat the Chicago Cubs four games to three.]

NOV. 5 **BRANCH BREAKS THE ICE:** Last week, after three years of scouting Negro leagues, Branch ("The Brain") Rickey called in reporters to tell the world that Brooklyn had broken the ice on hiring Negro players and had signed Jack Roosevelt Robinson as shortstop.

Rickey, as usual, had looked before he leaped. At U.C.L.A. Robinson won All-America mention as a halfback. Later, with the Kansas City Monarchs of the Negro American League, he hit a healthy .340 and fielded sensationally. No one knew better than 26-year-old Jack Robinson how high a barrier he had to scale. Wrote Ludlow Werner in a Negro newspaper, the New York *Age*: "I'm happy but sorry for Jackie. Unlike white players, he can never afford an off-day." Said Robinson: "There is no possible chance I will funk it for any other reason than that I am not good enough."

NOV. 12 **ARMY'S SUPER-DUPERS:** This week the football season reaches an early apogee: unbeaten Army and Notre Dame, rated No. 1 and 2 in the nation, are set to beat each other's brains out in Yankee Stadium. By almost any gauge, Notre Dame has worked up enough steam to press West Point's pants. But the 1945 Cadets look and act just as unbeatable as 1944's unbeatables.

Army has the two best backs to come down the pike in years. One is a human blockbuster named Felix ("Doc") Blanchard. The other is a jet-propelled gent named Glenn ("Junior") Davis. They make Army's cream-smooth T attack bubble and boil like no other T in the land.

Once in the clear, Blanchard's beef-trust legs dance on egg-shells. He has a 14-game average of 6.6 yards for every time he has carried the ball. Halfback Davis carries a special kind of speed that is all his own. After a brief show of hippiness, enough to get around the end, he simply leans forward and sprouts wings. Mister Inside and Mister Outside are guaranteed to drive a rival defense nuts. To South Bend, where the week's defense problem was to try and find a way of stopping

Blanchard and Davis, a Notre Dame scout dispatched a one-word suggestion: ropes.

NO CONTEST: Army's football wonders blew down Notre NOV. 19 Dame, 48-0.

BLANCHARD, DAVIS & CO. **(CONT'D):** The experts who NOV. 26 thought that Pennsylvania might at least slow down Army thought wrong. Score: Army 61, Penn 0 (touchdowns: Blanchard three, Davis three, others three).

THE CHAMPS: Calmly confident, Army's cadets bet that their DEC. 10 wonder team would collect a touchdown in four plays. Said Navy's grim Coach Oscar Hagberg: "Army can't call its shots against us. We're not that bad." To find out, President Truman and 102,000 other fans last week jammed Philadelphia's Municipal Stadium.

Navy's underdogs charged hard. But Army scored in seven plays. The day's touchdown total, five (Blanchard three, Davis two). The score: Army 32, Navy 13.

MILESTONES

DIVORCED: Staff Sergeant Joe Louis Barrow, 30, deadpan heavyweight boxing champion; by Marva Trotter Barrow, 27, nightclub singer; after ten years of marriage (one child).

DIED: Robert Charles ("Bob") Benchley, 56, a sly wag with an inexact mustache, a burbling laugh and one of the world's warmest wits; of a cerebral hemorrhage; in Manhattan. Though no mean cracksman ("I've got to get out of these wet clothes and into a dry martini"), he shunned the out-&-out gag, preferred to get his laughs while puttering among the minor catastrophes and major banalities of everyday life.

MISCELLANY

HANDLES: In Columbus, Ohio, Sergeant Mitchell Combs married Madeline Curl. In Bronte, Ont., Dr. William Deadman announced that he had conducted 7,000 autopsies. In St. Joseph, Mo., competing real-estate agents tried to get ahead of one Earley D. Bird.

THE WAY IT IS: The American Hotel Association made it official: the odds against getting a steak dinner in a Midwest hotel or restaurant these days are 400-to-1.

FOILED: In Cincinnati, Samuel Brown left his girl friend in his apartment when he went to get some beer, took her dress so she wouldn't run out, returned to find that she had— with his other pants and $196.

FESTIVE: In Jersey City, six Army veterans invited the entire staff of their draft board to dinner, served nothing but cold C and K rations.

THE THEATER

JAN. 8 **"ON THE TOWN"** is a youthful high dive that hits the water with a terrific splash and is one of the freshest, liveliest, most engaging musicals in many years. It is an enlargement in color of the sock ballet, *Fancy Free,* that Choreographer Jerome Robbins and Composer-Conductor Leonard Bernstein did for the Ballet Theater. Best of all, it has the oldtime touch it needs: under George Abbott's direction, youth has made hay without going haywire, and a lot of slightly off-Broadway talent has been given a sharp Broadway spin.

JAN. 22 **"A LADY SAYS YES"** is a $200,000 musicomedy blunder redeemed only by the shapely figures of Carole Landis and Christine Ayres. The critics said no.

APRIL 9 **"THE GLASS MENAGERIE,"** by Tennessee Williams, has its faults and needless frills as a play. But in the role of the mother, Laurette Taylor gives the most fascinating and memorable performance of the season.

Actress Taylor plays a middle-aged, down-at-heel former Southern belle, nagging, grandiloquizing about her mint-julepy, porticoed youth, absurd in her foolishness, pathetic in her pretensions. Her devices are those of a superb performer: with mumbled words, fluttery gestures, unpredictable movements, small changes of pace and stress, she bit by bit reveals what she is, was, thinks she was, pretends to be, vaguely dreams of yet becoming.

APRIL 30 **"CAROUSEL"**–All *Oklahoma's* horses and all *Oklahoma's* men have put another charmer together again. But *Oklahoma's* and *Carousel's* Composer Richard Rodgers, Librettist Oscar Hammerstein II, Choreographer Agnes de Mille have not repeated themselves. *Carousel* is not a musicomedy but a lovely and appealing "musical play."

Composer Rodgers has swathed it in one of his warmest

and most velvety scores. But it is still in tunes that Composer Rodgers' real magic lies—the tender *If I Loved You,* the light, murmurous *This Was a Real Nice Clam Bake,* the full-throated sweetness of *June Is Bustin' Out All Over.*

"HAMLET" brought Maurice Evans back to Broadway in the DEC. 24 shortened, sharpened version with which he wowed G.I.s in the Pacific. It cuts boldly across whole scenes—there are no grave diggers, no "Alas, poor Yorick," no obsequies for Ophelia. It cuts boldly across time: Actor Evans has laid it in a 19th-Century Denmark of waltzes and tight trousers.

A tough-guy convert to *Hamlet* on opening night was Toots Shor, whose Manhattan restaurant is the sports world's second home. Toots's tribute: "It's real cops & robbers stuff, with class." And during the intermission Toots remarked: "I'm the only bum in the audience that's going back in just to see how it comes out."

MILESTONES

MARRIED: Private Red Skelton, 31, limber-legged, extroverted radio and cinema comic; and Georgia Maureen Davis, 23, ex-photographer's model; in Beverly Hills. Second item on the bridegroom's furlough schedule: having his tonsils out.

DIED: Alla Nazimova, 66, Russian-born actress who specialized in Ibsen *(A Doll's House, Hedda Gabler)* and Chekhov *(The Cherry Orchard),* one-time silent screen glamor girl *(Salome),* lately featured in character roles *(Since You Went Away);* of coronary thrombosis; in Hollywood.

DIED: Jerome David Kern, 60, dean of American show-music composers, whose half-a-hundred musicomedies since 1912 have kept the nation humming such lilting melodies as *Make Believe, Smoke Gets in Your Eyes,* and *The Way You Look Tonight;* of cerebral thrombosis; in Manhattan. A mild, owl-eyed little man with a head for business, he strove to make his songs "charming rather than spectacular, popular without being vulgar," succeeded in making the best of them *(e.g., Ol' Man River)* internationally loved.

MISCELLANY

"C'EST LA GUERRE": From France, Staff Sergeant Paul Lobel notified his family in Middleboro, Mass., that a French girl tried to kiss him, pulled him from a Jeep, broke his rib.

KIDDIES' MATINEE: In Etna, Pa., a little boy stepped up to a captured Japanese machine gun on display in a movie lobby, pressed the trigger, chattered a stream of bullets into the opposite wall.

FACT: In Indianapolis, American Legion officials solemnly ruled that members of the K-9 Corps could not become Legion members, because dogs aren't people.

MUSIC

JAN. 15 **FOUR-WAY FLASH:** The brightest young man in the U.S. musical world was just practicing last week. Leonard Bernstein was brushing up on Ravel's *Piano Concerto,* and getting ready to go on the musical warpath. He was about to leave Broadway—where his rollicking musical, *On the Town* is packing them in—for a triple-threat appearance with the Pittsburgh Symphony as conductor, composer and piano soloist. Leonard Bernstein can do more things than most musicians and he can do them better.

Four-ring Musician Bernstein would probably have been equally successful in his father's Boston beauty-parlor supply business. But his Aunt Clara's old upright piano attracted him first. Lenny Bernstein took to the old upright like a duck to a puddle, went on to major in music at Harvard. After that, he roamed Broadway as a would-be songwriter, advertised for piano pupils, taught singing at $2 a lesson, finally got a $25-a-week job doing routine orchestrations for a music-publishing house. Summers he spent studying conducting with Sergei Koussevitzky at the Tanglewood school. There he caught Conductor Artur Rodzinski's eye, was offered the assistant conductorship of the New York Philharmonic-Symphony. [It was during his assistant conductorship that he walked onstage in 1943 to replace guest conductor Bruno Walter, suddenly stricken ill. He scored a sensational success. Appointed director of the orchestra in 1957, Bernstein went on to conduct more concerts than any other man in Philharmonic history.]

MARCH 12 **THE CREAMER:** Eager adolescents jampacked Paris' gilded, rococo Opera House. They had come to hear the shy, Detroit-born, 24-year-old Sergeant Johnny Desmond who has been spreading havoc among European bobby-soxers since he first sang over BBC five months ago. Before he enlisted in 1943, black-haired, velvet-eyed Johnny sang with Bob Crosby and

Leonard Bernstein can do more things better than most musicians. Page 205.   *Sgt. Johnny Desmond makes young Parisians squeal "Bis! Bis!"*

Gene Krupa. Then he signed up as a drummer—the Army does not admit "singer" as a musical classification—with Glenn Miller's Air Forces Band.

Last week Sergeant Desmond—variously known as the "G.I. Sinatra" and "The Creamer," because of his smooth, creamy baritone—was getting fan mail in three languages: English, German and French. His *I'll Be Seeing You* and *Long Ago and Far Away,* in phonetic French, make young Parisians jump up & down, squal "Bravo! *Bis! Bis!*" and clutter up the stage-door alley for a closer look at *Le Crémair.*

100-YEAR-OLD HIT: APRIL 9

> *The little man felt ill at ease,*
> *and said, "Some bread, sir, if you please."*
> *The waiter's voice roared down the hall,*
> *"You gets no bread with* ONE MEAT BALL!"

The plaintive ballad about the man who dared ask a war-time waiter for one meat ball is fast becoming a fad with U.S. bobby-soxers. The adolescents have no idea how old-fashioned they are: their latest musical hero was well known to Boston in the 1850s. Almost a century ago, a shy Harvard professor named George Martin Lane tried to buy a single fish ball in a restaurant, heard his order bellowed out by a surly waiter.

The professor preserved his humiliation in a song called *The Lone Fish Ball,* which was published in *Harper's Monthly* (1855). It was later plugged by the Harvard boys, taken up by Boston's Irish societies, and even translated into Italian for an opera co-authored by James Russell Lowell. For the new version, the bouncy music of *The Lone Fish Ball* has been discarded for a minor-keyed tune.

NOV. 19 **"THE GREATEST MUSICIAN":** The Polish offensive of January 1945 had begun. In the Great Hall of the Moscow Conservatory, a woman stepped to the platform. Said she: "In the name of the fatherland there will be a salute to the gallant warriors of the First Ukrainian front who have broken the defenses of the Germans—20 volleys of artillery from 224 guns."

As she spoke, the first distant volley shook the hall. A lank, bald-headed man in white tie and tails mounted the podium and stood with bowed head, facing the Moscow State Philharmonic. He seemed to be counting off the rumbles of artillery. At the 20th, he raised his baton and began the world's première of his newest symphony. The bald-headed conductor was Russia's greatest living musician, Sergei Prokofiev.

Last week in Boston's Symphony Hall, that same music, Prokofiev's *Fifth,* had its U.S. première. It was a great, brassy creation with some of the dynamic energy of a Soviet power plant and some of the pastoral lyricism of a Chekhov countryside. The Boston Symphony's famed Russian-born Sergei Koussevitsky was ecstatic. He called the *Fifth* "the greatest musical event since Brahms and Tchaikovsky! It is magnificent! It is yesterday, it is today, it is tomorrow. Prokofiev is the greatest musician today!"

It is for the charming little musical fairy tale, *Peter and the Wolf,* which he wrote to help children identify orchestral instruments, that Prokofiev is mainly known to the U.S. man in the street. He brought that piece to Koussevitsky, tartly recommending it as suitably infantile for Boston. It has since become so popular that in U.S. phonograph-record sales Prokofiev now rates above Mozart.

DEC. 3 **"CHICKERY CHICK":** In the 1870s, collegians at Amherst set a 100-year-old jingle to music and sang it over pots of ale, when they wanted to prove that they could walk a musical straight line. One of the many versions ran like this:

> *In China there lived a little man*
> *His name was Chingery-ri-chan-chan,*
> *His feet were large and his head was small,*
> *And this little man had no brains at all.*
> *Chingery-rico-rico-day ekel tekel happy man.*
> *Kuan-a-desco canty-o gallopy-wallopy-china-go.*

Last week this old tongue twister, with new and even less intelligible lyrics, was the fast-climbing No. 2 seller in *Billboard* magazine's poll of record sales and was well on its way to join *Mairzy Doats* and the *Hut-Sut Song* in the jabberwocky Valhalla of the jukebox. Twenty-nine-year-old Jo Proffitt had changed the Chinaman into a chick, and called it *Chickery Chick*. Now it describes a chicken who got bored with saying "chick chick" all day, astounds his companions with some jived-up poultry poetry:

> *Chickery-chick cha-la cha-la,*
> *Check-a-la-romey in a ba-nan-i-ka.*

Tin Pan Alley actuarians estimate that the U.S. will need about three months to get over it.

MILESTONES

MARRIED: Gloria Vanderbilt di Cicco, 21; and Leopold Antoni Stokowski, sixtyish; he for the third time, she for the second; one day after her divorce from Pasquale ("Pat") di Cicco; in Mexico.

REPORTED MISSING: Major Glenn Miller, 39, begoggled, popular trombonist and bandsman, leader of the Army Air Forces Band; while a passenger on a military flight from England to Paris. [Miller's body was never found.]

DIED: Newell Converse Wyeth, 62, famed mural painter and book illustrator, whose colorful, romantic depictions have given many Americans their conceptions of such fictional and legendary figures as Long John Silver, Deerslayer and Odysseus; in a grade-crossing accident near Chadds Ford, Pa., in which his three-year-old grandson was also killed.

MISCELLANY

HABIT: In Mattoon, Ill., Golfer John W. Preihs, who had made a hole-in-one in 1925 and saved the lucky ball ever since, was forced by the current shortage to take it out and use it again, promptly made another hole-in-one.

ART

JAN. 29 **PRAISE FROM PABLO:** Pablo Picasso got down on his knees to look. What he was looking at was a firmly painted picture of a red brick Riviera villa, at a Paris exhibition. The charming villa rose from a brilliant green meadow dotted with gnarled olive trees. When he had finished looking, Painter Picasso said: "If that man were a painter by profession, he would have no trouble earning a good living." The signature on the canvas: Winston Churchill.

MARCH 12 **A STRIP TEASE PAYS OFF:** One of the nation's fattest cash prizes for art was copped last week by a grossly satirical picture of unbuttoned sensuality. For *Strip Tease in New Jersey,* the Corcoran Gallery of Art in Washington, D.C. handed over its $2,000 First Prize Award to blond, balding Reginald Marsh, 46.

Reginald Marsh's "Strip Tease in New Jersey" is—by a broad bottom's width— the raciest picture ever honored by the Corcoran.

"Reggie" Marsh made his reputation in the late '20s with Hogarthian studies of city low life ("Well-bred people are no fun to paint"). His *Strip Tease* was easily, by the width of a broad bottom, the raciest picture the staid Corcoran had ever thus honored. It showed a slightly idealized, if muscular, ecdysiast in mid-routine. The brooding faces of seven balding burlesque-addicts include the artist's own. Artist Marsh found inspiration for it in a Union City, N.J. burlesque house.

DRIVEN TO ABSTRACTION: The abstractionists have had a major impact on U.S. typography, advertising layout, architecture. And by now, the layman, whether he knows it or not, owes a good-sized debt to the non-objective painters. Nevertheless, the unwary gallery-goer whose eye lights on an abstract painting immediately suspects that someone is trying to pull his leg. Last week in Manhattan, three famed abstractionists were on display, to give the layman that old feeling. APRIL 2

Of the three, the canvases of Swiss-born Paul Klee were the most recognizable. Concealed in his childlike scrawling was many a suggestion of reality; much of his work possessed simplicity, sharpness and humor, and a spontaneity as fresh as a candid camera shot.

Russian-born Wassily Kandinsky, whose designs are both whirling and geometrical, hated the thought of painting "dogs, vases, naked women." To him "a circle is a living wonder" and a blob of color is enough to convey a mood (blue, "the typical heavenly color," stands for rest; blue-black for grief; violet, the echo of grief; green is "the bourgeoisie—self-satisfied, immovable, narrow").

Dutch-born Piet Mondrian, pioneer of purest abstractionism, also felt fettered by objects. But where Kandinsky went off in a whirl, Mondrian drew nothing but horizontal and vertical lines, convinced that the right angle was the purest "expression of the two opposing forces which constitute life." To the uninitiated, the result might look something like a linoleum pattern, but Mondrian spent days shifting colored Scotch tape around a canvas, hoping to achieve a perfect harmony of balanced rectangles.

GÖRING'S BEAUTIES: In a little Bavarian village near Berchtesgaden the American 101st Airborne Division has put on MAY 28 display Hermann Göring's fabulous $200,000,000 collection of art works, the *crème de la crème* of the loot of Europe.

This fantastic treasure was discovered by a Seventh Army counterintelligence task force which was scouring the countryside for hidden stores of bullion. They first found an empty cave built into a hillside. One room had been walled up. The wall was broken down, and there, in dripping darkness, was the Göring treasure.

Lucas Cranach, an early 16th-Century German master, was a Göring favorite, and he had some Cranach beauties—about 50 in all. There are five Rembrandts. Even more dazzling than the paintings are the gold and jewelry of Göring's collection. There are stacks of tableware made out of solid gold. There are gold candlesticks by the dozen. There is also a silver cup presented *by* Hermann Göring, Reich Master of the Hunt, *to* Hermann Göring, Reich Master of the Hunt. Yes, that is what the inscription says.

JULY 2 **HARDY MASTERPIECE:** Last week the Allied Commission announced that Leonardo da Vinci's faded, dusty masterpiece on the refectory wall of Milan's convent church, Santa Maria delle Grazie, *The Last Supper,* had survived time, bungling repairs and bombs.

The convent's roof had been destroyed in August 1943, but the huge fresco, no longer protected by sandbags and steel scaffolding, was again on view. Only one retouching job would be necessary: a four-inch square in the tunic of St. James the Greater.

JULY 9 **AMERICANS IN PARIS:** G.I.s visiting Paris want to see the Eiffel Tower, the Folies Bergère, and Pablo Picasso. Their interest in art generally and Picasso in particular has astonished Artist Picasso and the Red Cross, which handles their entertainment requests.

The first to find their way to Picasso's huge, messy duplex studio at No. 7 rue des Grands Augustins were two cherubic-looking 9th Air Force sergeants. French phrase books clutched in their hands, they clattered in with a musette bag full of gifts, dumped their presents happily onto a canvas which lay on the table—a Paris street scene which would probably later sell for 150,000 francs ($3,000). Picasso was delighted. He admired the K rations and the Velvet tobacco, kissed one G.I. on both cheeks.

Since then the Red Cross has been running tours to the studio. Hundreds of G.I.s have heard that Picasso is a swell guy and that he can be seen any day between eleven and one. Picasso finally began to feel like an exhibit in a zoo. And he got sick & tired of K rations. So he called a halt. Said the Red Cross: "We don't know what to do. All the boys want to see him. We just give them his address and tell them to try to get in on their own!"

Even if they cannot see Picasso now, the G.I.s in Paris can and do buy prints of his pictures. One shopkeeper said that he sold American soldiers from one to six Picasso prints a day. (Next in order of popularity: Matisse, Gauguin, Bonnard, Goya, Toulouse-Lautrec.) "I am surprised," he said. "They know a lot about painting, just as much as the Germans, if not more."

SIMPLE LINES: Color is perhaps Henri Matisse's chief claim to NOV. 12 fame—he paints with colors that are as loud as a Marine band, as subtly harmonious as a Bach cantata. But "what counts most in a picture," says 76-year-old Matisse, "is a drawing and composition." Last week 22 of his black & white pen & pencil drawings went on view at the Manhattan gallery of his son, Pierre Matisse. It was the first show to come out of France since the war, and it revealed the French master at his joyful best.

The drawings, made during the Nazi occupation of France, were simple, linear statements of the things Matisse likes most to see—flowers, faces and figures. He believes art should be a "mental soother devoid of troubling or depressing subject matter." The pictures look as though Matisse had been looking at the model, not the paper, and acting out what he saw with fine, free-swinging gestures of his right hand. "When you draw a tree," he explains, "you should have the feeling to reach up with it."

SCIENCE

JAN. 15 **NAZI RESEARCH:** It has been rumored that Nazi scientists have used civilian prisoners as guinea pigs for macabre biological experiments. Last week the rumors were documented. A French investigating commission reported on a huge prison camp in Alsace where hundreds of men & women had been tortured and killed under carefully controlled conditions in order to supply data for Nazi science.

Near the camp's rows of dark green huts was a "laboratory" equipped with gas and torture chambers, a crematorium, a vivisection room. There some 20,000 people (mostly Jews) were used and killed. Some were inoculated with plague and leprosy germs. Thirty women were blinded, then given a 15-day "treatment" during which they screamed incessantly. All were put to death. In another experiment, a doctor led 84 young women in batches to the gas chamber. German professors watched their dying reactions through a window.

JUNE 11 **BALLOON BOMBS:** They were on a fishing trip in the woods of Oregon's Lake County: the Rev. Archie Mitchell, his wife, and five children. Joan Patzke, 11, spotted a strange white object. Another child tugged at the thing. Suddenly there was a tremendous explosion. Only the minister survived.

Thus, announced the War Department last week, death came early last month to the first victims of Japanese balloon bombing on the U.S. mainland.

The balloons are kept in the stratosphere by a device which jettisons a sandbag whenever they begin to drop. Blown along by the prevailing easterly wind at some 125 m.p.h., the balloons reach the U.S. in an estimated 80 to 120 hours. When the last sandbag has dropped, Japs calculate, the balloon should have reached its goal. Another automatic gadget then starts it dropping, one by one, its load of incendiary bombs. When the last egg has been laid, another device permits the Jap balloon, in true Nipponese style, to blow itself up.

THE SHAPE WE'RE IN: How the average U.S. girl looks with her clothes off was shown last week by Manhattan's American Museum of Natural History. The name of the girl is "Norma." She is a sculptured composite of 15,000 present-day U.S. women, aged about 18.   JUNE 18

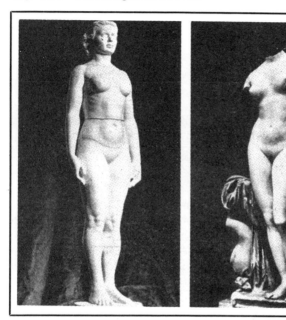

A model named Norma (33.9-26.4-37.4) shows what the average U.S. girl looks like with her clothes off and is less voluptuous than Aphrodite (right).

The modern girl is taller (5 ft. 3½ in.), longer in the leg, thicker in the waist (26.4 in.), and has slightly heavier hips (37.4 in.) and legs than the 1890 girl. But thanks to a bigger bust (33.9 in.) and torso, her figure looks better proportioned, at least to the anthropologists. And compared to the Greek ideal (*e.g.,* Aphrodite of Cyrene), Norma is relatively slim-hipped and less voluptuously curved; the trend in development of her figure seems to be toward the "high fashion" or dress-model type—a tall (5 ft. 7 in.) triangular shape with broad shoulders, very slender hips and long legs.

WORST-KEPT SECRET: The Institute of Radio Engineers was closeted to discuss military secrets. President W. L. Everitt   JULY 30 leaned forward with a conspirator's expression and solemnly announced: "Gentlemen, the Army & Navy have now finally given permission to use the word *radar*—provided you spell it backwards."

Washington has been grinning over this story for weeks. For censorship officers, the story has a double sting: they are well aware that radar has been one of the worst-kept secrets of the war. A favorite gag pictures a mother remarking to her husband: "John, don't you think we ought to tell Junior about radar, before he picks it up in the street?"

AUG. 20 **RADAR:** Hard on the heels of the atomic bomb, World War II's other incredible invention—radar—was this week released from military secrecy. The U.S. has spent half again as much (nearly $3 billion) on radar as on atomic bombs. As a military weapon, either in combination with atomic explosives or as a counter-measure, radar is probably as important as atomic power itself.

An electronic supergadget which "sees" as well in the dark as in the light, radar projects a radio beam which, on striking an object near or far, returns an echo that is translated into a visual image on the radar screen. Radar can see the flight of a shell, the wake of a ship, the explosion of a target, the fall of a hit plane. At sea, it can detect buoys, reefs and other ships more than 20 miles away. From the air, by night or day or through the thickest cloud, it lays open the terrain below like a relief map, showing coastlines, ships, harbors, jetties, mountains, lakes, rivers, bridges, cities. And it was a radar operator who gave the tragically ignored warning of approaching Japanese planes at Pearl Harbor.

The British say that radar and 300 R.A.F. pilots won the Battle of Britain. Radar opened the roof of Hitler's Europe for the day & night, all-weather body punching that crippled the *Wehrmacht.*

SEPT. 10 **MAN'S PRIME:** Composers, athletes, authors, philosophers, explorers, painters, scientists all achieve their top performances in their early thirties. This discouraging news for ambitious oldsters of 40 was reported by Psychologist Harvey C. Lehman of Ohio University in the current *Scientific Monthly.* Talented men, he reports, keep up the quantity of their output fairly well until about 50. But the peak of greatness occurs much earlier. Averaging up the age at which most of the great operas, novels, paintings, scientific discoveries, etc. have been produced, Professor Lehman arrived at a precise figure for the average man's prime of life: 33.

FISH OUT OF WATER: For years, the Robert Ripleys confi- DEC. 24 dently affirmed the fact. At last the sober, scholarly Smithsonian Institution solemnly confirmed it: some fish do climb trees. According to recent Smithsonian Bulletin 188, *The Fresh-Water Fishes of Siam,* Siamese fish frequently set out on overland treks. One capricious *clarias batrachus,* apparently bored with captivity, jumped out of its bowl, wriggled down two long corridors, was caught high-tailing it out the front door. A Danish scientist named Daldorff once saw a fish leering at him from five feet up an Indian palm tree.

MILESTONES

MARRIED: Artie Shaw, 35, bandleader; ex-husband of Cinemactress Lana Turner; and Ava Gardner, 21, starlet, ex-Mrs. Mickey Rooney; he for the fourth time, she for the second; in Hollywood.

DIED: William Phelps Eno, 87, inventor of the one-way street; in Norwalk, Conn.

DIED: Heber Jedediah Grant, 88, President and Prophet of the Church of the Latter-day Saints (Mormons) since his succession (by seniority) in 1918; in Salt Lake City. One of Utah's shrewdest, most successful insurance men and bankers and only son of the fifth wife of Salt Lake City's first mayor, Grant outlived two of the three wives he married before the Church outlawed polygamy.

MISCELLANY

STRIP TEASE: In Red Bank, N.J., a bus-load of soldiers heard a female voice ask the driver, "Will you wait a minute, please, while I get my clothes on?", twisted their necks out of joint, saw a laundress lift aboard a load of linen.

HAPPY BIRTHDAY: In Brazil, Ind., entered on the court calendar for February 22 was the divorce case of George Washington *v.* Martha Washington.

FOR THE EARS: In New Mexico, when an airline hostess passed out chewing gum with the routine instruction "For the ears," a lady passenger later complained: "It worked all right, but couldn't you use something not so sticky?"

PERSUADER: In St. Paul, a proposed bill to outlaw air rifles met violent opposition from one farmer who wanted to know how, if the bill were passed, he could get his stubborn bull into the barn.

RADIO

JAN. 1 **HEALTH *v.* BEAUTY:** Hollow-cheeked Frank Sinatra made people listen, but he just didn't move them to go out and buy vitamins. So Vimms canceled its year-old contract. But there was solace for the swoonmaster: a new sponsor wanted him enough to raise the weekly ante from $12,500 to $13,500. Beginning next week, Frankie will sing for Max Factor Cosmetics—on the not unlikely assumption that even if his voice didn't sell vitamins, it will probably send women straight out to the drugstore to buy lipsticks and pancake powder.

JAN. 22 **WHO WON:** Radio tastes of 1,000-odd magazine and newspapermen were reported by the trade paper *Radio Daily*. The journalists voted *Information Please* their favorite commercial and quiz show; Bob Hope, favorite entertainer (and comedian); Bing Crosby and Dinah Shore, favorite popular songsters; Lowell Thomas, favorite commentator; New York Philharmonic-Symphony, favorite symphony orchestra; *One Man's Family,* favorite soap opera.

MARCH 26 **WORLD-WIDE GROANER:** A man who was christened Harry Lillis Crosby last week won Hollywood's Oscar for the best cinemactor of the year. But it had just become apparent that he could boast of a far rarer distinction: his voice had been heard by more people than any other voice in history.

For the past ten years "The Groaner," now 41, has averaged a new record every other week. Number of copies sold since he first began recording two decades ago: about 75 million. The Crosby voice has been heard oftener and by more people than even these figures hint at. Most U.S. radio stations play about twelve hours of recorded music a day. Day in & day out, from coast to coast, the singing voice heard oftenest in canned concerts is Crosby's. His best-sellers: a ballad (*White Christmas,* 1,700,000 records), a hymn (*Silent Night,* 1,500,000), a cowboy song (*Don't Fence Me In,*

LISTENER TALKS BACK

Harold Tucker Webster, cartoonist-creator of lifepecked Caspar Milquetoast ("The Timid Soul"), has been performing a notable public service with another cartoon series, "The Unseen Audience." In it, Humorist Webster has jabbed away at radio's more vulnerable excrescences like the example shown here. But he still has faith that radio will grow up some day, has six radios in his own home, is a constant listener. – TIME, July 9 issue

1,250,000), a romantic love song (*Sunday, Monday and Always,* more than one million).

IN MEMORY: Thanks largely to radio, no public figure had APRIL 23 ever seemed quite so close to so many citizens as Franklin Roosevelt. Reporting the death of the President, who made his own radio history, radio, too, made history of a sort. For four days it was not itself, and for one full minute it was silent.

The news was announced at the White House at 5:48 p.m., and the flash broke into the regular time for juvenile adventure stories. Thus in many thousands of U.S. homes the first to hear the news were the children. That was the end of most commercial radio for four days. Out went the commercials, the comedy shows, the soap operas, the blood & bluster dramas, the gay music. Radio listeners heard little besides reminiscences and tributes to their late President, newscasts, comment, prayers, and the sort of music (Gounod's *Ave Maria*; Tchaikovsky; *Home on the Range*—Roosevelt's favorite song) that radiomen considered suitable to the nation's mourning mood. Many stations broadcast old records of Roosevelt speeches, and listeners heard with a kind of shock the long-familiar voice of the outstanding radio personality of his time.

Then, for one minute, at 4 p.m. on Saturday, the U.S. radio was silent. To many, this was the most memorable moment in radio's strange four days.

DEC. 31 **CLAGHORN'S THE NAME:** Every Sunday evening on the Fred Allen program, many a U.S. radio listener lends his ear to a loud-mouthed, platitudinous, corn-cackling character who calls himself Senator Claghorn. The "Senator," played by Announcer Kenny Delmar, is a broad burlesque of the worst in Southern statesmen. On the air for less than three months, he is already being mimicked by children at school, businessmen at luncheon clubs, drunks at bars.

Claghorn, who carries professional Southernhood about as far as it can go, tells how he was weaned on mint juleps, drinks only from a Dixie cup, sees only Ann Sothern movies, never listens to *Mr. & Mrs. North,* avoids the Lincoln Tunnel. His hat is a Kentucky derby. He naturally hates compasses for the way they point.

Typical script:

Claghorn: Claghorn's the name, Senator Claghorn, that is. Ah'm from Dixie. Ah represent the South.

Allen: Look, Senator, I. . . .

Claghorn: Thanksgivin', Ah only ate the part of the turkey that's facin' south.

Allen: Yes, I know, but I. . . .

Claghorn: No man livin' can make me wear a Union suit.

Allen: Well, I. . . .

Claghorn: What's on your mind, son? Speak up. This is America, son. You got free speech. Go ahead and talk, son—talk, that is.

(**RELIGION**)

PRAISE YE THE LORD: Though millions heard the great news MAY 14 of victory in Europe this week without changing expression, they prayed in silence, wherever they happened to be. And for millions who did not even know they were praying, their tears were prayers.

THE GERMAN HITLER FEARED: The man whom Adolf Hitler MAY 21 dared not kill stood in the chancel of a little church in the Alpine village of Cortina d'Ampezzo, Italy. Only a few hours before, Pastor Martin Niemöller, leader of Germany's Confessional Church—and one of Christianity's most effective anti-Nazi weapons—had been liberated by the U.S. Fifth Army. His first public act after eight years of imprisonment was to conduct a religious service.

Pastor Niemöller was a staunch early-Party member. But when he saw how the wind was blowing, he stood up in his Dahlem pulpit and denounced Hitler's mumbo-jumbo racial theories. He also refused to put the will of Der Führer above the will of God.

Last week Niemöller said that his defiance had cost him four years of solitary confinement at Sachsenhausen and Dachau. But unlike most other concentration-camp prisoners, he was given permission to have books. His wife was allowed half-hour visits with him twice a month—always in the presence of the *Gestapo.*

In the fifth year, the *Gestapo* relaxed a bit, locked him up with three Catholic priests. Last December he was permitted to hold services at Dachau. During his entire imprisonment, he said, the guards treated him "correctly"—but "I can't say why I was allowed to survive." One likely reason: an ex-U-boat commander in World War I, Niemöller was known to Germans as a good German.

Now Pastor Niemöller is anxious to get back to work. He is certain that the church holds Germany's only hope for the future: "Our people now know that all false idealisms are worthless. There is only one way in the future. It is a tremendous challenge not to let our people down at this moment."

SEPT. 17 **PARALYZING PRAYERS:** *And these signs shall follow them that believe; in my name they shall cast out devils; they shall speak with new tongues; they shall . . . take up serpents and if they drink any deadly thing it shall not hurt them.* Mark 16: 17-18.

Among many Southern hill sects this Biblical injunction has been taken literally. Some brethren catch and baptize snakes, drape them over their necks and arms with only the paralyzing power of prayer for protection.

Occasionally the prayers are not sufficiently paralyzing, and there are mortalities. Last week two believers died. In Wise County, Va., a snake leaned out and bit the wife of the Rev. Harve Kirk of the Faith Holiness cult. Though Mrs. Kirk was pregnant, she refused medical aid. Harve prayed as never before, but Mrs. Kirk's hand swelled up and turned black. Her baby was born prematurely and died in 20 minutes. Mrs. Kirk kept shouting "Precious God" and "Glory to His Name." Six hours later she died too.

The other casualty was Lewis Francis Ford, a truck driver and lay preacher of the Dolly Pond Church of God in the

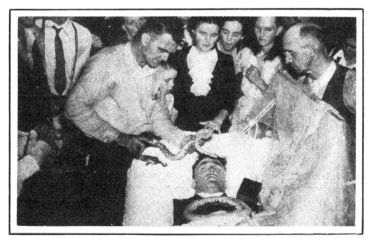

At the funeral of Lay Preacher Lewis Francis Ford, who died after handling a snake, the Rev. Raymond Hayes places the errant serpent in Brother Ford's coffin.

hamlet of Grasshopper, Tenn. Brother Ford was a new man with snakes; he had handled them only since last July 22. He was bitten before he really started praying. His father explained afterward:

"He took three snakes out of the box and laid them over his arm. Then a fourth, a rattler, bit him on the finger. He brought his arm up and the snake was hanging by his fangs in Lewis' finger. He went on preaching for ten minutes and he got a good victory over the serpent. The snake was laying over the pulpit like he was dead when Lewis stepped down."

As soon as Lewis Ford had died, his wife requested snake handling at the funeral. Almost 3,000 people came to watch. The brethren played guitars, cymbals and tambourines and when they got to shouting good, the snake handling began. The Rev. Raymond Hayes of Grasshopper put the serpent that had bitten Brother Ford into the coffin. It coiled up quietly on Brother Ford's chest.

BOOM: With over half the U.S. population belonging to one church or another, the Federal Council of Churches tallied the reports of religious bodies, found that their membership had reached the alltime high of 72,492,669—a jump of four million in two years. SEPT. 17

MERELY PLAYERS: In Oberammergau, in the foothills of the Bavarian Alps, plans for next spring's revival of the world-famed Passion Play had hit a snag. Stars Alois Lang (the Christus), and Anni Rutz (the Virgin Mary) and Willy Bierling (St. John) had been refused American Military Government permission to play their respective roles and were being held in Allied prisons as active members of the Nazi party. Only one leading character, Hans Zwink, a regular member of the anti-Nazi movement, was ready to go on stage. His role: Judas. OCT. 8

MEDAL FOR A PACIFIST: Like his Master, he was a carpenter. He was also a Seventh-Day Adventist, and a pacifist. Desmond T. Doss, of Lynchburg, Va., refused to bear arms in World War II. He explained simply: "It is right there in the Ten Commandments. Thou shalt not kill." But Doss did not object to serving as an Army Medical Corpsman. When he OCT. 22

was sent overseas he asked for assignments in the front lines. He felt that God would not let him perish by the sword if he did not live by the sword, and he had a deep sense of duty to his fellow man.

Like most other soldiers, he knew terrible fear. He conquered it with prayer. During the fighting on Guam and Leyte he became famous among the hard-bitten men of the 77th Division for his serene recklessness in the face of death. In the nerve-racking weeks of the Okinawa campaign, his fame grew. He climbed a 400-foot escarpment with an assaulting infantry battalion and stayed at the exposed summit for hours, lowered 75 wounded men down the rock walls to safety before descending. Twice he was wounded. Grenade fragments ripped his legs, knocked him down and out of action. Then a shellburst shattered his arm. He lashed a rifle stock to the arm, managed to crawl hundreds of yards to safety.

Last week 26-year-old Corporal Desmond T. Doss stood at attention on the White House lawn. President Harry Truman placed a pale blue ribbon around his neck, shook his hand warmly. As he stepped back—the first conscientious objector in U.S. history to receive the Congressional Medal of Honor —generals, admirals, Cabinet members, his proud parents and his pretty wife applauded.

DEC. 31 **THIRTY-TWO NEW HATS:** The College of Cardinals looked as though it had been raked by a machine gun. Of its full complement of 70 cardinalates, only 38 were filled. This week a special edition of *L'Osservatore Romano* announced that Pius XII had called a consistory for Feb. 18 to name 32 new princes of the church.

The U.S. will get four new red hats: Archbishops Francis Joseph Spellman of New York, Samuel Alphonsus Stritch of Chicago, Edward Mooney of Detroit, John Joseph Glennon of St. Louis. The U.S., which has had seven American Cardinals in its history, never had more than four living at the same time, will now have five—with present Cardinal Dennis Dougherty of Philadelphia.

MEDICINE

TRENCH FOOT: Europe's mud and slush of October and November caught the U.S. Army with its feet unprepared. Result: up to Dec. 12, 17,500 G.I.s had developed trench foot, something no one expected in World War II (partly because no one expected the war to settle down into mud and trenches). JAN. 1

Trench foot is a sort of mild frostbite that results from letting feet stay cold and damp for a long time. Circulation slows or stops, feet turn white and numb, sudden warming causes painful burning. The devitalized tissues may recover if kept cool and dry for a few days or weeks. But in some cases blisters develop and become infected, even cause gangrene, amputation or death. Many victims who emerge with feet intact can never fight again because their feet ache on long hikes and are very sensitive to cold.

The British have no trench-foot problem, even though they have been actually wading through Holland. Their stout workmen-type boots and gum boots have turned out to be drier than anything the U.S. has produced. But the most important factor is that British soldiers are required to keep their boots waxed, to massage their feet with oil and change frequently to dry socks. In contrast, most U.S. soldiers have tramped the mud in rubber-soled, rough-side-out leather combat boots; some had only ordinary G.I. boots with legging extensions (an extremely soggy combination).

The G.I.s are now learning to dry their socks on bushes or in their jackets or helmets. In some areas, dry socks are issued along with rations. And improved boots are on the way.

HEARTSICKNESS: *"Dear Jim: I have been thinking the whole thing over and I now see that it wasn't wise for us to be married. I don't want to hurt you, but. . . ."* JAN. 29

A serviceman's wife writing thus to her husband probably

suffers from a condition whose other symptoms include severe depressions, colitis, heart palpitations, diarrhea, frequent headaches. Described as a "new disease" by Dr. Jacob Sergi Kasanin, chief psychiatrist at San Francisco's Mt. Zion Hospital, this psychoneurotic condition by last week had become so prevalent among service wives that San Francisco psychiatrists were begging county authorities for the use of hospital wards to treat their patients. An estimated 2,500 women in San Francisco alone have undergone treatment for psychoneurosis during the past 18 months.

Says Dr. Kasanin: women are paying the same war penalties as men, many of whom crack up long before they reach combat. Those who have followed their husbands to embarkation ports often find themselves spiritually stranded. Many stay simply because they somehow feel closer to their husbands there.

Those women who have the sense to stay home or go back to it and keep busy, preferably at a war job, are apt to find adjustment easier. But others, particularly those recently married or childless, often develop such pathological reactions as resentment against the husband, inability to recall the husband's face or to sense the reality of the married state, vague fears of infidelity. Most susceptible are "orally demanding" women, those requiring constant assurances of their husband's devotion.

Many such neurotic women find escape in throwing off marriage ties, becoming floozies or barflies. Many find a complete cure in receiving their husband's first letter, or even his allotment check, either of which can serve to reaffirm the idea of marriage in the wife's mind. In any case, under simple psychotherapeutic treatments, says Dr. Kasanin, "most cases get over their depressions very quickly."

NEWEST WONDER DRUG: Antibiotics, of which penicillin is the most famed, are now the objects of the most exciting search in all bacteriology. Last week came news of a new antibiotic that may be as great as penicillin. Called streptomycin, the drug was discovered by stocky, energetic Selman A. Waksman, 56, Russian-born microbiologist and dean of U.S. antibiotic researchers.

In test tubes, streptomycin has destroyed the bacilli of tuberculosis and leprosy, the bacterium of tularemia. It has saved mice from dying of salmonella infections. Tested on human beings for toxicity, it has proved not dangerous. [In 1952, Dr. Waksman was awarded the Nobel Prize in medicine for his discovery.]

MORE WOMEN DRUNKS: Since the repeal of prohibition, MARCH 26 U.S. women have made great strides toward alcoholic equality with men. In last week's *Journal* of the American Medical Association, Dr. David Benjamin Rotman produced a chart showing that the ratio of female to male alcoholic addicts (meaning people whose drunkenness gets them in trouble with police) in Chicago climbed from 1-to-5 in 1931 to 1-to-2 in 1943.

ATOMIC WOUNDS: The first trustworthy account of the after- SEPT. 17 effects of the atomic bomb came last week from a Dutch surgeon who was in a Nagasaki prison camp when the bomb fell. The surgeon challenged one Jap claim: that anyone entering an atom-bombed city afterwards would suffer from radioactivity. But he verified the fact that many of the bomb victims who seemed to be recovering collapsed and died several weeks later. Their symptoms:

"At first I thought it was simple lockjaw. There was swelling in the back of the throats, light hemorrhages under the skin, fever and a high pulse rate. Then I noticed a rapid consumption of white blood corpuscles. Finally there was internal bleeding in the intestinal tract."

THE MENTALLY UNFIT: U.S. citizens last week got some OCT. 15 shocking statistics about themselves. Roughly 12% of all those examined by the armed services were mentally unfit (most of them are not crazy, but just too neurotic, inept, stupid, or illiterate for the Army or Navy). Rejected at preinduction physicals: 1,750,000. Discharged: 524,000. Total number mentally unfit for the armed forces: 2,300,000.

THE CHILDREN OF DACHAU: Doctors know what to do about NOV. 5 the undernourished bodies of European children. What to do about their war-warped personalities is not so simple. Last week UNRRA workers described some 200 stick-legged,

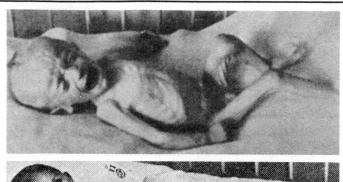
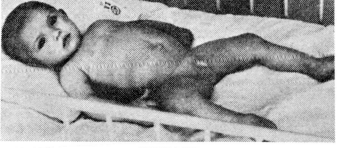

BELSEN BABY

This is one of the 48 starving, nearer-dead-than-alive babies UNRRA rescued from Belsen concentration camp and turned over to Sweden for nursing care. In the first picture he is about four months old. The lumps along his ribs indicate rickets. In the second picture, taken five months later, he is a healthy but still solemn baby. UNRRA thought that all 48 of the waifs picked up at Belsen would probably die, but the Swedish workers managed to save 40.

spare-ribbed children now housed at a monastery. All are under 16 and all were former inmates of Dachau.

The 18-month-old babies could not sit up at first—and they never smiled. Those old enough to remember anything remember most vividly the separation from their parents at railroad sidings where their parents were crowded into trucks. When first released, the starving children wanted to talk more than they wanted to eat; they seemed to need a sympathetic listener more than food. Talking steadily, they followed workers around, telling their stories. Two Polish boys kept wanting to tell how they had stoked crematorium fires at Auschwitz. A Jewish boy insisted on telling again & again how he used to cut down the bodies of the hanged.

In the British medical journal *Lancet*, Lieut. Colonel F. M.

Lipscomb wrote: "The most conspicuous psychological abnormality was a degradation of moral standards characterized by increasing selfishness more or less proportional to the degree of undernutrition. Children who had grown up in concentration camps were almost unmoved by the sight of these horrors."

Even when they learned that there was plenty of food at the monastery, the children stole it from the table; they explained that they couldn't help it. Some still steal. Others who have broken themselves of the habit leave the dining room proudly with their open hands held ostentatiously out from their sides.

MORE DEADLY THAN WAR: The Census Bureau reported last DEC. 31 week that nearly twice as many U.S. citizens died of cancer during 1942-44 as were killed by enemy action in World War II.

MILESTONES

DIED: Geraldine Siebolds Pyle, 44, War Correspondent Ernie Pyle's twice-married (both times to Ernie) widow; after an attack of influenza; in Albuquerque, N.M.

DIED: William Eugene ("Pussyfoot") Johnson, 82, genial, world-famed prohibition zealot; in Binghamton, N.Y. Boozebuster Johnson admittedly lied, bribed, even downed drinks to pile up evidence against the Demon Rum. Appointed by Theodore Roosevelt in 1906 to combat bootlegging in Indian Territory (now Oklahoma), he got 4,400 convictions, lost five deputies, shot. On a teetotaling world tour in 1919, he lost an eye but won admirers in a free-for-all slugfest with unregenerate London tipplers.

MISCELLANY

BILINGUAL: At Fort Benning, Ga., the mystery of strange sounds in the night was finally solved when it was discovered that Officer Candidate George Chew speaks perfect English in the daytime, perfect Chinese in his sleep.

INITIAL INVESTMENT: In San Diego, Petros Protopapadakis made application to change his name to Petros FDR Protopapadakis.

MALE ORDER: In Harlan, Ky., Miss Ioma Creech read that the Army had taken over Montgomery Ward & Co., promptly mailed her order for a "staff sergeant of 5 feet, 9 inches height, dark hair with brown eyes." Said Miss Creech: "I never noticed them in the catalogue."

COOLER SWEATERS: In Pittsburgh, a matron sent sweaters for the native girls living on the Pacific island where her husband was stationed, was horrified to hear that the girls had made them cooler by cutting two big holes in the front.

BUSINESS & FINANCE

FEB. 26 **LIGHT ON LIGHTS:** The U.S. smoker, taking any kind of cigaret he could get last week, found himself also short of
matches.

The free matchbook that once went with every pack of
cigarets had gone, and the smoker was hard put to it to buy
matches of any kind. Reason: the military has taken all the
safety (penny-box) matches, and 35% of the paper-folder
kind. U.S. civilians get what is left.

Kitchen matches, the strike-anywhere type, will be mainly
what the civilian smoker will get. There will be 175 billion
of them available this year, plus 125 billion book matches.
Thus, statistically, each of the 100 million civilians old enough
to play with matches could get 3,000 for the year.

MAY 7 **V-E DAY FOR INDUSTRY:** Last week the War Production Board
decided that the time had come for a return to civilian production. This meant that as fast as plants finish up their war
contracts they can get into production on a limited number
of civilian goods.

¶ The bans on the making of dozens of civilian items (*e.g.,*
telephones, sunglasses) were lifted.

¶ WPB doubled its estimate of the amount of steel which can
be used for civilian production. There may be 3,000,000 tons
—enough to start mass production of cars, refrigerators, etc.

AUG. 6 **KAISER & FRAZER:** From his West Coast summer home on
Lake Tahoe, Shipbuilder Henry J. Kaiser last week long-
distanced an old friend, Joseph Washington Frazer, president
of Detroit's Graham-Paige Motors Corp. As reporters listened in, Shipbuilder Kaiser rumbled: "Congratulations,
Joe." To which Joe replied: "Thanks for the flowers, Henry."

In this cozy fashion, Joe & Henry let out the best kept
financial secret of the year. They have formed a new company
to invade the dog-eat-dog auto business. With Kaiser as

board chairman and Joe Frazer as president, the Kaiser-Frazer Corp. will build two cars, the Kaiser and the Frazer.

THE WINNER: Marshal Stalin's famed Teheran toast to U.S. AUG. 20 industry—"Without American production the United Nations could never have won the war"—was never more appropriate. The war was ending, and the record was in.

In the five years since the fall of France, U.S. industry and labor had turned out:

¶ 299,000 combat planes (96,000 last year)
¶ 3,600,000 trucks
¶ 100,000 tanks
¶ 87,620 warships, 5,200 merchant vessels
¶ 44 billion rounds of ammunition.

THE FIRST TARGET: In determined and confident tones, the SEPT. 24 powerful United Automobile, Aircraft and Agricultural Implement Workers (C.I.O.) read out the declaration of war. Said the union: the auto industry must raise wages 30% to make up for the loss in take-home pay caused by the return of peace, *i.e.,* the loss of overtime when the week was cut from 48 to 40. If the pay raise is not granted, said the union, it would strike one automaker and close all his plants and keep them closed.

Which automobile company would be the target for this all-out assault? For a day, the union kept mum on its choice. Then wily, redheaded Walter Philip Reuther, U.A.W. Vice President, announced the first objective: General Motors Corp.

The union could hardly have picked a better time for itself, a worse one for G.M. Swamped by $2 billion in contract cancellations immediately after V-J day, it had the biggest job of all U.S. industry; some 35% of the entire reconversion job of the nation. By working night & day, G.M. had cleared acres of tools from its plants, nearly completed installation of hundreds of miles of conveyors, set up dozens of assembly lines. Now the back-breaking job was almost done. The new assembly lines were running in Detroit.

But the crisis between the world's biggest union and the world's biggest automaker would not be settled in Detroit. It would be settled high up on the 24th floor of G.M.'s building near Manhattan's Columbus Circle. There, in the paneled office of G.M.'s board chairman, Alfred Pritchard Sloan Jr., all G.M. problems eventually come home to roost.

At 70, Sloan carries the load of running G.M. with remarkable ease. He still dresses with a touch of the dandy. In his tie, he usually wears a pearl stick pin. A silk handkerchief always cascades from his breast pocket. The running of G.M. is his work, hobby and dissipation. He does not smoke, takes only an occasional cocktail and has never played golf or any other sport. Sports, Mr. Sloan firmly believes, are an unprofitable waste of a man's time. Once, when friends insisted that a man in his position should own a yacht, he bought a 236-ft. boat for $1,000,000. But he rarely used it. When a friend asked him how things were aboard, he gave a businesslike reply. Said he: "The crew of 43 is eating regularly and appears to be healthy."

OCT. 8 **NEW DAY AT FORD:** Young Henry Ford II, barely settled in his new chair as president, gave his billion dollar empire a shaking that rattled its teeth. The first shake tumbled Harry Bennett out of power. Bennett, the apple of Old Henry Ford's eye, has long been second in command of the company. Young Henry removed "the little giant" from his potent position as boss of Ford's labor & industrial relations. Then, in two days, he demoted or fired nearly a dozen Bennett-men. From now on, said Young Henry, in unmistakable tones, everyone would be responsible "directly to me."

As usual in the tight-lipped company, no one would say what had caused the earthquake. But this time the silence was doubly significant. When Young Henry moved into the presidency a fortnight ago on the retirement of his grandfather, automen watched sharply to see how much power Old Henry would let him have. (In all the years the late Edsel Ford was president, Old Henry kept tight control in his own hands.) Now they knew. In allowing his old favorite's downfall, Old Henry had made it pikestaff plain that Young Henry is now absolute boss.

The harsh fact was that Harry Bennett had outlived his usefulness to the empire. The things which he had spent his life protecting it against were now dead issues. He was hired by Old Henry in 1917 to guard the Ford plants against saboteurs. Then he took over the job of guarding the Ford family from kidnapers. Often, when Mr. Ford blurted something to reporters which might get him in hot water, Bennett would step in with a "Now what Mr. Ford meant was—" and tone down the statement.

Bennett fought hardest to protect the empire from unionism, yet when he lost he was the first to advise Old Henry to sign up. In his long role as guardian, squat, flint-hard, bow-tied Mr. Bennett (he never wore a four-in-hand for fear someone would use it to choke him) was shot at, beaten up and stoned. He took all this as part of his watchdog job. Said he: "I believe in the things that Mr. Ford wants done. Believing in them has made them easier to do."

POP GOES THE CORN: In his small movie theater in Hugo, NOV. 19 Okla. (pop.: 5,909), Owner Allen L. Blunt was checking his books one night. He was astonished to find that the popcorn machine in the lobby earned almost as much as the box office. So with his twin brother Almer L. he decided to try his hand at popcorn growing. (Among others once astonished by popcorn: Christopher Columbus, who found the Indians popping it and using it for necklaces.)

The Blunts discovered that the hot, dry Oklahoma climate produced corn with little moisture content, that they could therefore capture the all-important early market (elsewhere, popcorn must go through a long and expensive dehydration process). They built a $25,000 processing plant, began urging Oklahoma farmers to plant popcorn instead of cotton or peanuts. The war brought new markets: popcorn substituted for scarce candy, went overseas to lend a homey touch to military life, was eaten in bars and cocktail lounges by a nation which was drinking with both hands. Result: unprocessed corn soared from the prewar price of $1.57 (for 100 lbs.) to $3.86.

Last week the Blunt twins were cashing in also. Their company started to process eight million pounds of popcorn this year, and will ship 90 carloads all over the U.S.

CINEMA

FEB. 26 **"OBJECTIVE, BURMA!"**–At the rate Errol Flynn & Co. knock off the Japanese, it may make you wonder why there is any good reason for the war to outlast next weekend.

MAY 14 **"BILLY ROSE'S DIAMOND HORSESHOE"** generally hits the dirt short of the peg; but it clangs out ringers whenever Betty Grable is pitching. It is the loudest and most energetic Grable vehicle in some time. As the *Horseshoe*'s fastest filly, Miss Grable socks out *A Nickel's Worth of Jive,* and demonstrates the fact that motherhood's extra pound or so of flesh can improve even the screen's most unimprovable body.

JUNE 11 **"WONDER MAN"** is a temperate enough description of Danny Kaye. Barring Kaye, and the pretty hoof-&-mouthing of the flea-sized, dainty screen newcomer Vera-Ellen, the picture is about as short on drive, sparkle and resourcefulness as a Sam Goldwyn production can be. But fortunately, there is no such thing as barring Danny Kaye. He is a one-man show and at his frequent best, a howling good one.

At the straight comic setpieces—the dancing and impersonation of a Russian baritone struggling between his hay fever and *Otchi Tchorniya,* and in a glistening little imitation of a pet shop in full cry, including goldfish—Kaye is great.

JULY 2 **"A BELL FOR ADANO"** has a crack in it.

JULY 23 **"STORY OF G.I. JOE"** is an attempt to picture the infantryman's war as the late Ernie Pyle saw it. Pyle himself (played in the film by Burgess Meredith) vouched for the movie's hard-bitten authenticity. The result is far & away the least glamorous war picture ever made and General Eisenhower called it "the greatest war picture I've ever seen."

Some of the individual soldiers (notably Captain Walker,

who is played by Robert Mitchum and whose death inspired one of Pyle's most moving dispatches) are well known to Pyle readers. Among other things, war is a craft, and *G.I. Joe* does an excellent job of explaining it.

"ANCHORS AWEIGH" is easily the pleasantest couple of hours JULY 30 that can be bought currently in a movie theater. Its standard-bearers: Gene Kelly, described as the Sea Wolf; his sidekick Frank Sinatra, a shy type but eager to learn. Kelly dances beautifully and Sinatra sings the roof off.

"ISLE OF THE DEAD" is one of the best horror movies ever SEPT. 17 made. Quarantined on a tomb-haunted island off the Grecian coast, after one of them dies of the plague, is a strange crew, including a Greek general (Boris Karloff), a sinister peasant woman, a genteel Englishman, his sickly wife, their full-blown servant girl. Tensions grow as the characters develop a pervasive fear of death. The wild laughs, blown leaves, scrawks and tongue-swallowings of jittery nightbirds would have pleased and scared the daylights out of Poe himself.

"BLITHE SPIRIT" is 99.9% Noel Coward and as light-spun and OCT. 15 unsubstantial as a cornucopia full of cotton candy. For people who like that kind of thing, it will be just as tasty.

A British novelist (Rex Harrison) lives stylishly in the English countryside with a stylish wife (Constance Cummings) and is badgered by the unladylike ghost of his first wife (Kay Hammond). The brightly brittle script now & again drowses slightly. But one violent stimulant never fails to wake everybody up: Margaret Rutherford's unceasingly funny impersonation of Madame Arcati, the medium who bounces through the proceedings with all the healthy hilarity of a Girl Guide while she raises hob with the spirit world and her own.

"SARATOGA TRUNK" has been packed by expert hands with NOV. 26 practically everything a film needs for a triumphant box-office tour. In the top drawer of this expensive portmanteau, Ingrid Bergman is wonderfully bewitching in a black wig and bustle, and Gary Cooper drawls and sprawls in his best skin-tight cow-pants.

Ingrid Bergman is that rarity in Hollywood—a good-looking

woman who can change her personality to suit her part. As Clio, freed from the virtuous nobility of her usual roles, her brilliant act of sexy razzle-dazzle makes most of Hollywood's glamor girls look like bobby-soxers. Most exciting shot: Bergman at the piano singing French-Creole songs to Cooper in a manner to make less stalwart he-men wilt.

DEC. 3 **"THE LOST WEEKEND"** is a nightmarish look at the life of a specialized urban type: the fear-paralyzed writer turned alcoholic. Ray Milland is convincing and often disturbing in his hangovers, his delirium tremens, his melancholy. By telling an interesting story in the straightest possible way *Weekend* becomes one of the year's best pictures.

MILESTONES

MARRIED: Judy Garland, 23, snub-nosed cinemingenue; and Vincente Minnelli, 38, who directed her in *Meet Me in St. Louis*; in Los Angeles; one week after she divorced Bandleader-Composer David *(Holiday for Strings)* Rose.

DIVORCED: Humphrey Bogart, 45, cinema bad man already engaged to his current leading lady, Lauren ("The Look") Bacall; by his third wife, onetime Cinemactress Mayo ("Sluggy") Methot Bogart; after nearly seven years in the marriage ring; in Las Vegas, Nev. Sluggy's official charge: "Extreme cruelty."

DIED: Thomas Joseph Pendergast, 71, most notorious political boss of the century; of heart disease; in Kansas City. Son of a teamster, old "T.J." ruled Kansas City in its bawdiest, gaudiest, era, hired ghost voters by the thousands, bet millions on the ponies, hand-picked Governors and Senators, started Vice President Harry Truman up the political ladder. In 1939 he was caught red-handed with a whopping $430,000 bribe from insurance companies, went to jail for income-tax evasion.

MISCELLANY

SPECIAL DELIVERY: In Arlington, Va., expectant mothers requiring the services of the Red Cross were instructed to telephone one Mrs. Willis Stork.

SAFE DEPOSIT: In Mountain Home, Idaho, slot machines at the local air base bore this sign: "In case of air raid stand near these machines. They haven't been hit yet."

PANNED: In Milwaukee, a little boy on a bus tugged at the scarf wrapped around his head, finally uncovered a shiny aluminum pan clamped fast to his head. His embarrassed mother explained to the other passengers, "It's stuck, and we're going to a doctor to have it removed."

AN AKRONISM: In Akron, a thoughtful bus driver drew up at a grocery, announced, "They've got cigarets today," waited while all 16 passengers made their purchases.

IN THE SWIM: In Topeka, Kans., Gage Park swimming pool reopened with a request to bathers to hang onto their bathing suits this year, because the last time the pool was drained employes found ten suits.

```
┌─────────────────────────────┐
│         THE PRESS           │
└─────────────────────────────┘
```

STORY OF A PICTURE: By last week, the picture of the Iwo MARCH 26
Jima flag raising [see page 104] had already made almost
every front page in the land and was turning up again in
fancy, full-page color in U.S. Sunday papers. It was easily
the most widely printed photograph of World War II. One
Senator proposed it for a 3¢ stamp; a Congressman wanted
it used as a model for a national monument. A lyrical Roch-
ester, N.Y. art critic compared it to Leonardo da Vinci's *Last
Supper.* The less erudite Danville (Va.) *Register* was reminded
of *Washington Crossing the Delaware.*

Navy Secretary James Forrestal called Joe Rosenthal, who
took the picture, "as gallant as the men going up that hill."
In San Francisco, Rosenthal's draft board switched him from
4-F (bad eyes) to 2-AF (essential deferment) because the picture entitled him "to a classification better than 4-F." Along
with the praise came inevitable murmurs that the sculptural
symmetry of the picture was "too good to be true." Last week
short (5 ft. 6 in.), bespectacled, mustached Associated Press
Photographer Rosenthal, 33, camera veteran of Guadalcanal, Guam and Peleliu got back to the U.S. Said he: the picture was taken without one word of direction by him, was
completely unposed.

ERNIE: "It's not that I have a premonition that death's going APRIL 30
to catch up with me. It's nothing more than any foot soldier
in the lines feels. You begin to feel that you can't go on forever without being hit. I feel that I have used up all my
chances. And I hate it. I don't want to be killed."

It was Ernie Pyle, talking to a fellow newsman three months
ago. Like many correspondents, and more than most, he had
certainly used up chances. He had covered London in the
blitz, slugged across North Africa, landed with the troops in
Sicily. He had been bombed, wounded and awarded the Purple Heart at Anzio. He had gone into Normandy on D+1

and later watched in horror as Lieut. General Lesley J. McNair and other Americans were killed by off-target bombs from their own planes at Saint-Lô.

"War to an individual is hardly ever bigger than a hundred yards on each side of him," Pyle wrote. That 200 yards was his beat. In articles home to 393 daily and 297 weekly newspapers (total daily circulation: 13,390,144) Ernie Pyle covered that 200-yard view, its terrors, fatigues, laughs and heroism, more vividly and more simply than any other U.S. reporter. After 29 months of it, he wrote from France last September:

"I have had all I can take for a while. All of a sudden it seemed to me that if I heard one more shot or saw one more dead man, I would go off my nut."

He returned to the U.S., not unaware of the fame he had attained but unready for its demands. Paulette Goddard, Olivia de Havilland and Jinx Falkenburg kissed him, all in one afternoon. Hollywood made a movie with Burgess Meredith playing Ernie Pyle [see page 233]. Ernie's earnings reached a half million dollars.

After three and a half months of being lionized, he got ready to go to war again, this time to the Pacific:

"I'm certainly not going because I've got itchy feet again, or because there's any mystic fascination about war. I'm going simply because I've got to—and I hate it."

It was harder than ever for this skinny (110 pound) little man, with grey-fringed balding head and offside grin, to be his simple self. From Okinawa he wrote to his wife on March 31: "I've promised myself and I promise you that if I come through this one I will never go on another one." But there was a sideline invasion coming up, on the ten-mile square isle of Ie Jima, three miles off Okinawa, and Pyle went along. Last week on Ie Jima, Ernie Pyle, 44, met death from a Jap machine-gunner's bullet.

Big men paid him tribute. Said General Eisenhower: "All of us have lost one of our best and most understanding friends."

The G.I.s he wrote about paid their respects too. On Ie Jima, Corporal Landon Scidler fashioned a handmade wooden casket for him. Soldiers nailed Pyle's dogtags on the top, and buried him beside the G.I. dead.

HEADLINE OF THE WEEK: In bold black type, the Geneva (Switzerland) *Tribune* admitted:
EVENTS SEEM TO BE SUCCEEDING ONE ANOTHER WITH GREAT RAPIDITY.

SAN FRANCISCO SPECTACLE: The United Nations Press Secretariat had handed out San Francisco credentials like tickets to a two-bit political clambake; accredited correspondents outnumbered delegates six to one. Legmen, pundits, gossip columnists, hatchetmen, trained seals and freaks—1,600 of them, all classified as newsmen—fought for seats in a press section big enough for 600.   MAY 7

Newsmen and pseudo-newsmen who couldn't get into the conference sessions, or didn't want to, mobbed the Palace Hotel's Pied Piper bar, interviewing each other, exchanging rumors.

Legitimate newsmen heard Hedda Hopper cooing in a hotel lobby: "My dear, if this thing doesn't pick up pretty soon, it's going to be the dullest clambake ever held." They read Elsa Maxwell's astute comments on the Russians: "a bunch of magnificent he-men." Worst of all, the New York *Post*'s self-styled Saloon Editor Earl Wilson, whose usual preoccupation is with movie stars' brassières and derrières, interrupted Soviet Premier Molotov's press conference to ask whether vodka was pronounced "wodka" and whether it could "be consumed without fear of internal injury." Obviously annoyed, Mr. Molotov broke off the interview, with a number of other more important questions still unasked.

SCOOP: The voice was faint, muffled: "This is Paris calling."   MAY 14
The Associated Press deskman in London, answering the telephone, then heard: "This is Ed Kennedy. Germany has surrendered unconditionally. That's official. Make the date Reims, France, and get it out." Then came the details, dictated slowly and carefully. Dark-haired, alert, Brooklyn-born Edward Kennedy, 39, chief of A.P. war coverage in Europe, had the scoop of a lifetime.

Across the Atlantic the story sped. In Manhattan, where it arrived at 9:27 a.m., top A.P. executives huddled for eight minutes at the cable desk, debating whether to send the bulletin on to the A.P.'s 2,500 clients. They considered the risks if

Saloon Editor Earl Wilson asks Molotov how to pronounce vodka.   *Ed Kennedy of the A.P. is ordered home for a "disgraceful" scoop.*

the story didn't stand up. (After last fortnight's false armistice bulletin from San Francisco, Britain's Newspaper Proprietors Association recommended a Fleet Street boycott of A.P. news.) They also considered Kennedy's dependability during his 13 years of reporting for the A.P.

Weighing all this, and satisfied that Kennedy's story had too many details to be suspect, A.P. Assistant General Manager Alan Gould gave the go-ahead. Then the A.P. sat back, waiting for the U.P., I.N.S. and SHAEF to catch up. Instead SHAEF called the story unauthorized, clamped a news embargo on the A.P. The ban was later lifted for all A.P. men except Kennedy. He did not have to worry: his superiors were claiming for him "one of the greatest beats in newspaper history."

MAY 21 **WHOSE FAULT?** Who fouled up the peace news? The full story was slow in coming out. On Sunday afternoon at an airport outside Paris, 16 newsmen had been assembled—on 15 minutes' notice—and told they were to cover an important out-of-town assignment. After their big C-47 was in the air, Brigadier General Frank A. ("Honk") Allen Jr., SHAEF press chief, shouted above the engines' roar: "Gentlemen, we are going to cover the signing of the peace. This story is off the record until the respective Governments announce it. I therefore pledge you on your honor not to communicate the results of this conference or the fact of its existence until it is released by SHAEF."

No one objected—not even the A.P.'s Edward Kennedy—but back in Paris that afternoon Ed Kennedy broke his word. He first made some attempt to warn SHAEF (but not his colleagues) of what he was up to. He tried to reach General Allen by telephone, but was told that the General was too busy. According to Kennedy, he then warned Allen's aide, who said: "Go ahead and try to get it out, Ed; it's impossible." Then Kennedy sneaked his story to London by telephone. Kennedy gave as his reason for breaking the peace news that there was no military security involved. General Allen had told him, he said, that the surrender story was being held up only for Big Three political reasons.

Fifty-four correspondents signed an angry 500-word protest, calling Kennedy's action "the most disgraceful, deliberate and unethical double cross in the history of journalism."

As for Kennedy, SHAEF "disaccredited" him and ordered him back to the U.S. Said Kennedy: "My conscience is clear."

PEACE, IT'S WONDERFUL: Big type flashed from London SEPT. 17 newsstands: THIS IS THE FIRST UNCENSORED DAILY EXPRESS FOR EXACTLY SIX YEARS. The New York *Times* announced happily that for the first time since Sept. 1, 1939 no war communiqué was issued anywhere in the world.

WHO'S LOONY? The Washington *Times-Herald's* vitriolic, NOV. 12 red-haired Publisher Cissie Patterson, 61, who publishes the biggest but not the best paper in the capital, has had insanity on her mind recently. Last week she spread her thoughts across eight columns, under the heading CRAZY—CRAZY LIKE FOXES. They added up to some of the most vicious personal slander since the days when all journalism was yellow. Examples:

❡ "Henry Wallace . . . crystal-gazing crackpot. . . . A harmless kind of a nut."

❡ "Walter Winchell: Hard to tell just what's biting this middle-aged ex-chorus boy. False shame of his race may be at the root of it all. Anyhow he suffers from a chronic state of wild excitement, venom and perpetual motion of the jaw." As Cissie's scurrilities go, these were mere warm-ups. The worst she saved for her ex-son-in-law Washington Columnist Drew Pearson, whom she mortally hates. Wrote Cissie: "Ah, Drew, rose-sniffing, child-loving, child-cheater, sentimental Drew. . . . Vicious and. . . ." (Eleven more lines, reflecting on Mr. Pearson's personal habits, have been deleted by TIME. To publish them might put TIME into court for disseminating a libel.)

A minute later, Mrs. Patterson was talking about Winchell, Pearson "and Quislings, who manage to get paid big money for their treachery." Their crime, as Cissie saw it: "of plotting, planning, sneaking, lying, spying, cheating, stealing, smearing, in the mere HOPE of one day overthrowing our American form of government."

Said ex-son-in-law Drew Pearson, in his Sunday night broadcast: "The British have organized a society for protection against mothers-in-law, but what we really need in this country is an organization for protection against ex-mothers-in-law. I would like to be a charter member."

Said Winchell, on his program two hours later: "Very special bulletin! The craziest woman in Washington, D.C. is not yet confined at St. Elizabeth's Hospital for the insane. She is, however, expected any edition."

MILESTONES

MARRIED: Shirley Temple, 17, cinema's dimpled goldilocks who grew up to bobby-sox roles *(Kiss and Tell)*; and Sergeant John Agar, 24, tall, handsome A.A.F. physical instructor; in Los Angeles.

DEATH REVEALED: The Rev. William T. Cummings, 42, famed Army chaplain ("there are no atheists in foxholes") whose calming voice was heard above the bomb bursts in a Bataan hospital, and later by starving men on a Jap prison ship; of starvation and exposure.

DIED: Technical Sergeant Torger Tokle, 25, towheaded, Norwegian-born ski-jump champion of the Western Hemisphere (289 feet); from German shell-fragment wounds; near Monte Torraccio, Italy, as his 10th Mountain Infantry Division made a four-mile advance.

MISCELLANY

POWER OF SUGGESTION: In Arkansas City, Kans., City Clerk James Clough lay ill in bed, was visited by a friend, the sexton of the Riverview Cemetery, who was soon followed by the pastor of the Central Christian Church. When another friend, who was also an undertaker, dropped in to cheer him, Clough got up, rushed back to work.

BOOKS

"CANNERY ROW"–The Monterey, Calif. of John Steinbeck's JAN. 1 imagination is the easiest-going community in American literature. On Cannery Row, in addition to the sardine canneries, stands Dora's house of prostitution, the "Bear Flag Restaurant," with twelve girls, a bouncer, a bar, a flawless reputation and a steady trade from the fishermen who come in at the front door and the leading citizens who sneak in at the back. There is also the Western Biological Laboratory, dealing in snails, spiders, rattlesnakes, Gila monsters, barnacles, crabs, starfish, frogs, cats, sharks, octopuses. Its proprietor, a bearded beer drinker named Doc, is "half Christ and half satyr," a benevolent California intellectual who plays Gregorian chants on his phonograph, and brings tears to the eyes of the girls from Dora's with his readings of translations from the Sanskrit.

The achievement of *Cannery Row* is that Author Steinbeck makes all this credible and some of it funny. It is brief, episodic, formless, and Steinbeck suggests that he just opened the pages and let the stories crawl in by themselves.

"THE THURBER CARNIVAL"–Since his birth in Columbus, FEB. 12 Ohio on "a night of wild portent and high wind in 1894," James Thurber has seemed to live in a world where the edges of reality are fuzzy, the edges of fantasy insanely sharp. The focal character of most Thurber prose and drawings is a reticent, befuddled, thwarted little man who tries sadly to preserve himself and his reason against a practically worldwide onslaught. Grim psychiatrists, gadgets that "whir and whine and whiz," erratic servants, domineering women, unfriendly dogs, ghosts, foreigners—all are in league to crush the Thurber Male. To Thurber's devotees, who rate him the greatest U.S. humorist since Mark Twain, his blankly exaggerated reports of their own qualms and misadventures are recognizable and (since nobody considers himself quite as badly off as a Thurber character) reassuring. *The Thurber Carnival* is a well-edited selection of Thurber's stuff (he selected it himself).

Occasionally, a Thurber Male copes with dreadful reality by fleeing from it. Walter Mitty *(The Secret Life of Walter Mitty)* is, in his escape, the dauntless Commander Mitty ("Throw on the power lights! Rev her up to 8,500! We're going through!"). He is also the world-famed Dr. Mitty, taking over the crucial operation when other specialists are baffled.

The author supplies readers of his *Carnival* with an illuminating biographical sketch. "Not a great deal," says the autobiographer, "is known about his earliest years, beyond the fact that he could walk when he was four." Because of his dim sight (one eye was ruined in boyhood), he is forced to draw on huge sheets of paper, wearing special glasses.

FEB. 26 **"STEPHEN HERO"**–Mrs. James Joyce has hitherto been noted chiefly for her comment after reading *Ulysses*: "I guess the man's a genius, but what a dirty mind he has, surely!" Now Joyce's admirers find themselves deeply indebted to this quiet woman for *Stephen Hero,* a fragment of the first draft of Joyce's autobiographical *A Portrait of the Artist as a Young Man.* After it had been rejected by 20 different publishers, Joyce flung the 914-page manuscript into the fire. Mrs. Joyce risked her own skin to retrieve pages 519-902.

Stephen Hero was written when Joyce was 19 or 20, rewritten into the *Portrait* when he was about 30. The two books are significantly different. The *Portrait* is masterfully compressed and polished; *Stephen Hero,* covering Joyce's college years, is comparatively diffuse.

The passage in *Stephen Hero* (omitted entirely from the *Portrait*) which throws most light on Joyce's artistic origins deals with epiphanies. "By an epiphany [Stephen] meant a sudden spiritual manifestation, whether in the vulgarity of speech or gesture or in a memorable phase of the mind iself." Stephen felt that it is the artist's duty to record epiphanies.

MARCH 5 **"BLACK BOY"**–This is the autobiography of Richard Wright, 36, generally accounted the most gifted living American Negro writer. [His powerful novel, *Native Son,* was published in 1940.] Wright's new book makes it clearer than ever that he has one of the most notable gifts in U.S. writing, black or white: a narrative style that is simple, direct, almost completely without pretense or decoration, yet never flat. In *Black Boy,* that narrative tells the story of his first 18 years, in Natchez and Jackson, Miss., Elaine, Ark. and on Beale Street in Memphis. The story is a brilliant account of how it feels to be a sensitive Negro growing up in the U.S. South.

Richard sold papers, worked in a drugstore, a credit clothing store, a brickyard, an optical factory. He was hopeless at each job. He could not cover up his feelings. He forgot to say "Sir," or said it too slowly. Moreover, in crises—as when a white man hit him in the mouth with a whiskey bottle—his old immobility came back and left him paralyzed.

Richard Wright. The naked white prostitutes would pay no attention.

C. S. Forester. "I recommend him," says Hemingway, "to every literate."

He did better as a bellboy. The naked white prostitutes paid no attention to him when he delivered bootleg whiskey to their rooms. He saved his money, stole everything he could lay hands on, pawned it, and fled to Memphis. There he began to read Mencken and Sinclair Lewis, and to see the white men around him in a different light.

His reading also gave him a profound awareness of his people's plight. "I used to mull over the strange absence of real kindness in Negroes, how unstable was our tenderness, how lacking in genuine passion we were, how void of great hope, how timid our joy, how bare our traditions, how hollow our memories, how lacking we were in those intangible sentiments that bind man to man, and how shallow was even our despair. After I had learned other ways of life I used to brood upon the unconscious irony of those who felt that Negroes led so passional an existence!"

MAY 28 **"COMMODORE HORNBLOWER"**–C. S. Forester. "Get out my best uniform and sword! Have the horses put to in my chariot!" bellowed Captain Sir Horatio Hornblower when the Admiralty summoned him back from shore leave. "It will take me away from you," he told his gorgeous wife Barbara (the future Duke of Wellington's sister). "Darling," she answered, "six months of the kind of happiness you have given me is more than any woman deserves."

That the fate of Europe hung upon the fictional Sir Horatio and his little squadron will come as no surprise to Hornblower fans. The series has made the Captain's creator, C. S. Forester, one of the most popular adventure writers alive. ("I recommend Forester to everyone literate I know," said Ernest Hemingway.) And bluenoses who find his plots and action too outrageously farfetched have no business reading historical romances.

SEPT. 24 **AMBER IN ENGLAND:** Kathleen Winsor's *Forever Amber,* U.S. sex-seller (nearly a million copies), appeared this month on London's bookstalls. English critics thumbed through and condemned it as tedious, bad writing and worse taste. Typical was the reaction of the *Evening Standard*'s reviewer: "Miss Winsor has attempted an erotic novel on a grand scale, swoony with ill-defined sex, written in a style that rasps the nerves like a Brooklyn accent. I gave up on page 272, by which time Amber had reached her eighth man."

OCT. 8 **"CASS TIMBERLANE"**–On Main Street one day last week George F. Babbitt, Booster, ran into Honest Jim Blausser, Hustler. Said Honest Jim:

"I certainly was astonished in the streets of our lovely little city, the other day—a knocker!"

"Who d'ya mean?"

"Harry S. Lewis from Gopher Prairie—I mean Sauk Centre

—this writing fellow that calls himself Sinclair Lewis."

"Well now, Jim," said George Babbitt, "maybe you hadn't ought to be too hard on old Red Lewis. You don't want to forget he made me and you and. . . ."

"Sure, how can I forget it? And he made us and this Great Country the laughing stock of the whole world, didn't he?"

"Well, now, Jim, did you hear that Lewis got nearly 500,-000 smackers for this new book of his before it was even published?"

"Five hundred thousand bucks! You mean they gave him all that money just to write a book? Why, that's half a million dollars!"

"Yes, sir."

The man whose literary killing was of such inflaming interest to George F. Babbitt was in Manhattan last week. He had breezed in to attend to sundry pressing business matters. Among them: the sale to M-G-M of the movie rights to *Cass Timberlane,* which, together with The Book-of-the-Month Club and the magazine serial rights, would certainly boost the total take for his new novel well up toward the half-million-dollar figure.

As fiction, *Cass Timberlane* is a good many cuts below *Dodsworth* and will add little if anything to Lewis' literary stature, which was clearly established with *Babbitt.* But it is of special interest as Novelist Lewis' first try at a love story uncluttered with large social concerns and as an indication that the Scourge of Sauk Centre is moving toward a reconciliation with his origins and an unusual preoccupation with sex.

"THE AGE OF JACKSON"–Once upon a time, when the Yew- OCT. 22
nited States was just a little shaver among the nations, there lived younder in Tennessee a lovable old man with a tongue like a rat-tailed file and a face so hard they called him Old Hickory. He was a great hero. In the War of 1812, he licked the British in the Battle of Noo Orleens. Everybody loved him because he had come up the hard way from nothing, but he never forgot the COMMON MAN. Sitting on his plantation porch of an evening, he would say: "I still love the COMMON MAN," and, with a jet of tobacco juice slanchwise between the Ionic columns, would drown a doodlebug at five yards.

They called him the Sage of The Hermitage (his plantation).

Now, in the big city of Philadelphia, across the mountains, lived a very wicked man. His name was Nicholas Biddle. He was president of the Yewnited States Bank, which was a wily scheme to get hard money away from the COMMON MAN and give him scraps of paper in exchange. This Biddle was a bad actor. He did not eat with his knife and he foregathered with cronies who drank soup in silence so they could hear each other plot against the COMMON MAN. They were called Federalists.

One day Old Hickory got so mad he roared: "My name is Andrew Jackson, fresh from the backwoods, half-horse, half-alligator, a little touched with snapping turtle. Come on boys, let's get Nicholas Biddle."

So all the peckerwoods and rednecks and the big planters from the South and the farmers from the West, they voted Old Hickory to be President of the Yewnited States. Then they went to the White House for free grog and climbed over the fancy chair with muddy boots. Everybody got jobs with the Government because, as Old Hickory said: "To the victors belong the spoils!"

So runs the Jackson legend. Now Arthur M. Schlesinger Jr., in a brilliant justification of the New Deal disguised as a history of the age of Jackson, says that the legend and the facts do not jibe at all. The election that broke the Federalists and made Old Hickory President brought entirely new social forces into political power in the U.S. They were the same kind of forces that made the New Deal powerful.

Says Schlesinger: "The Jacksonians believed that there was a deep-rooted conflict in society between the 'producing' and 'non-producing' classes—the farmers and laborers on the one hand, and the business community on the other. The business community was considered to hold high cards in this conflict through its network of banks and corporations, above all, its power over the state."

DEC. 3 **BEST SELLER:** University presses rarely get one of their books on the best-seller list. But last week Professor Henry DeWolf Smyth's authoritative *Atomic Energy for Military Purposes,* popularly known as "the Smyth report," had sold more than 77,000 copies, was outselling Bennett Cerf's latest jokebook.

"STUART LITTLE"–"When Mrs. Frederick C. Little's second son was born, everybody noticed that he was not much bigger than a mouse. The truth was, the baby looked very much like a mouse in every way. He was only about two inches high; and he had a mouse's sharp nose, a mouse's tail, a mouse's whiskers, and the pleasant shy manner of a mouse. Before he was many days old he was not only looking like a mouse but acting like one, too—wearing a gray hat and carrying a small cane. . . . The doctor was delighted with Stuart and said that it was very unusual for an American family to have a mouse."

DEC. 31

With this musine bow, Stuart Little pops out of the pocket of his creator, *New Yorker* writer E. B. White, and begins his adventures. When Mrs. Little lost her ring down the bathtub drain, Mr. Little suggested that they lower Stuart into the drain on a string. Soon Stuart came up with the ring around his neck. "How was it down there?" asked Mr. Little, who was always curious about places he had never been to. "It was all right," said Stuart. *Stuart Little* is a tale of few laughs and many smiles. Adults may read into it any meanings they like. Children will read and reread it for fun.

MILESTONES

DIVORCED: By Ernest Hemingway, 47, masculine, monosyllabic author; his third wife, Martha Gellhorn, 37, author of social novels and Hemingwayesque short stories; after five years of marriage, no children; in Havana. Grounds: desertion.

KILLED IN SERVICE: Major Richard Ira Bong, 24, U.S. ace of aces (40 Jap planes); in the crash of a Lockheed P-80 jet fighter; at Burbank, Calif. The round-faced, snub-nosed flyer returned from the Pacific last January, married his Wisconsin sweetheart and was assigned to test-flying.

DIED: Lord Alfred Douglas, 74, scholar, sonneteer, son of boxing's famed rulesmaker, the late eighth Marquess of Queensberry, whose letter denouncing young Alfred's friend, Oscar Wilde, was the cause of Wilde's libel suit and subsequent imprisonment for pederasty; after long illness; in Lancing, Sussex, England.

MISCELLANY

ANIMAL KINGDOM: In Providence, R.I., State Labor Director William L. Connolly reached for an aspirin, swallowed a pill for his wife's petunia plant instead, grew panicky, was calmed by an agricultural expert who informed him that he had merely taken the equivalent of 18 bushels of horse manure and had nothing to worry about.

OUT OF CONTROL: In Washington, OPA announced that it would no longer regulate the prices of bird cages, aluminum horseshoes, sleigh bells, artificial grass, poker-chip racks, cat & dog beds.

Numerals in italics indicate an illustration of subject mentioned.

PICTURE CREDITS

X

PRODUCTION STAFF FOR TIME INCORPORATED
John L. Hallenbeck *(Vice President and Director of Production)*,
Robert E. Foy, Caroline Ferri and Don Sheldon
Text photocomposed under the direction of Albert J. Dunn and Arthur J. Dunn

QUOTES OF THE YEAR

Vice President Harry S. Truman
(to reporters on learning of President Roosevelt's death—p. 19): "Did you ever have a bull or a load of hay fall on you?...Please pray God to help me carry this load."

Brigadier General Anthony McAuliffe
(answering a German demand to surrender Bastogne —p. 90): "Nuts!"

General George S. Patton
(to an Army chaplain during the Battle of the Bulge— p. 94): "I want a prayer to stop this rain. If we got a couple of clear days we could kill a couple of hundred thousand of those krauts."

War Correspondent Ernie Pyle
(three months before he was killed by a Japanese sniper—p. 236): "I feel that I have used up all my chances."

Assistant Secretary of State Nelson Rockefeller
(on being handed a $1,449 bill for a diplomatic party— p. 195): "Who do you think I am, Rockefeller?"

ANSWERS TO PICTURE QUIZ—1: General Dwight D. Eisenhower; 2: President Harry S. Truman; 3: British Prime Minister Clement Attlee; 4: Secretary of State James F. Byrnes; 5: King Ibn Saud of Saudi Arabia; 6: Labor Leader Walter Reuther; 7: Ex-dictator Adolf Hitler; 8: Cartoonist Bill Mauldin's cartoon character, "Willie"; 9: Admiral William F. Halsey; 10: General Motors Chairman Alfred P. Sloan Jr.; 11: Army football stars Glenn Davis and Felix ("Doc") Blanchard; 12: Japan's Emperor Hirohito; 13: New York Giants Manager Mel Ott; 14: Generalissimo Chiang Kai-shek; 15: Novelist Sinclair Lewis; 16: Air Force General Curtis LeMay.